ADOLESCENTS IN CRISIS

Other books by G. Wade Rowatt Jr.:

Pastoral Care with Adolescents in Crisis
with Mary Jo Brock Rowatt (Westminster John Knox Press)

The Two-Career Marriage
with Mary Jo Brock Rowatt (Westminster Press)

ADOLESCENTS IN CRISIS

A Guidebook for Parents,
Teachers, Ministers, and Counselors

G. Wade Rowatt Jr.

Westminster John Knox Press
LOUISVILLE
LONDON · LEIDEN

Book design by Sharon Adams
Cover design by designconcepts/Kevin Keller

First edition
Published by Westminster John Knox Press
Louisville, Kentucky

This book is printed on acid-free paper that meets the American National Standards Institute Z39.48 standard. ∞

PRINTED IN THE UNITED STATES OF AMERICA

01 02 03 04 05 06 07 08 09 10 — 10 9 8 7 6 5 4 3 2 1

Library of Congress Cataloging-in-Publication Data
Rowatt, Wade.
    Adolescents in crisis : a guidebook for parents, teachers, ministers, and counselors / G. Wade Rowatt Jr.
        p.   cm.
Includes bibliographical references and index.
ISBN 0-664-22334-6 (pbk.)
    1. Teenagers—Counseling of. 2. Teenagers—Pastoral counseling of. 3. Crisis intervention (Mental health services) I. Title.
HV1421 .R69 2001
158'.3'0835—dc21
                                                                2001016237

*Dedicated to my three children
and their families:
Wade and Tammy Rowatt;
Brock, Cindy, and Lindsey Rowatt;
and Ashley J. Rowatt*

Contents

Acknowledgments

*C*ountless persons have contributed in a professional and personal way to the development of this book. Wayne E. Oates consulted with me just weeks before his death. His suggestions rang clear as this book unfolded. From the probing questions and careful dialogue of my teaching, ministering, and counseling colleagues, Clarence Barton, Tom Bloxam, Mary Burks-Price, Joan Clagett, Dianna Garland, Jan Cox-Gedmark, Bruce Hardy, Ted Hodge, Walter Jackson, Isaac Nygunga, Kwanjik Lee, Andrew Lester, Elizabeth Millazotto, Edward Thornton, and Valerie Vincent, this book received numerous ideas, redirections, and revisions.

A research grant from the Eli Lilly Foundation through the Union Theological Seminary in Richmond Youth Project funded portions of the social research for this book in 1988. Sara Little and Dan Aleshire offered encouragement along with their support. G. Randolph Schrodt, M.D., and Barbara A. Fitzgerald, M.D., codirectors of the Adolescent Treatment Program, Norton Psychiatric Clinic, and professors in the Department of Psychiatry and Behavioral Sciences, University of Louisville School of Medicine, provided a clinical setting and professional critique that deepened my understanding of the multidimensional nature of adolescent crises. The outstanding nursing, educational, and other staff members of Six East at Norton Hospital provided wisdom and were models of professional care. Their work with teenagers was an inspiration.

The professional staff at Menninger in Topeka guided my study for an additional year's sabbatical study and continued education. I offer special thanks to Walter Menninger, M.D.; Glenn Gabbard, M.D.; Kathryn Zerbe, M.D.; Bede Healy; and Marc Des Lauriers, director of continuing education. In various ways they changed my thinking about the world of adolescents in crisis.

By their sharing and example, a number of teachers informed this work. Helen Barnett, Carol Garrison, Robert Gilbert, John Locke, Carol Reitze, and Geoffrey Wygand set high standards for creatively reaching out to teenagers. Over one hundred ministers discussed the needs of teenagers and shared how they attempt to minister in crises. James Appleby, Patricia Bailey, Jamie Broom, Gwynn Davis, Mori Hiratoni, Mark Hogg, Vickie Hollon, John Lepper, Malcolm Marler, Don McMinn, Richard Ross, Barbara Robbins, Bob Tallent, T. Scott Wiggington, John Willingham, and Joel Wayne are but a few to whom I owe a debt of gratitude.

Six graduate students spent one or more semesters ministering with adolescents in crisis and offered their insights for our supervision and seminar context. Thank you Vance Davis, Mariam Anne Glover, Val Gonzollas, John Gray, Karen Lovett, and Brian Williams.

The courageous youth of Norton Psychiatric Clinic who permitted me to join in their struggle for wholeness sustained me as I walked alongside them during their hospitalization. The teenagers who came for counseling to St. Matthew's Pastoral Counseling Center and gave me their poems, letters, and diaries have also been my teachers. All these adolescents touched my heart as we journeyed toward health. Confidentiality prohibits my sharing their names. Special thanks are extended to the youth who swim for Kenyon College.

I am grateful to Victoria Moon, Wade C. Rowatt, and Tammy Rowatt, who assisted with the statistical research. They focused and challenged my thinking.

I offer thanks to Angela Jackson of Westminster John Knox Press, who provided words of affirmation, suggestions for expansion, friendship, and appropriate confrontation as this project unfolded. She redirected the scope of this work and expanded its vision. Her contribution goes beyond her helpful editorial suggestions for the final production.

As always, my wife, Jodi, gave loving support and a professional exchange of ideas. Wade C., Tammy, J. Brock, Cindy, and Ashley, our sons and daughters, challenged and enlightened the concepts in this volume. Ashley, our nineteen-year-old, brought to this book new perspectives, diverse friends, and cyberspace thinking. Lindsey Marie, our granddaughter, provided moments of joy to punctuate the laborious task of writing. I thank God again for my family.

Introduction

*H*elping adolescents in crisis looms as a challenge for contemporary society. If this book assists you in that task, then it has served its purpose. Parents will find suggestion for guiding their teenagers through the white-water rapids phase of development. When their life seems to capsize, you will find guidance in these pages. Teachers, ministers, and counselors will discover how to work as a team and how to sustain and channel adolescents through developmental predicaments and emergency catastrophes. Specific suggestions flow from foundational concepts for caring and counseling. Teachers will encounter ideas for changes at school as well as approaches to adolescents in crisis. Student teachers will find this book a trustworthy resource for understanding the teens in their schools. Ministers will come across ideas for sermons, programs, and interventions at church and in the community. Students in training for the ministry (who frequently finance their education by part-time youth work in churches) can be introduced to deeper levels of crisis ministry that may otherwise go unnoticed in the youth program. Chaplains, pastoral counselors, and family counselors will acquire specifics in working with teenagers and their families. School counselors can uncover ways to counsel teens in the midst of their attention to academic agendas. We can all better understand the context of care for troubled adolescents.

A variety of research avenues and methods have yielded insights, apprehensions, interventions, and theories that blend together in the pages that follow. A literature search revealed exciting new reading in fields that exist in near isolation from one another. Legal, medical, psychological, educational, and religious research reflected limited interaction in addressing the problem of adolescents in crisis. Social research on young people provided intriguing summaries that suggest that many teens are at risk of major crises.

Interviews with teenagers (aged twelve to nineteen) yielded rich, personal, but often pain-filled stories. The needs of Hispanics, African Americans, Caucasians, Asians, and those of mixed race surfaced as sometimes different but more often similar. Social-class differences, not racial ones, loomed large. Teens shared different views of home, school, and church. Urban, suburban, and rural teens told of varied pressures. Interviews with those who work with adolescents (psychiatrists, social workers, psychologists, pastoral counselors, family therapists, attorneys, ministers, group-home staff, public- and private-schoolteachers, parents, and police) underscored the complexity of the issues facing our youth and demonstrated how training and orientation condition both the definition of the cause of their crises and the preferred treatments, responses, and solutions.

This book attempts to summarize reflections from a wide range of sources, to provide understanding for the comprehensive picture of youth crises, and to offer practical, psychological, and theological clarifications that inform the process of care and counseling with adolescents in crisis. Although many readers will no doubt be familiar with the adolescent psychosocial developmental issues described in Chapter 1, Chapter 2 integrates religious insights, developmental issues, and the effects of current social pressures. Chapter 3 discusses foundational principles of care and counseling with teens, and Chapter 4 suggests methods for interventions. The implementation of the principles and methods unfolds in a variety of common problems: family crises (Chapter 5); sexual problems (Chapter 6); academic and peer problems (Chapter 7); school violence (Chapter 8); depression, grief, and suicide (Chapter 9); and substance abuse (Chapter 10). A concluding section reflects on our selves as gifts to teenagers.

Chapter 1

Adolescents in Crisis

*A*dolescence, the tough and turbulent transition between childhood and adulthood, holds a fascination for children and adults. The romanticized images in teen magazines, on MTV, in action movies, and general television shows induce school-age children to dream of magic futures with love, leisure, and lusty luxury. Elementary-school girls no longer dress up only like Mom; they copy the "teen model" look with designer clothes, name-brand makeup, and, as soon as possible, cell phones of their own. Their male counterparts emulate rock stars, sports idols, military heroes, and video action icons. They stay in touch using pagers and cell phones of their own. Preteens crowd Internet chat rooms and flood radio call-in programs. While children daydream of that magic thirteenth birthday, many adults frantically attempt to preserve their own vanishing youthful images and dread each passing year. Franchised health clubs, diet supplements, and plastic surgeries entice men and women alike. We color our hair. We dress like the youth. We walk, run, dance, pump iron, ski, and swim to tone our bodies. We pour on wrinkle-fighting cosmetics in hopes of appearing younger. We search for the right diet and the right sleep cycles to support a prolonged, youthful body. Western adults, like their preteen children, are lured by the adolescent image. I have early-twenties adults asking if they look old. Although it is great to take better care of ourselves, we need to reexamine our worship of the teen culture.

Moreover, adolescence also stimulates fears and generates anxieties. Fifth- and sixth-graders frequently dread leaving elementary school and graduating to new pressures in junior high or middle school. Although the level of academic expectations frightens a few, more resistance stems from alarming reports of drugs sold on campus, school shootings, sexual advances, and peer rejection. Panic attacks regularly emerge among early adolescents unprepared for the stress of the teen world. One intimidated girl voiced it this way: "I don't want to grow up. I like being protected by Dad and Mother. I'm afraid of what will happen to me." A fifth-grade boy told his parents that he would rather be home-schooled than face the hassles of middle school. Parents, teachers, ministers, and counselors face new concerns each year as the world of adolescents transforms to keep pace with this ever-changing, cyberspace culture. Disadvantaged preteens and teens grow increasingly frustrated and discouraged as they endure the widening gap between their world and the world of their rich peers.

In reality, many teens ordinarily find their lives frustrating and disappointing. The Hollywood portrayal of teenage fun, fame, and friendships eludes them, and they experience depression, isolation, confusion, grief, anxiety, rejection, anger, and loneliness. They feel betrayed when their aspirations turn into terrifying reality:

- They cannot get dates.
- Their steady dates dump them.
- A romantic evening turns into a pregnancy.
- A hot car wrecks and someone special dies.
- The substance-induced high crashes.
- They are busted for shoplifting or possession of a substance.
- Their parents devastate them with unfaithfulness.
- Trusted friendships turn sour.
- Their grades plummet toward failure.
- Deadly violence erupts at school.
- Ugly prejudice mars personal victories.
- A beloved teacher gets arrested.
- The counselor quits for a better position.
- They get "cut" after the first day of tryouts.
- A single parent finally gets married, but to someone they despise.
- Their bodies fail to develop into what they anticipated.
- Dreams become nightmares, and they conclude, "Life sucks!"

Although adults long for feeling young again and desire personal interaction with teenagers, many frequently resist dealing with teen issues and despairingly decry the day their own offspring reach these tumultuous years. "In this day and age, a parent can be thankful just to get them through alive and in one piece," said the father of two high-school girls. Not only do parents struggle with teens in their homes, but many helping adults also avoid teens if they can. Teachers, social workers, counselors, physicians, attorneys, and ministers often disdain youth work. One has only to look at the burnout rate for teachers, juvenile officers, and youth workers to be convinced that it takes a special person to love working with adolescents over the years.

Preteens and adults may view adolescence with strong ambivalence and attempt to understand while avoiding actual contact, but teenagers do not have a choice in the matter. They must face the stressful, shifting, and perplexing youth culture. It is theirs!

Concerns of Today's Youth

Fifty percent of today's youth may experience a major crisis before reaching the age of eighteen. They will be hospitalized, appear in court, have major parental conflicts, be crippled in an accident, attempt suicide, abuse alcohol or drugs, drop out of school, get pregnant, contract a sexually transmitted disease, be arrested, be raped, pay for or have an abortion, witness an act of violence, or experience something else of this magnitude. Many will endure multiple crises!

With each new level of solutions (mechanical, electrical, atomic, DNA decoding, cyberspace) comes a higher, more complex level of problems. The teens of the twenty-first century face a complex web of continuing social problems, new ethical decisions, and radical life-style options. As teens, their parents thought little about safety at school, animal cloning, body piercing, e-mail security, porn web pages, and Internet copyrights for music. The information age of the twenty-first century, although promising seemingly unlimited opportunities in a shrinking world, introduces an unheard-of level of temptations for teens cruising the town square, hanging out at the stables, skating on the plaza, playing on the beach, or surfing the web.

Contemporary Western society offers decreased support while at the same time it contributes to the increased stress level placed on the adolescent generation. More young people grow up in one-parent families. Those who do have both parents in the home spend less time there, and almost all teens are isolated from their extended family of grandparents, aunts, uncles, and cousins. One survey found that the major complaint of teenagers was not enough time with their parents. They are less likely to be friends with a caring adult neighbor, teacher, minister, or coach. Parents report that they do not have time to get involved in their kid's schools (*NEA Today*, September 2000, p. 10). The network of supportive, caring people with whom teens can interact diminishes, deteriorates, and in some cases disappears.

Not only does this decrease normal relationships; it also means significantly less support in times of adolescent crisis. A resulting remoteness, isolation, detachment, and loneliness creates anxiety for teens, and that in turn fuels more "angry acting out" and "depressive withdrawing" behavior. Seemingly normal teenagers turn to missing school, at-risk thrill seeking, substance abuse, and casual sex. Depression, anxiety, and isolation climb to new highs!

However, the major additions to the stress level in the lives of adolescents are the social problems in their world. The following list of typical real-life issues of today's youth illustrates this fact:

- AIDS and sexually transmitted diseases (STDs) continue to spread in the teen generation.
- Party drugs promise safe fun and deliver brain damage.
- Date rape soars to all-time highs.
- Mandatory testing for graduation finds more students lacking the basics.
- Suicide among teenagers grows.
- School violence reaches epidemic levels.
- Sexual predators use the Internet to arrange rendezvous with teens.
- Poverty haunts many youth in "the land of plenty."
- Hazing becomes crippling or deadly on some campuses.
- Ethnic diversity challenges identity formation.
- Automobile accidents claim the lives of beloved peers.

Teens' parents and in some cases grandparents may have demonstrated in the streets for social justice, sung for Farm Aid, protested for gay rights, fought for racial equality, and insisted on equal pay for females, but today's youngsters have little or no forums. They have no voice. Make no mistake; they search desperately to be heard. "Where do we cry 'help'?" asked a sensitive fifteen-year-old girl in Miami, Florida. She went on to say, "I'm afraid of so many things: AIDS, being kidnapped, and terrorist attacks, not to mention that we will all be nuked by someone pushing the wrong button." A bright seventeen-year-old boy confessed, "I'm afraid of a terrorist attack every time I attend a big meeting in my city." A young girl lamented, "I never take a drink of anything at a party unless I fix it myself. You never know when it might be fixed." A biracial sixteen-year-old grumbled, "Where do I fit? Neither world sees me as theirs." Their cries redefine the sound of silence.

Larger numbers feel the suffocating pressure of being number one. Parents push for stellar grades, outstanding achievement test scores, star performances, athletic accomplishments, and well-rounded resumes to ensure acceptance into the right magnet or private high school long before the buildup of stress of seeking admission to the right college. Peers pressure each other with new levels of competition in music, drama, sports, art, and even x-games. One thirteen-year-old told me, "I suck as a kid," because he lost a dirt-bike competition in his hometown. Charles Whited reflected: "Today's world is tough on both parents and kids. At one extreme, the nation's prisons overflow with the offspring of parents who failed. At the other extreme among upward-striving yuppies, you find a fierce drive to create super-kids, geared to win honors, be rich, run things" (Whited, p. 1). That was over a decade ago! Now, decades later, the prison population has doubled, and the push for perfection reaches fever pace in some prep schools. Nearly a third of teenagers in one study reported they would cheat on their college admissions application to get into the right school.

The concerns expressed by the young people I talk with reflect new social worries as well as typical adolescent struggles. Dating and sexuality still top the most-often-mentioned list. Tensions with parents continues as teens strive to find their own identities and struggle for independence by testing the limits, challenging the rules, and checking out the sincerity of parental love bonds. Although some parents, teachers, ministers, and counselors relate well with youth, others feel that the generation gap has become a canyon. A number of teens report years of taking care of themselves because their parents devote their time to other things. Adolescents of workaholics suffer the most. Their parents climbed the ladder of success but left them unattended. Other typical adolescent concerns are body image; vocational decisions; academic and athletic competition; racial tensions; spending money; curfews; telephone, television or Internet time; physical illness; friends who are unacceptable to their parents; adult tensions at school or in church; and getting a car or a driver's license. The list goes on and on.

You can add your own observations to this list of gripes. One teacher complained that a majority of today's teenagers lack character, commitment, and ambition. "They lie, cheat, avoid homework, care mostly for themselves, and expect to be taken care of by someone else," he complained. Another pointed to the increased disrespect in the classroom as her major concern.

A new group of social concerns includes fears of being abducted, AIDS, school safety, strict dress codes at school, depletion of oil resources, homosexual and heterosexual rape, abandonment by parents through divorce or desertion, pollution of the environment, and growing up to find a bureaucratic society that has no place for them. "I'm afraid that I'll either never grow up or that, when I do, the world will be so messed up I can't lead a normal life," complained a fifteen-year-old boy in Miami. Parental disapproval of interracial dating seems to be an increasing complaint of today's teenagers. They fear that the world has reached its peak and that things will only get worse. "Why try?" echoes loudly from this generation of school dropouts. Two teenage joggers passed me on the beach, wearing matching T-shirts that summed up the contemporary anxiety level. They read, *Save Our Planet*. Hopelessness spreads like a fungus among many teenagers.

Economic shifts, downsizing, losses of manufacturing jobs, closings of family stores, racial prejudice, and waves of third-world refugees are creating a larger group of newly poor families. Teenage girls who become mothers seldom escape the poverty cycle. Young people in extremely poor families feel angry and frustrated to be doing without in the "land of opportunity." The middle class of America is shrinking as the rich get richer and the poor get poorer. Some wealthy teens seem to be wandering in meaningless fashion as they search for happiness in designer clothes, beach and ski trips, fast cars, recreational sex, substance abuse, and world travel.

Special pressures abound. Some poverty-stricken teenage females are said to have children for the sake of additional welfare support; some young Asian Americans report excessive family pressure to excel academically. Sons and daughters with athletic, dramatic, or musical talent are pushed to excel in ways that harm their psychosocial development. As the social pressures on young people mount and the support network diminishes, the anxiety level increases. As the anxiety level increases, the number of adolescents in crisis begins to soar.

As the number of nonwhites grows in most states, the pressures of intercultural adjustments abound. Change means learning from each other, but it can also bring the weight of living in two worlds. Bicultural concerns focus on maintaining one's racial heritage and living in the "American" world. Theologian Edward Wimberly suggests that balance is the key. Families should maintain a relationship with their cultural roots and a relationship to the culture of their new environment (Wimberly, p. 28). We must become aware of the impact that dual cultural participation has on ethnic teenagers. An "achievement gap" between the test scores of white and black students can best be explained by the lack of accumulated wealth in black families. Children get a sense of ownership, hope, and trust in the resources that impacts their school attitude more than any amount of preaching, according to one researcher (Jehlen, p. 33).

For decades, social institutions have tried to support parents as they responded to young people in trouble. These trends reflect the need for more solid, sustaining networks as well as increased levels of crisis counseling. High schools, for instance, offer child-care services for teenage mothers and fathers. Some cities have separate schools (grades 6–12) for teen mothers. Because most teen-related crime occurs between three and seven o'clock, many communities are providing after-school programs and activities. Psychiatric treatment centers for adolescents have grown around the nation but are closing because of insurance shifts. The federal government has a missing-and-exploited-children's agency and has launched major initiatives to fight school violence, reduce smoking, and combat drug use among teenagers. These efforts have had mixed success. Substance-abuse programs for teens are increasing, although there are long waiting lists. Churches and denominational agencies are responding with special materials and new youth-oriented programs. It takes a cooperative effort among parents, teachers, ministers, and counselors to address the wide array of issues facing present-day teenagers.

Self in Body, Mind, and Soul

The teenage years consist of a quest for the self. Teens long to discover a satisfactory answer to the age-old question "Who am I?" Adolescents emerge like butterflies from larva, evolve like frogs from tadpoles, and grow like oaks from acorns. They unfold according to an ancient biological code that interacts with elements of their unique current surroundings. They are a reflection of both their parents' bodies and their psychosocial, cultural environment. Teens take clues from their bodies and often conclude, "I'm not OK." I frequently hear things like "I'm just too plain"; "I'm ugly"; or "I wish I were taller (thinner, stronger, faster, or shorter)." Some like their bodies and grow positive internal images. Those who have regular physical activities or belong to mutually supportive sports teams seem to have enhanced images of their bodies. They enjoy taking care of their physical selves. Another major factor is how they think their friends evaluate them.

Teens sometimes surmise from their grades, "Others are smarter than I could ever become." Even 4.0 students tell me that they do not feel bright. They discount their achievements with, "I just worked more" or "Those others are real geniuses." Students who actually fail a subject frequently give up trying. Perhaps 20 percent do feel competent and intelligent. They thrive in a peer climate where doing your best means popularity. "It is neat to be in classes where we help each other learn and think it is cool to make good grades," chirped one high-school senior.

Teens conclude from their own actions, media images, and critical feedback, "I am a bad person." A fifteen-year-old group member confessed, "I really believe that I am evil because so many bad things come my way." Thinking that they have a sick soul is perhaps the most devastating conclusion for teenagers. This can cause them to give up hope, become depressed, and turn to destructive behavior. A growing number of teens find an authentic faith experience that encourages feelings of self-love and loving care for others. They give back in meaningful service hours and creative mission projects.

Parents, teachers, ministers, and counselors stand outside the process as guides or shepherds on the journey from childhood to adulthood. However, we also become a part of the environment that interacts with their particular process of becoming. We mirror their images back to them by how we relate. This is especially true in crises. We provide nurture and confrontation to point toward wholeness, support, and guidance to influence choices; and we provide instruction, information, and education to prepare them for self-reliance. We offer faith, hope, and love as fuel for their revolutionary journey into transformation. As they eventually put off an old self, a new self emerges all grown up.

We cannot protect adolescents from the revolution within their bodies and brains, but we can be a safe place for testing whatever emerges. They will be different, albeit good or bad, pretty or ugly, active or passive, strong or weak, trusting or doubting, able or incapable, free or bound up, directed or confused, organized or jumbled, extroverted or introverted, accepting or rejecting. Accepting them as "works in progress" paves the way for their becoming more mature. Teens are not yet who they will be. One private school principal urges parents to respect the man their boy will become (Kelly, *Respecting the Man the Boy Will Become*). At best, we shepherd the process of developing strong bodies, effective minds, and passionate souls.

Parents, teachers, ministers, and counselors know that those awkward young teens might emerge as competent, capable, talented, and accomplished high-school seniors. But the teens do not know this yet. We are like shepherds leading a flock of lambs on a long journey into the high-mountain pastures where only mature sheep can survive. We know they will be grown by the journey's end and strengthened by each step in the journey, but they need the trip time to become ready.

Parenting, teaching, and counseling, from a religious viewpoint, can best be understood through this image of shepherding. Shepherding is the basic historical model for pastoral care and religious counseling (Hiltner, *Preface to Pastoral Theology*). Teenagers need a continuing relationship of support and/or confrontation with a "shepherd" (a caring parent, teacher, minister, and/or counselor) in times of developmental or emergency crisis.

Shepherding is first and foremost a relationship. The relationship may be informal, such as casual hallway conversations or across-the-table discussions in a youth lounge. Or it may be more formal, "in the classroom" instruction, "at the church" religious study, or "in the office" counseling. In formal teaching and counseling, a specific time, place, and agenda are planned around a helping or therapeutic conversation. In both the formal and informal context, the primary key is the relationship.

Although modern instructional methods and materials, professional pastoral care, and clinical counseling are twentieth-century phenomena revised in the twenty-first century, this shepherding stance toward persons in crisis is an ancient biblical concept. Perhaps the shepherding principles are most clearly articulated in Psalm 23 and in Matthew's Gospel (25:40), where Jesus promises that "as you did it to one of the least of these my brethren, you did it to me," as he speaks of the poor, the naked, the sick, the imprisoned, and the hungry. Healing, guiding, informing, sustaining, confronting, and reconciling are approaches that appear throughout the scriptures as the shepherding of suffering persons.

These six dimensions—healing, reconciling, sustaining, confronting, guiding, and informing—are to be woven together in the care and counseling approach to adolescents in crisis. For the sake of clarity, these dimensions will be analyzed separately; however, in practice one can hardly label a particular response to a change or crisis as *only* sustaining or *only* confronting or *only* guiding. One of these dimensions may dominate, but the others remain. Caring for teens in transition and crisis reflects some of all six dimensions. The shepherding approach assists teenagers to face crisis and to experience the richness and fullness of a holistic relationship to themselves, to their environment, and to the future because of the hope they find in God.

Dimensions of Shepherding

A brief definition of the six dimensions of a shepherding relationship builds a foundation for a discussion of their interrelatedness. Think of how each of these might be visible in your relationships with the teens in your life:

- *Healing* is a process of assisting persons to move toward wholeness, especially in the light of the brokenness brought about by crisis.
- *Reconciling* is a process of assisting persons to move toward restoring wholeness in broken or strained relationships with those who constitute their social environment.

- *Sustaining* is a process of supporting persons by standing by them and bearing burdens with them while responding to the crisis.
- *Confronting* is a process of moving against the thoughts, feelings, assumptions, or behavioral patterns of persons in response to the crisis.
- *Guiding* is a process of assisting persons to make decisions by drawing from within them what was potentially available in their own decision making.
- *Informing* is a process of clarifying alternatives for persons by providing specific new information and data.

Reconciling and Healing

The foundational question in a shepherding response to a teen in crisis involves a polarity between reconciling and healing. What is the goal? The parent, teacher, minister, or counselor holds healing and reconciliation in dynamic tension and responds by suggesting the possibility of both. Although healing is the ultimate goal for the individual in crisis, reconciling is the primary objective for the individual's relationships to others in the crisis. We want them to get well and get back into healthy relationships with others.

Healing means seeking to find a sense of wellness in the teenager's sense of self. Both healing and reconciling carry biblical significance as a perspective for relationships. The four Gospels record twenty-six cases, excluding the parallels, of individuals who were healed by Jesus. The language of salvation itself blends with the language of healing throughout the New Testament. Jesus frequently intertwined the dimensions of physical healing and personal wholeness or salvation in his ministry. For instance, as he healed the palsied man who was lowered through the roof in the midst of the crowd (Mark 2:1–2), Jesus performed the healing miracle there as a prerequisite for the faith necessary for healing *and* salvation. Also in the epistles, Paul's work in healing supports the view of the early Christians that physical and spiritual wholeness are interwoven.

Adults concerned with healing and reconciliation with adolescents in crisis are cautioned to avoid two common errors. On the one hand, adults might inappropriately push the question of the adolescent's relationship to God in a way that angers the adolescent enough to break the caring relationship.

On the other hand, we need to avoid the assumption that no examination of faith is appropriate. A crisis will raise questions of one's faith stance (particularly in reflecting). One girl asked if her parents' divorce because of infidelity meant that what they had taught her about God was somehow invalidated. Another blamed God for allowing her to be molested by a teacher. A young man decided to embrace satanic readings after he was physically abused by his stepfather. Ultimate questions for reflection come after the crisis has passed its critical point and will focus around one's relationships, around one's view of self, and around the future. All involve a theological dimension. Relationship to the self begins with a belief in the goodness (or the evil) of creation and continues with understanding the meaning of redemption and incarnation. The relationship to self is ultimately asked: "Am I a person of worth, created in the image of God, loved by God, and therefore of value?" Questions about relationships are basically faith queries: "Can one's environment be trusted? Are the powers of light able to sustain the battle against the powers of darkness?" The response of persons of faith is that "the light shines in the darkness, and the darkness has not overcome it" (John 1:5). Facing one's environment is ultimately a question of faith. Facing the future is fundamentally a question of hope. The foundation of hope from a religious perspective is in the working of a Being greater than all personhood, but it is not devoid of the responsibility of persons and the goodness of persons. Although shepherds are cautioned against prematurely and inappropriately pushing religious questions into a crisis situation, they must also be cautioned not to ignore the impact of faith questions on the response to the crisis.

Healing of the teenager, a primary goal, cannot be understood apart from reconciliation with one's environment. No youth can be whole and remain isolated from meaningful relationships. Crises can result from broken relationships, but more frequently crises *produce* broken relationships.

Reconciliation, a major theme of Christian scripture, is a process of restoring broken or strained relationships between persons, individuals, and God. Reconciliation is bridge building over the troubled waters of crisis. Reconciliation is the caring adult's response to the teenager's disunity and brokenness. The incarnation has at its heart reconciling persons to God. Paul appeals for reconciliation many times but most notably in the dispute over the different spiritual gifts (1 Cor. 12:21–26). Reconciliation attempts to assist adolescents to see their place in the family, with their peers, at school, and in society at large, and to equip them to live in growing, mutually enhancing relationships.

Reconciliation is more than "shaking it off" with a casual comment. It involves awareness of the brokenness, confession of one's own participation in the brokenness, however large or small that might seem, and the giving and receiving of forgiveness. Sometimes a ritual of acceptance such as the verbal pronouncement of a blessing on the adolescent serves as a powerful symbol of reconciliation in times of crisis. However, most often a hug, a handshake, a gift, or a shared moment of laughter becomes the unlabeled ritual of reconciliation.

Sustaining and Confronting

Healing the self and reconciling with the environment remain in tension as the shepherd responds to a crisis. Two relationship stances can be taken toward both healing and reconciliation. They are confronting and sustaining. In the proper context, confrontation may lead to healing and reconciling. At other times, sustaining may be the avenue to healing and reconciling. These two stances must also be held in dynamic tension. When do we hold them in comfort, and when do we confront them with a "hold on there" attitude?

Confronting means speaking out against the teen's thoughts, feelings, values, or actions. Like healing and reconciling, confronting and sustaining are biblical models for shepherding. Confronting is the application of "the law," whereas sustaining is more an "expression of grace." Confronting occurs throughout the scriptures and can mean moving against the environment as well as against a person's assumptions, thoughts, feelings, or behavioral patterns. The prophets spoke boldly, not only to individuals, as in the confrontation of King David for his involvement with Bathsheba, but also to environments, as the prophets Jeremiah and Amos spoke to the culture of their time.

Furthermore, in Matthew's Gospel, Jesus provides a model for confronting. In Matthew 18:15–22, the disciples are instructed to confront a "brother" if they feel wronged. Jesus confronted not only individuals but also the culture of his time, seeking reconciliation between individuals and their environment. You can see as Jesus speaks to oppressed and persecuted persons (such as the woman taken in adultery) that he seeks reconciliation in the environment. Paul, reflecting upon this ministry, writes in Galatians 3:28 that in Christ there is no male or female, no Jew or Greek, no bond or free. Confrontation has its ultimate goal—total reconciliation and healing.

Parents, teachers, and ministers must be careful to note that the authority of confrontation does not come from one's own personality and perceived superior ability but from one's role and personal integrity. Authority in confrontation means more as a representative of something larger than one's self. We must take care not to risk rejecting individuals through unrealistic private confrontations. Ultimately, the confrontation should be such that persons feel they have encountered a truth larger than themselves. The truth of confrontation produces hope and respect when shared in the context of love.

Sustaining means supporting the teen's thoughts, feelings, actions, or values. Sustaining exists in dynamic tension with confrontation as the fourth shepherding dimension. Sustaining, like confrontation, is an approach of bringing wholeness to a self and reconciliation to the environment. Sustaining consists in supporting persons by standing by them in their quests for healing and reconciliation. Understanding, feeling with, and accepting an individual moves them toward wholeness and is at the heart of the sustaining process.

The sustaining aspect of shepherding is also seen throughout the Old and New Testaments. God is with the bewildered and lost slaves in Egypt and sustains them in their pilgrimage through the wilderness as they move toward their future. Galatians 6:2 instructs us to "bear one another's burdens." Sustaining, a continuing process of seeking to preserve hope, encourages self-acceptance. In the face of a crisis, adolescents sometimes overgeneralize and magnify problems out of proportion. Sustaining teens as individuals maintains a degree of self-respect and hope.

In a time of crisis, sustaining the environment may also be needed. The adolescent's parents, siblings, extended family, peers, teachers, and others all need a word of encouragement during a crisis. The shepherd advocates for the adolescent, thus sustaining efforts toward reconciliation.

Confronting and sustaining are maintained in tension without either excluding the other from the context of shepherding. Wayne Oates, the minister who coined the word "workaholic," used the analogy of hand surgery in discussing his approach to shepherding. Early surgeons would literally hold the hand of the patient in one hand while performing the surgery with the other hand. The underneath hand symbolizes the sustaining, while the hand with the surgical instrument represents the confrontation. Both are necessary.

In a team approach to adolescent ministry, it is not unusual for some members to take a confronting, hard-line, maintain-the-rules, "stop and think" approach to a given adolescent in crisis, whereas other members of the team take a supportive, understanding, "I'm-your-friend" approach. These representations of law and grace are easier to make when a team is responding to the crisis. Parents, teachers, ministers, and counselors will need clear communication to coordinate such efforts. A single caregiver cannot easily maintain the tension between confronting and sustaining as the process of responding to a youth in crisis unfolds.

Guiding and Informing

A third set of shepherding polarities, guiding and informing, are similarly to be held in tension. Both guiding and informing are ways of confronting or sustaining. An attempt to provide new information produces confrontation. At other times, guiding the person's thoughts and reflections leads to self-confrontation. Likewise, in sustaining individuals, informing will be the approach at times. In other situations, guiding individuals to examine their own thoughts and reflections will lead to sustaining.

Guiding—the process of helping persons discover within themselves the resources for making decisions—involves reflection upon thoughts, feelings, attitudes, and behaviors. Adolescents in particular may need assistance in differentiating between their thoughts, feelings, and attitudes. *Feeling Good: The New Mood Therapy,* by David Burns, provides excellent information on the process of examining and differentiating thoughts, feelings, and attitudes. Guiding is an integral part of shepherding when choices are discovered by the person in crisis and examined in light of potential outcomes. In direct contrast to guiding, informing brings information from outside the individual to bear upon confrontation and sustaining.

Like confronting, sustaining, reconciling, and healing, guiding finds a foundation in scripture. Guiding is seen throughout the Old Testament, where both the prophets and the priests proclaim and teach the word of God in hope of a response from their listeners. Furthermore, as Jesus talks with the accusers about to stone the woman taken in adultery, he draws out of them the criteria for making their decision. In John 8:7 he demands, "Let him who is without sin among you be the first to throw a stone." As the hearers reflect on the implications of his statement, they turn one at a time to leave. They have been guided in the process of making their own decision, but never directly told what to do.

Informing, a process of clarifying alternatives by providing specific new information, provides hope for a way out of the crisis. Teenagers do not know resources and procedures for finding the help they need. Parents, teachers, ministers, and counselors can supply relevant data and open new channels for recovery (healing or reconciling). For example, adolescents might need a list of free counseling services in the community or a resource book on "How to . . ." They might need to know the facts about sexually transmitted diseases, smoking, alcohol, or drugs. They just may need help in anger management, communication styles, managing money, or a host of other informational topics.

Informing also has a broad foundation in scripture. In Isaiah 40:28–31, the prophet questions his listeners: "Have you not known? Have you not heard? The LORD is the everlasting God. . . . He does not faint or grow weary. . . . Even youths shall faint and be weary, . . . but they who wait for the LORD shall renew their strength, they shall mount up with wings like eagles, they shall run and not be weary, they shall walk and not faint." This information is provided as a form of sustaining individuals and their environment in a time of crisis. In the New Testament we see an example of informing as a means of sustaining individuals and confronting their time of grief when Paul, writing to the church at Thessalonica (1 Thess. 4:16), addresses their concern for family members and friends who have died before Christ's return. Their grief over the loss is both confronted and sustained by Paul as he writes, "The dead in Christ will rise first." The shepherding response of informing involves input of new data. Sometimes a teen just needs a clear, wise, direct explanation of how things work in the real world.

Informing has long been a part of the work of teachers and parents. However, ministers and counselors can also provide basic, practical information to teenagers. The good shepherd leads the sheep to find the truth. Perhaps in the way questions are asked, information voids can be revealed and appropriate responses made. For example, a young man in a substance-abuse crisis can be asked about the substance's effects; then information can be provided if he does not have accurate data. Informing may also focus on the consequences of behavior and pointing adolescents toward information from other resources that can be applied in a particular crisis.

In some ways, adolescents are better off today than ever before. They have better resources in their schools. They are offered more exciting youth-focused church programs. Today's youth spend more discretionary money to enjoy movies, music, and the magic of an automobile. They are healthy, drug use is down a bit, smoking is down, and more youth go on to college. However, new, pressing crises haunt the lives of numerous teenagers. There are plenty of problems to go around. The gap between the bright and the dropouts is widening. Parents witness more rebellion. Technology brings new promises but offers new problems.

When parents, teachers, ministers, and counselors work together with community leaders, they can address the problem areas of today's youth, provide comprehensive preventative programs, and offer wide-ranging helping services. In some communities, parents organize and take the initiative to coordinate responses to adolescents in crisis. Other areas have schools or churches taking the lead. A few localities have extensive services offered by health care and government agencies. In some communities, like

Littleton and Paducah, parents, schools, churches, counselors, and agencies are working together to address the needs of teenagers in crisis. Shepherding is a primary model for bringing wholeness to individual teens and reconciliation to their environment. Our goal in shepherding is healing and reconciling. Our interventions might involve sustaining, confronting, guiding, and informing. As we work together, we can assist teenagers in crisis to reach higher ground and greener pastures.

Chapter 2

Understanding
Developmental Issues and Crises

*T*eenagers come in all sizes, shapes, and styles. How do you know if your teens are basically normal? Take a wide view of the modern adolescent scene. Teens reinvent their fads almost annually. Teenagers have similar pathways of development, but unique ways of traveling those pathways. They face common physical changes during puberty, but demonstrate distinctive self-adaptations and social reactions to those changes. They confront predictable family struggles for independence, but cope with these in radically diverse behaviors. They meet common academic challenges, but deal with school in incredibly different fashions. They meet head-on with new philosophical and faith questions, but they support or reject religion with numerous approaches. They encounter numerous challenges (driving, dating, working, etc.), but with varied amounts of success and distress.

Adolescence, a recent development, reflects the long-drawn-out time needed to prepare for independent living. Ancient peoples went directly from childhood into adulthood. The concept of adolescence as a prolonged transition between childhood and adulthood does not appear in ancient writings. Children receive focused attention; however, after puberty persons are addressed as young men and women. Adolescence as a psychosocial moratorium between childhood and adulthood appears to be a relatively recent concept. It arises from the increased occupational demands for more advanced skills during the rise of capitalism and the industrial revolution (Anthony, p. 318). A lack of well-defined periods of adolescence in some undeveloped and primitive societies calls into question the assumption that adolescents are tied primarily to biological changes. Teens have adult bodies and expanded brains, but they have no adult roles. As one adolescent researcher proclaimed, they are all grown up with no place to go (Elkind, p. 3).

The period of adolescence begins earlier and lasts longer for many of today's young people. Ten-, eleven-, and twelve-year-olds often feel pushed into dating and attending parties and social functions that were once reserved for teenagers. This creates a stage of preadolescence, when children aren't permitted to be children but are rushed into teen activities. Fourth- and fifth-graders are experimenting with sex, alcohol, pot, and violence. One twelve-year-old boldly told me, "I have a right to kill somebody if they mess with me." Parents often wait too long to discuss handling anger, to begin sex education, and to discuss substance-abuse issues. Preadolescents are frequently experimenting with danger and tearing at the apron strings in an attempt to be free from control.

At the other end of adolescence, many adults in their early twenties remain dependent on their parents and have trouble leaving the protection, care, and comfort of parental support. Parents of overly dependent, early-twenties children fret over getting them "out of the nest." My social research focuses primarily on thirteen- to nineteen-year-olds, but my counseling includes children, teens, and young adults. Role and relationships, not age, define adolescence. Parents are advised to treat each child according to her or his rate of development, not age expectations. Some eighteen-year-olds are not ready to make responsible decisions away from home. Perhaps they should live at home and work or commute to college. Some seventeen-year-olds can function and care for themselves. Adjust the freedom and support according to the level of responsibility.

Although adolescence represents a term of delayed adulthood, it also provides an opportunity for personality growth, expanded education, and social development. The building blocks of personality such as trust, autonomy, initiative, and industry become set during childhood. Work attitudes, intimacy styles, and self-image normally grow naturally through the teen years. However, adolescence represents a second chance for teens to revisit earlier, childhood issues and then reach mature development (Derek Miller, *Adolescence,* p. 436). This chance comes at a time of major cognitive advancements and greatly increased verbal skills. Recently, *Newsweek* reported on MRI research that shows that puberty brings actual brain growth. A neuronal growth spurt is followed by a loss of circuits that are not used (Begley, p. 58). In the early teens, sudden change may be triggered by new brain cells.

You will be familiar with the teen developmental process (having experienced it), but a brief review is provided here, along with considerations for each stage's impact on typical crisis needs. Parents get surprised with their first teenager's changes and are shocked that those of the teen's siblings are so different. Teachers soon learn the patterns of their grade level; however, new issues arise almost monthly. Ministers know the teens that attend their place of worship, but may be bewildered by other groups. Counselors understand troubled teens, but may not be as tuned in with other adolescents. Physical, emotional, intellectual, family, social, and spiritual dynamics join in distinctive patterns during each period of adolescence.

Preadolescence

Not all ten- to twelve-year-olds enter this preadolescent stage. Children who act like teenagers but have not begun puberty fall into this grouping. Frequently they copy adolescents on television and adopt oppositional attitudes toward parents, teachers, and ministers. They have not yet experienced the physical changes; however, they think and act like early teenagers. Of course, some youth do experience physical changes before the age of thirteen. Often these early teens are in conflicted relationships with at least one parent. Sometimes the parents have not provided enough structure, limits, rules, and guidance. Other preadolescents follow older siblings or peers into the adolescent culture ahead of their time.

Changes

Preadolescence begins with a change in focus on appearance, social relationships, and independence. The main **physical changes** are external. They dress like the teens they admire. They may change their hair and their jewelry, and desire to wear makeup. A few beg for a "first piercing." Some choose to go "grunge," whereas others opt for a "prep" appearance. They want to give the impression of being teenagers. Parents will want to discuss these changes and gently guide early experimentation with teen appearances. There will be time enough for testing the limits after puberty assaults their glands.

Preadolescents want attention. Their actions may signal a need for more time with parents. **Emotional changes** focus on increased frustration with parents, growing concerns for social activities, and a preoccupation with sexual excitement. They may become resentful about parental supervision of parties and may even attack the basic family rules. Elementary school parties can become too much pressure for them. They worry over not being invited or not being liked by the right people. Some preadolescents seek sexual knowledge from the wrong places. They turn to porn and older teens. Parents, ministers, counselors, and teachers should provide clear, accurate, and complete sex education opportunities for them that includes more than biological information. Discuss the emotional, cultural, and relational aspects of males and females. Teach them about their feelings.

The **intellectual changes** for these teenage wanna-bes reflect a shift in attitude toward education. Some push too hard and attempt to become super students. They dream of becoming the next outstanding scientist, poet, or broadcaster. Others lose focus and begin to devalue learning. They daydream of instant fame as a renowned teen-band star, a legendary movie superstar, a notorious x-game hero, or a celebrated model. Parents and teachers need to work together to maintain a healthy, balanced approach to learning. For the most part, preadolescents still lack the capacity for abstract thinking and cannot reflect on the reality of their dreams. They need to build effective work habits and productive study routines. Their job is to learn how to learn.

Social changes for preadolescents may be painful. They become insecure about acceptance and easily misinterpret a friend's actions as rejection. They want to hang out at the mall with older kids, but might be ridiculed and excluded. These "big children" want the social freedom of older adolescents, but lack the ability to cope with the pressures. New friends might be less known to their parents. A sense of discomfort may grow between childhood friends who segregate on issues of social inclusion. There is often a reshuffling of friendship groups. Painful exclusions often outnumber thrilling new relationships. Regularly these pretend-teens express loneliness, fear, and frustration. They need clear rules and close supervision as they venture into the jungle of adolescent social organization.

Faith changes are usually not internal for this group. Ten- and eleven-year-olds lack the reflective ability for philosophical questioning. For them faith is commonly a matter of following the rules and living up to parental expectations. They tire of the rules and lack the abstract thinking to view religion intuitively. This preadolescent crowd habitually scoffs at the rules and delights in shocking parents and ministers with talk about not needing religion. They know what to say to get a response of distress. Patiently listen to their questions and doubts. Become their friend and demonstrate mature faith in your relationship to them. Lecturing may not help, but providing case studies and "what if" situations might affect their stance toward faith issues.

Crisis Issues

Preadolescents can have major crises. Two of the shooters in the rash of school shootings during the late nineties were preadolescents. Take rebellion and threats seriously, even from preteens. Their biggest need is for more structure and adult involvement in their lives. They need the reassurance that grown-ups still care for them. Too much freedom is read as not showing an interest in them. School uniforms appear to reduce discipline problems for this group.

Preadolescents also need structured activities, groups of friends, a forum for questioning issues, and a rationale for learning at school. Planned, organized activities give them a forum for relating. Organized sports, music groups, formal hobbies, and school clubs provide organization for relationships to grow. Too much free time leaves these children bored and looking for excitement outside of normal limits. Friendship constellations band together for reinforcement. Parents need to support gatherings of buddies by providing transportation, time, and a safe place to congregate. These older children acting like teens are often brighter than average. They may have serious questions and real concerns. Stop and listen to their responses. Although their outbursts may seem harsh and even disrespectful at times, they provide an avenue for productive discussions. Often these youngsters are trying to find affirmation and answers in nonconforming ways. They get upset and act out when an outburst does not produce real concern in their parents. Premature rebellion is not just kids' play. Take it seriously!

Early Adolescence

Early adolescence, usually the period of twelve through fourteen years of age, may begin slightly earlier for girls than for boys. It begins with puberty and is a time of rapid physical change and relationship adjustments. This is easier to note for girls because their menstrual cycles begin. Boys may become sexually mature, and the parents do not notice. Alert parents take note of the changes and notice even the subtle alterations. Caring adults can provide both reassurance and freedom for these "ill at ease" teens.

Changes

Early adolescence, introduced formally by the onset of puberty, demands adjustment to a multitude of resulting **physical changes.** Both girls and boys are likely to experience uneven spurts of growth. Their sexual organs mature, and body hair begins to appear. These changes bring a sense of awkwardness and lack of graceful movement. Boys sometimes have difficulty accepting their new body image, and girls may react with either shyness or pride. It is not uncommon for both boys and girls to experience an increase in appetite, perhaps resulting in chubbiness for those who do not get enough exercise. Parents and teachers should encourage physical activity, artistic training, academic preparation, and spiritual inquiry. Ministers need to create an openness to questioning of faith issues and practices. Sensitive counselors will include physical, artistic, academic, and spiritual dimensions in assessment models and in ongoing conversations during treatment.

Because girls may develop somewhat more quickly, they are likely to be taller than the boys. This can create new envy on the part of the boys and confusion in the relationships between boys and girls. Chemical changes in the body are likely to lead to acne or other skin problems, which add to concerns about peer acceptance. Attention to cleanliness and body odor will need to be increased. Social acceptance relates to body image. Tall, muscular boys and thin girls are more highly valued and rewarded in Western society. Caring adults are wise to promote tolerance and acceptance at this age. Remind them that in a few years their bodies will be different again. That ninety-pound weakling might be the captain of the team in three years. Pushing teens can lead to compulsive exercising or even eating disorders. Maintain balance.

These physical developments precipitate a multitude of **emotional changes.** Basically, early adolescents react to chemical and physical changes by being on an emotional roller coaster. They go from sullen withdrawal, despondence, and vegetation to excitement, angry outburst, and hyperactivity for no apparent reason. One girl lamented, "I never know how I will feel by the end of the day. It is as if my body has a mind of its own." Although body adjustments are expected, emotional change is more often tied to confusion around role changes. Their relationships with their parents are shifting, their relationships to their own bodies are changing, and their relationships with their peers undergo transformations. Junior high and middle school introduce a new world of self-directed learning, changing classes, and shifting friendships. All of this can lead to self-doubt, negative thoughts, and depression.

Depression in early adolescents is difficult to assess because of their natural mood swings. They can be down for no real reason. Early adolescents may find warmth and intimacy difficult as they pull back from the parent of the opposite sex and awkwardly befriend the parent of the same sex. Younger juveniles often have difficulty handling angry feelings, which surface because of a multitude of unmet expectations, disappointments, embarrassments, and perceived attacks on their self-images. They need coaching in facing fears and handling anger. One mother complained that her thirteen-year-old could erupt over any little disappointment. "She won't take 'No' for an answer," she moaned.

While these physical and emotional changes are taking place, a number of **intellectual changes** are also occurring. Early adolescents move out of the concrete stage and into what the noted psychologist Jean Piaget has called "informal operations." Basically, early adolescents are beginning to differentiate between opposites and to understand gradations of meaning. They will see not only the positive and negative but also many alternatives on a variety of issues. They can see the gray areas between the black and white thinking of children. They are capable of understanding principles of substitution and reciprocity as characterized mathematically by the understanding of algebra and socially by understanding the complexities of their social, family, and political environments.

Nevertheless, little of this ability gets applied. They seem unable to plan their time, to organize complex tasks, or to demonstrate much self-control. Their instability has long been attributed to hormonal surges, but Dr. Jay Giedd of the National Institute of Mental Health reported in 2000 that growth of new brain tissue may indeed be responsible for the instability in thinking for younger teens (Begley, p. 58). Dr. Elizabeth Sowell of UCLA's Lab of Neuro Imaging believes that indeed the adolescent brain undergoes dynamic changes much later than we had thought (Ibid., p. 59). What may seem like not paying attention and outright mutiny may be the brain in transformation and expansion. The adolescent brain grows new cells, and that causes thinking problems for a while.

As might be expected, these physical, emotional, and intellectual changes interact to bring about a number of **social changes.** The early adolescent's relationship to family, teachers, peers, and other adults undergoes sweeping changes. While the early adolescent is still physically dependent on his or her family, a dramatic shift toward dependence on peers for emotional reinforcement begins. Teachers and ministers become major players in the young teenager's world. Family is still the primary determinant of moral values and is responsible for setting limits. However, this is a desirable time for the family to begin shifting the responsibility of setting limits from the parents to the adolescent. The family's values, structures, and rules have been a type of shell around the developing offspring. Limits, like the shell of a lobster, protected the child. Transferring the setting of limits to the young person means removing the shell and developing an internal, moral skeletal system. Parents are encouraged to discuss decisions more openly with young adolescents and to anticipate some input from them about limit setting. For example, curfews will still need to be set by the parents, but in dialogue with the young person. Parents will find that at social gatherings their offspring want more independence.

Early adolescent peer relationships also begin to undergo a transformation. Although most stay primarily in groups of the same sex, some heterosexual pairing off begins. If this does not receive adequate supervision and guidance, sexual crises can arise when emotions and temptations get out of control. On the other hand, if there is not enough opportunity for heterosexual relationships to develop, some adolescents will begin to rebel. "Latch-key" youth with too little supervision are prime candidates for sexual crises, like the fourteen-year-old who told of being made pregnant in her home after school by a nineteen-year-old neighbor.

Early adolescents need responsible peer groups to begin providing opportunities to develop independence from their parents. These groups need supervision by other adults and are likely to be the source of affirmation, education, and new questions. Early adolescents need opportunities to relate to these adults (coaches, teachers, ministers, etc.). Obviously, these relationships need to be characterized by responsibility on the part of these adults, who reinforce the parents' authority but also provide opportunities for young people to ventilate their pent-up emotions, question parental viewpoints, and begin the formation of personal authority.

Changes in the **faith development** of early adolescents begin as they question the borrowed faith from their childhood, which was primarily comprised of a list of hero stories, unexamined assumptions, and rules to be followed. They gain information about new areas of moral choices, find their own role models, and test the old rules. Early adolescents need education in a variety of moral values as they move from a rules-keeping ethic to an ethic of justice and love in the areas of substance abuse, relationships, world hunger, ecology, internet use, shoplifting, and general interpersonal morality. Early adolescents still find the locus of authority for their belief system in their parents and ministers. However, they will be keenly aware of any inconsistencies in the thinking of these persons and will be personally damaged by any lapses in moral behavior that they perceive in the lives of their authority figures. The early adolescent's faith takes on a personalized dimension. Hope becomes a new friend for combating depression. Faith becomes less the practice of habits and more a matter of personal experience of the Holy. The circle of expression of love is expanded to include persons outside of one's own social circle. However, sin is still primarily seen as breaking the rules or not keeping one's promises.

Crisis Issues

Having considered these developmental issues, let us say by way of summary that early adolescents need a sense of **positive self-identification** in the face of the changes brought on by puberty. They need avenues of success in their social encounters, physical activities, and intellectual endeavors. They need the support of both parents as caring adults in finding these moments of success. Well-adjusted early adolescents develop an expanded sense of appreciation for humor and celebration, especially in their religious activities. They need religious and educational spaces to celebrate and to let down their hair, so to speak. Teens deserve room to grow and freedom to explore their new ideas.

Early adolescents are also beset by a multitude of eruptive **developmental crises** that come from within themselves. For instance, early adolescents would experience anxiety from a reshuffling of their peer group. They might consider it a crisis the first time they were aware of the full force of their anger toward their own parents. They might experience it as a crisis if they were ahead or behind their peer group in physical or psychosocial development. They need permission to discuss these changes and find support for the persons they are becoming. They need forgiveness for awkward mistakes and impulsive outbursts in the family system. Some rigid parents mistake this growth as disrespect. Others get tired and disengage too soon. Some early adolescents have so little family, peer, and other adult support that they are besieged by a number of emergencies. A recent national study by the YMCA reported that the number one complaint of twelve- to fifteen-year-olds was "not enough time with their parents" (Parent and Teen Study, April 2000).

Obviously, early adolescents would perceive the death of a parent, an accident to themselves, the divorce of their parents, or a forced move to a new school as a **disruptive crisis**. In such times, early adolescents especially need information about the crisis, a sustaining environment characterized by hope, and avenues of forgiveness for real or imaginary guilt. Younger teens need parents, teachers, ministers, and counselors who offer a supportive relationship that encourages the discussion of uncomfortable questions. They warrant access to adequate sources of information and counseling. They need permission to speak of previously taboo topics. Also, early adolescents in a time of crisis deserve concrete information about their situations and future plans. They ought to be included in discussions about the years ahead. They want a voice in major decisions.

Although early adolescents need opportunities to participate in personal and family decisions, they need the reassurance that their parents are still in charge. Limits signal security. If their parents are not present, youngsters need the reassurance of knowing who *will* be in charge. Perhaps a caregiver in crisis intervention will be the only person who looks out for an early teen's well-being. Different teens need varied amounts of freedom and limits at school. Finding schools and teachers who match their needs ensures opportunities for learning. Finding appropriate places of worship encourages faith growth.

Middle Adolescence

Middle adolescence usually encompasses fifteen through seventeen years of age. It is a time of expansion, independence, and experimentation. Teens start to question and rebel in major ways. Middle adolescents are characterized by continuing physiological changes, independent thinking, and the questioning of authority. They venture into new, expanding, adventurous peer relationships. The dependent, shy ones may feel further isolated from peers and slip into depression and/or anger.

Changes

Like early adolescence, middle adolescence often occurs earlier in American girls than in boys. Some researchers suggest a lack of meaningful contact with the father as a contributing factor; in societies where both father and mother participate in child rearing, boys and girls mature at the same rate. Middle adolescence, a time of experimentation with ideas, feelings, and behaviors, brings an expansion of social relationships.

The **physical characteristics** of middle adolescence involve fewer abrupt changes, but a general expansion of physiological development consolidates a unique body image. Teens may experiment with strange clothes, tattoos, or body piercing. For most, care for the body in terms of cleanliness, exercise, and diet reflects a new concern for self-image. A few give up and don't care how they look. Generally, as an adolescent develops a positive body image, a healthy overall self-image grows. However, dangers exist for those who become obsessed with body type. Eating disorders are also a common teen crisis and are not easily hidden. Lack of self-care may reflect a dislike for self or indicate depression.

Adolescent females' preoccupation with thinness often leads to bulimia or anorexia (see Chapter 10). A desire to become extremely thin can distort one's self-perception and degenerate into a compulsive effort to lose too much weight. Girls who do not eat properly can retard their normal body growth. However, they apparently return to their growth rate when proper diet is resumed. Boys may become compulsive about muscle building and turn to steroids. This can lead to psychological disturbances and uncontrolled aggression. A balanced concern for growth expands interest from weight lifting to exercising and general body conditioning. Traditionally, girls concentrate on aerobic classes, running, or swimming, and boys choose jogging, pumping iron, and competing in sports with their peers. However, both sexes can now turn to a variety of physical exercises.

Middle teens develop almost adult bodies with new, powerful sexual urges. Peer groups seem to re-form, differentiating those who become sexually active from those who do not. Estimates vary widely, but from 30–75 percent of middle adolescents are likely to be sexually active, which sets them at danger for a number of crises, including pregnancy, sexually transmitted diseases (STDs), emotional rejection, abuse, rape, and homosexuality. Date rape accounts for most cases of rape. New odorless, tasteless drugs can render a teen defenseless and open to sexual attacks.

Furthermore, middle adolescence is a time of expanding **emotional development** that brings new depths of depression, anger, and anxiety. These are likely to develop alongside the social freedom that comes to middle adolescents. They also soar to new levels of excitement, joy, love, and happiness. Some live to party. The fluctuating highs and lows of early adolescence commonly stabilize in middle adolescence. However, there is an increased danger of sustained levels of depression. They may contemplate suicide. Not only does the intensity of negative emotions increase in middle adolescence; the range of those feelings expands. These confusing emotions relate to an expanded social involvement and new areas of experimentation. "I've never felt this way before" is a frequent complaint of bewildered middle teens. For the first time, they deal with new levels of sexual excitement, temptation, guilt, and perhaps even shame.

Time and again middle teens grumble about being lonely. Those who lack sustained care also develop new levels of fear. The loss of their earlier blind trust and a few bad experiences open their eyes to a multitude of dangers. Frequently, in their attempts to avoid negative emotions, adolescents will become chronically busy and form cliques for security. Some turn to the great escapes of alcohol, drugs, and partying. A few might develop hallucinations and fantasies to escape the agony and pain of their emotional conflict and turmoil. Although hallucinations might be drug related or very early psychotic signals, many are conversion reactions; that is, they develop as a block to any activity that produces uncontrolled anxiety. For example, a person who fears the temptation of peeking into windows may become functionally blind. A teen who fears a particular temptation may become immobilized by hallucinations.

Adolescents in this expanding time tend to think of themselves as the centers of their emotional worlds. They will be most concerned with what brings pleasure to them and will demonstrate only a limited capacity for sacrificing their own pleasure for the pleasure of others or for the benefit of their families or communities. Much of the motivation comes from a philosophy of "If it feels good, I want to try it." They attempt to avoid boredom at all costs. However, they need more than entertainment; they need challenges at deeper emotional levels. Teachers and ministers can help by providing stimulating programs. They still need clear, perhaps written, parental rules. Most can handle expanded freedom and deserve more trust.

Middle-adolescent thought patterns and **intellectual processing** are also in an expansive mode. Middle adolescents are more likely to have moved further away from concrete thinking into abstractions. They are able to think symbolically and give new meaning to their world and to their faith. Middle adolescents who continue to mature are less impulsive about decisions and can compare their views and conclusions to the responses of others. This new ability to think critically about alternatives and issues can be a positive resource for dealing with crises. A simple process of (1) differentiating problems so that each problem can be defined, (2) generating alternatives, (3) assessing the probable personal impact of each alternative, and (4) deciding on a plan of action aids many adolescents in developmental and emergency crises. Middle adolescents will be able to handle this process and seek less advice from their caregivers than will early adolescents. However, middle adolescents are egocentric; they still think more in terms of the effect of a crisis on themselves than on others, although this is not as pronounced as in childhood and early adolescence.

Middle adolescents also think in the present. Because they perceive time as moving slowly (a month is a long time), they fail to evaluate long-range effects of their decisions. Because of their increased capacity for critical and reflective thinking, middle adolescents are likely to challenge inconsistencies and injustices in their family, school, work, peer, and church environments. Although they are not as idealistic as late adolescents, they still tend to think in terms of *what* is right as well as *who* is right. Depressed youth can be naturally expected to focus their perceptions on themselves and to suffer an increase in cognitive distortions. Some stop trying at school and cut classes frequently. A few will think about dropping out of school. They need parents who push them to get an education or job training. Teachers of this age group should assist them to learn at some level. The true challenge is to get them interested, confident, and focused.

Middle adolescence is a time of expanded **social activities** and a further weakening of parental ties. As middle adolescents develop new friends, they pull farther away from the family group. They will spend much of their time with the peer group and will bring frustration to adults who try to maintain family time together. Parents who themselves are caught up in a hectic pace may be relieved by their children's lack of demands on their time and be lured into a false sense of security that their offspring no longer need them. Parents have to find time for these teenagers or loose them to "the world." Middle adolescents will have frequent sibling squabbles with younger children at home as they attempt to differentiate themselves from the family structure. Middle adolescents begin to develop relationships with other adult family members and nonfamily mentors. In settings where the extended family still lives in close proximity, aunts, uncles, older cousins, and grandparents may serve as adult friends who assist in beginning the movement away from the nest.

However, because of the rapid mobility of Western society, many young people do not have the luxury of extended family members who live nearby. Therefore, the middle adolescent must turn to the community or the church family to find a role model. This may be a coach, youth minister, teacher, counselor, a friend's parent, or a neighbor. Young people who have no positive mentor are prime targets for pushers, pimps, and perhaps gangs. A positive adult relationship serves as a transition object during detachment from the family and attachment to the external world. Parents need to bless their middle adolescent's friendship with an appropriate and respected adult. It is time to trust them with responsible adults.

Because of their new ability to think critically and to reflect on inconsistencies, middle adolescents develop an expanded capacity for **faith experience.** They will ask new questions about the scriptures, about their own church's doctrine, about other faiths, and particularly about justice issues. They find themselves blaming God for what seems to be unfair events or crises in their lives. They may blame God for letting a parent lose a job or for the death of a friend in a car wreck. Usually they cannot verbalize these feelings toward God without the assistance of a caring minister, teacher, or counselor. However, they will act out by drawing back from church and by becoming less involved in religious activities. Ministers need to keep pace with the ever-changing adolescent world and take action to make the effort to keep youth programs meaningful and relevant. Put youth on planning committees and listen to their input.

Middle adolescents develop and build new faith rituals and examine new belief issues. They become interested in new musical experiences. They enjoy expressing faith through the music of their day. Churched middle adolescents may be fond followers of Christian rock groups and Christian radio stations. Some will join school clubs like the Fellowship of Christian

Athletes, which is also open to nonathletes. Those who are on the outside often long to be included but do not know how to begin. Others experiment with cults and quasi-religious groups. They need places to vent their feelings about traditional beliefs and to see what they do believe. I ask them to "invent" a religion by writing down what they believe and disbelieve. What would be their "Greatest Commandments"? The freedom to not believe a particular statement coupled with an invitation to explore their ideals often leads to new depths of faith.

Crisis Issues

In a time of crisis, middle adolescents have needs to be assessed that differ from those of early adolescence. Middle adolescents, like early adolescents, face both developmental and emergency crises. The needs vary, but focus around these experiences:

- Driving
- Dating
- Distancing

Several common **developmental crises** illustrate these needs. One common adjustment focuses on accepting responsibility for transportation and driving a car. Gaining the necessary knowledge, skills, and attitudes about responsibility for transportation is essential before an adolescent can take part in Western society. Most teenagers need more supervision and instruction on the safe use of an automobile. Auto accidents are the number one killer of youth.

Dating is also a typical middle-adolescent developmental adjustment that brings its special needs. Obviously, there is a need for understanding oneself sexually as male or female and for developing an informed, safe, and responsible attitude about one's sexuality. Dating brings new levels of intense joy, excitement, and affirmation, but it also provides an equal potential for new depths of grief, rejection, and pain. A lost boyfriend or girlfriend frequently causes adolescent thoughts of suicide. Parents, teachers, and ministers should offer dating education stories and information. Have clear guidelines, expectations, and rules. Provide specific instructions, such as (1) do not close the bedroom door when a date visits or (2) no members of the opposite sex should be in the house when parents are away. Counselors need to be informed about teen dating problems and center in on their relationship issues.

Distance from parents, a third developmental issue for middle adolescents, is understood in terms of freedom. Middle adolescents typically express this need in such statements as "Why can't my parents understand that I can think for myself and make decisions by myself? My parents need to know that I have a mind of my own; I'm not a baby any more." Parents who are too strict urge their strong children toward rebellion, while they nudge offspring of lesser ego strength into a premature foreclosure on a compliant identity. However, parents who provide few stable values and resist limit setting push teens into experimenting. Adolescents with good ego strength will be able to set limits for themselves, but those with weaker ego strength may fall off either end of a continuum. Some will become so anxious and frightened by freedom that they begin to deteriorate emotionally, whereas others will become so enamored of freedom that they act out behaviorally.

In addition to developmental crises, middle adolescents have unique needs in times of **emergency crisis.** The major emergencies for them are related to the following:

- Family
- Substance Abuse
- School
- Sex
- Depression
- Illnesses

If the family system deteriorates, middle adolescents will frequently blame themselves and grieve deeply. Grief over the end of their parents' marriage and unbearable self-blame, for example, may lead to acting out sexually, to attempting to escape into alcohol and drug abuse, or to hedonistic pleasure seeking. Physical abuse and sexual abuse increase during middle adolescence. They are more like adults and get mistreated—more often by stepparents than biological parents. Abuse must always be reported to the police or proper social service agency!

Addicted adolescents may need out-of-home placement or a substitute family while they are repairing the relationships with their own families. Those with substance-abuse problems, including food and eating disorders, need programs not only to assist them in getting off drugs, perhaps a residential treatment program, but also to assist them in learning to manage the negative thoughts and feelings that have led to such behavior. Substance abuse will be explored in more detail later.

Middle adolescents more frequently become behavior problems in school or in the neighborhood. They need firm but loving control and discipline by persons who have previously established a caring relationship. They benefit from programs of value clarification that stress internalizing the value system. They usually are not motivated by fear of external reprisals.

Middle adolescents may have sexual crises such as the fathering or conceiving of a child out of wedlock. A few express fears of being sexually abused by an adult (and not always outside the family). Although adolescents need room to find their own sexual values, they need enough education and guidance not to abuse or be abused sexually. Always report any sexual abuse!

For middle teens, depression may mean that medical treatment is needed. They respond well to a combination of counseling and medications. Take all suicide threats seriously and refer the teen for professional evaluation. This subject also receives detailed attention in Chapter 9.

In this time of expansion and exploration, middle adolescents need time and space to reflect and learn from their emergency crises. They need some system of forgiveness for their own mistakes and also an experience of grace that accepts their attempts to discover themselves. Although they must admit their mistakes, they need reassurance that they did not cause all their problems.

However, experimentation often leads to accidents and illness. Young people need good medical care, but, even more, they need a place to talk about major concerns. Their worries are more likely to be developmental and social than physical and death-related. For example, a fifteen-year-old boy, hospitalized for tests for meningitis, did not share his parents' anxiety about his health but was very concerned about what the hospitalization would mean for his chances to make the high school football team that fall. Teens need the opportunity and space to talk about the impact of an illness on the rest of their lives. Some become easily discouraged and give up on recovery. Their flip attitude works against getting better. Parents need to secure accurate medical information and share it with the teens. Ministers can be agents of faith, love, and hope. Teachers can make adjustments for students absent with illness or accidents. Peer visitation in the hospital is essential.

Faith issues for middle adolescents provide the time to reexamine their own faith systems from a depth perspective and to make decisions about the faith systems of their peers. They need opportunities to ask questions about other religious groups, including unusual sects. Usually these questions indicate that they are looking for authority in an idealized value system in the face of disillusionment in their own families and faith. One sixteen-year-old boy announced on the way home from church, "I stopped believing today!" He needed to explore his doubts. Parents, teachers, and youth ministers who organize mission projects and meaningful service hours sustain middle adolescents in their spiritual growth. This group wants a chance to give back to society. They long to make a difference.

Late Adolescence

Late adolescence is not so much a matter of chronology as it is a shift from experimentation to a mode of refinement and consolidation. Although almost all early adolescents move into the experimentation issues of middle adolescence, not all middle adolescents mature enough to struggle with late adolescence issues. Some stagnate in the experimental stage of middle adolescence. Late teens often seem to take a turn toward maturity. They begin to focus on jobs, education, and life partners.

Changes

Although some young people never stop experimenting, one would normally expect eighteen- or nineteen-year-olds to move into adult-like processes of refinement and consolidation. It is time to refine the data gathered through their experimentation and to consolidate those data into a view of self, family, peers, society, sacredness, and the future. For persons not able to move into late adolescence, the experimentation stage may continue into the twenties and beyond. Adult daredevils still abound. Perhaps these persons need at some point a moratorium from responsibility of life, where they can back up and work through refinement and consolidation issues again. For some persons, experimentation in delayed adolescence becomes a life-style, uncritically adopted, until a midlife crisis forces the refinement and consolidation task upon them.

Physical changes occur as the late adolescent's body is consolidated into an adult image. Late adolescence usually ends the period of growth and body development and is the time for lifelong decisions to be made about diet and exercise. It is the time for developing attitudes and values about one's sexuality. Young people need to learn to care for themselves in independent living arrangements. This involves not only money but also the basic necessities of cleaning, cooking, and running a household. It seems apparent today that both men and women are expected to maintain themselves in independent living. The impact of the feminist movement seems greatest in young women's expectations, as they prepare themselves not so much to care for a man as to live their own lives. However, many late-adolescent males have not adopted complementary views; they still expect to find women to take care of them. They may be rudely awakened. Young marriages experience difficulty as conflicts over expectations arise. More males appear ready to embrace equality in marriage. Fewer females accept a husband who will not carry his part of the marriage contract. Unfortunately, some groups still attempt to create the image that men are privileged and have special privileges in the family. Men and women deserve to be treated as equals and should find marriage roles based on their talents, interests, gifts, and abilities, not on gender. More young adults are waiting to marry later.

Settling into an **emotional style** begins with discovering how one's identity impacts one's environment. The emotional "ups and downs" of early and middle adolescence level out. Late adolescents settle into patterns where they can effectively give and receive affirmation, affection, and love. They settle into conflict-management styles that permit them to deal with anger in constructive ways. They strive to "be angry but not sin" (see Eph. 4:26). As they learn to deal with aggression, they negotiate new relationships with their peers, parents, and persons of authority. They see teachers and ministers as friends and learning resources. Stabilization of anxiety, fears, and guilt often occurs alongside the anger issue. This is most effectively handled through development of a personalized faith and a reflective stance toward one's belief system that builds respect for persons of varied life-styles.

Late adolescents, capable of complex and intricate thought patterns, begin their most creative, imaginative **intellectual phase.** Their abilities, limited not so much by a lack of cognitive development as a lack of knowledge and educational training, vary widely from individual to individual. Their reflective powers and memories permit gifted late adolescents who pursue higher education to challenge even their best professors. Their capacity to think critically about their lives and their relationships to others seems almost limitless. However, intelligence, imagination, and a critical reflective process are not to be confused with wisdom, which the late adolescent frequently lacks but will develop through effectively processing life's journey with its mountains and valleys, light and shadow. The most mature ones look to parents for consultation and friendship. Teachers become their learning guides and encouragers. Ministers take on spiritual director roles, and counselors become assets for growth. The immature ones may begin to crash and burn educationally. In rebellion, they toss about in a sea of job disillusionments. Some will take a second chance at training; others will not.

For those adolescents who do struggle with refinement and consolidation of **social relationships,** there is a questioning of values and the refining of a personal philosophy of life. This refinement usually brings a final consolidation of the peer groups. When older teens consolidate their peer groups, these become the basis for lifelong friendships. In the refinement stage, adolescents are more likely to develop friendships that are not necessarily of a dating nature with members of the opposite sex. Those who refuse to settle into responsibility often find bitter disappointments in unreliable relationships.

Furthermore, the refinement and consolidation process is seen in the area of academic studies and skill development. Vocation, a major decision facing late adolescents, becomes a serious social task. Interests, skills, and knowledge are refined and consolidated toward a given vocation, and peer support and feedback become important. Theological concepts of calling are very important for adolescents embroiled in a vocational struggle.

As late adolescents refine and consolidate their identities, they are able to make covenants and commitments with friends and peers that form lasting relationships. Likewise, as they are able to stabilize their identities, they are capable of making a covenant and commitment to a vocation. Some are ready for a career; others cannot hold a job.

Refinement and consolidation of dating relationships begin during late adolescence. Dating ceases to be primarily a way of learning social skills (early adolescence) and of recreation (middle adolescence), but becomes a way of selecting one's future spouse. Decisions about marriage and vocation are often delayed in favor of continued education. Young women are increasingly choosing to pursue a vocation or career rather than to marry. If marriage does not come toward the end of late adolescence, at least the decision *not* to marry at this time must be resolved. Parents should be patient and support their young adult's goals and decisions. Do not push! Teachers, ministers, and counselors can more objectively assist older teens to think through these tough decisions.

Late adolescence is also a time of refinement and freedom in the teen's relationship with his or her parents. Damage because of the generation gap can be immense during this phase if parents fail to bless not only the newly refined identity of their offspring but the teen's move toward independence. When parents support the journey into independence, they lay the foundation for interdependence where they and their adult child build more meaningful friendships. Moms and dads who refuse to untie the apron strings set the stage for them to be broken. Ministers and counselors can help families to face issues and reconcile their differences in mutual respect. Some parents make the mistake of attempting to overcontrol their older teens with money.

By late adolescence, young people will reject their childhood **faith systems** through one means or another. It may be in rebellion, rejection, redefinition, or refinement. Many teens turn from their childhood and early adolescent religiosity toward pursuit of personal faith. Those who rebel and reject their faith systems may prematurely adopt a philosophy of life that excludes faith from the realm of their conscious concerns. Others may seek to replace their childhood faith with the borrowed faith of a new religious leader. Although rejecting the authority of their parents' faith, late adolescents may blindly accept the authority of a cultic leader or a charismatic religious person. This faith will serve them no better than their childhood faith, but times of crisis, not lectures from their parents, will reveal this. Late adolescents who redefine and refine their childhood faith start on paths of religious enlightenment that can become lifelong pilgrimages, using this faith in a process that leads to decisions about marriage, vocation, and the constancy of friendships. This individualized belief system informs ethical decisions about their physical life-styles and facilitates their abilities to experience and maturely process a wide range of emotions. It provides an overall context in which to think critically about a variety of topics, including faith itself.

Remember that late adolescents develop independence, either through rebellion or with their parents' blessings. They not only socialize apart from their families; they may also live away from their families. In the West, socially acceptable ways of leaving the family include marriage, college, the military, and the pursuit of a job. In Asian societies, it is expected that young adults will stay in the parents' household and under the parents' authority for a longer number of years. In other ethnic groups, marriage may be accepted at an earlier age.

The failure to develop intellectual, economic, spiritual, and emotional independence will limit the young adult's capacity for social independence. There can be no refinement and consolidation of the social life-style until earlier issues have been settled. Prematurely striking out on his or her own can lead to problems. Late adolescents complain that their parents are still trying to run their lives, whereas parents bemoan the fact that their children are still dependent on them economically but desire too much freedom. Autonomy struggles dominate some late adolescents' concerns. However, without family support and an adequate foundation in early and middle adolescence, such autonomy is not likely to come. Teachers, ministers, and counselors often serve as sounding boards and become surrogate parents for floundering late teenagers.

Crisis Issues

Older adolescents need a value system that helps them interpret and make sense of the confusion and nonsense of their growing up. This includes sorting through and interpreting any sexual, physical, or emotional abuse from parents or others and winning the struggle for independence. They need large doses of the kinds of processes that began when they were younger. For example, they need a blessing from their parents like that received by Isaac and Jacob. They need to know that their parents affirm *who* they will become as well as their *right* to become. A young man named Brad sent his father a parable. The parable was of an Asian son who came in silence and stood until his father blessed him. When the father refused to bless him, the son stood in silence for a day and a half. Finally, the father returned and gave his son a blessing that said, "Go where you must go. If you are right in your pursuit, come and inform me. If you are wrong, come and I will still love you." Brad sought such a blessing.

Older teens need the freedom to make mistakes. They need the freedom to pursue their own paths as the father gave the prodigal his fair share and sent him on his way (Luke 15:11–32). Even with suspicions that trouble lay ahead, this freedom was granted. Such freedom enables growth for late adolescents. Similarly, as the father extended grace and forgiveness when the adolescent returned to beg a position as a servant, parents of older adolescents need to extend to them forgiveness and grace. Although the process of giving blessings, freedom, and forgiveness begins at the birth of the child, it reaches its highest point as the late adolescent prepares to leave the primary family system.

Developmental crises common in late adolescence focus around the three major tasks of developing an identity, deciding on a vocation, and forming intimate relationships with the opposite sex. Issues involving identity include choosing among finding a first job; enlisting in the military; enrolling for further training in vocational school, college, or university; and getting married. The big identity question is caught up with these job, school, and marital decisions. They are closely interwoven. Who am I? Am I student or employee, single or married, and does the type of job fit my ideal self? There are so many possibilities that choice itself becomes a typical and frustrating late-adolescent crisis.

Both parents and adolescents experience trauma around any decision of moving out. There is the grief of leaving home and the anxiety of independent living, but there is also the joy of newfound freedom and the excitement of new places and new faces. The final weeks may be filled with anger as grief is avoided. One twenty-year-old told his mother, "My life will be a lot better when I am away from you." A month later he was asking to return home. Moving from home, behaviorally, is symbolic of the shift in the relationship with the parents. Authority shifts from the parents to the adolescent. However, new responsibilities accompany this freedom. These transition issues cluster to form the major developmental needs and crises of late adolescence. Wise parents relax rules and discuss expectations when late adolescents return home for a visit.

Common **emergency crises** erupt, especially when developmental needs go unfulfilled. The three major emergencies involve pregnancy, legal issues, and substance abuse. However, minor crises can arise from illness or accident and unemployment.

Pregnancy is a crisis for late-adolescent males and females. Although there are alternatives that involve decisions about abortion, marriage, adoption, or single parenthood, there are no easy choices for most teens and their families. Frequently conflicts of values between the generations add to the disruptive nature of a crisis of pregnancy. Teachers, ministers, and counselors need to be prepared to listen to the pain, and to journey with these older teenagers through sexual crises.

Many late adolescents have their first encounter with the legal system through traffic violations—everything from parking tickets to driving under the influence of alcohol and reckless homicide. Others have drug-related arrests. They are winding up in prison at alarming rates. These are all crises of emergency proportions, and adolescents need the help of caring adults. They need guidance in the legal maze and in their emotional reactions to identify potential learning and growth points. They need someone with whom to reflect. They require expert legal assistance, a second chance, and counseling to reorganize life after the legal bind.

A third area of major emergency crisis is substance abuse. Drug and alcohol abuse may begin as excitement during early adolescence or through experimentation with other substances during middle adolescence, but it becomes a sick habit in late adolescence. Colleges in the twenty-first century are cracking down on binge drinking. The military puts an emphasis on controlling substance abuse. Most serious jobs require drug screening as a part of the interviewing process. Treatment programs are usually necessary for a late adolescent to kick a habit completely. Most large communities have dropped programs, and facilities are seldom available in smaller communities for adequate inpatient substance-abuse treatment. A caring referral system, however, can provide information to the adolescent and his or her family. Recent changes in the health-care field require more treatment to be outpatient. Counselors need to work with these adolescents and their families in fighting addictions. Peer pressure is a major factor in beginning alcohol and drug abuse, and peer support is a major factor in recovery.

Minor crises such as illness, an accident, or unemployment create much anxiety when first experienced by older adolescents trying freedom and independence. Although parents may want to rescue them, it is best if parents and caregivers can remain in supportive roles and permit the older adolescent to handle as much of the crisis as possible. A danger exists that a minor crisis may halt the growth toward independence. Parents can help but should not take over. Teachers can work with alternative learning contracts that meet older students at the level of their need. Counselors can defend older teens' right to become themselves. Ministers guide the process of reimaging faith and nurturing the search for vitality in faith.

When adults understand the multitude of changes for teens at various stages of development, they can then tell what is normal and what might be a warning sign. Changing is difficult. Teens need us to be a protective "cocoon" for their transformations. We will give more than we receive for a period of time. Seeing them embrace responsible adulthood makes it worth the sacrifice.

Chapter 3

Principles of Caring

Did he die from the fall? A young man had fallen asleep during the long-winded, late-night preaching of the apostle Paul. Perched in a third-story window, Eutychus sank down with sleep and fell from the open window. Bystanders had taken him for dead, but Paul "bent over him, and embracing him said, 'Do not be alarmed, for his life is in him.' And when Paul had gone up and had broken bread and eaten, he conversed with them a long while, until daybreak, and so departed. And they took the lad away alive, and were not a little comforted" (Acts 20:7–12).

This ancient story illustrates what should happen in the care of an adolescent in crisis. Notice how contemporary these events seem. First, the teen communicated his lack of appreciation for the traditional methods of adult education by falling asleep during the lecture. He was signaling, "Boring, boring, boring." Second, bystanders were quick to give up on him; they pronounced him dead and presumably returned to Paul for the important, adult stuff. They were signaling, "He cannot be helped." They were too quick to give up on the youth. Third, turning from his preaching, Paul stopped and attended to the young man. The leader embraced the teenager. Would a present-day teacher or minister or counselor stop a lecture to talk with a youth in crisis? The great ones would! Fourth, Paul turned to the community to comfort them about the young man's condition. A key role in caring for teens in crisis is to be a bridge between them and the community that has given up on them. Fifth, Paul did not return to his preaching but stopped for a meal and then talked until the sun came up. Some of the best conversations with teenagers take place at odd hours. Teens appear, like a desert cactus flower, to open up more fully during the deepest dark of the night. Teens may choose to discuss their crises during an all-night retreat, after the school dance, or when they come in from a date. Parents, teachers, ministers, and counselors need to stay alert for times to celebrate growth, progress, and recoveries with teenagers.

A survivor of an automobile crash was badly cut on her shoulders and chest. Her good friend died in the accident. After months of grief counseling and self-reassessment, she showed up for her session one day with a garment bag. "Would you like to see my prom dress?" she asked timidly. "Oh yes!" I exclaimed. This was a time of celebration! "I think it covers all of the scars, and it is my color," she added hopefully. Celebrate youths' steps in renewal.

Principles of caring create a framework and a context for parents, teachers, ministers, and counselors as we respond to a teenager in trouble. Principles provide a sense of direction in the maze of multifaceted problems that surround troubled adolescents. Furthermore, sound principles help us maintain our identities and roles as we meet together as partners on the healing team. These principles provide an overview as we define long-range goals. We need to stay focused on the big picture of helping the youth mature and develop in the face of the many here-and-now, intermediate issues in the ongoing care in a crisis. The principles that follow are not discussed in order of their importance. They are to be taken together as a whole and viewed as the skeletal structure of an organism. Nor are they intended to be all-inclusive; they are suggested for you to examine and integrate into your own efforts of caring for teenagers. Although there is a paradoxical side to several of these principles, I suggest they be held in dynamic tension to help maintain the strength of the total organism.

Relationship

The first set of principles focuses on the relationship between the adolescent and us. Our relationship might well be the essential factor in determining whether or not we successfully nurture an adolescent through a time of crisis. Many descriptive terms get at the ideal nature of a helping relationship. However, all fall short of fully describing it. Friendship, as suggested by Wayne Oates in *The Christian Pastor,* is one of the first levels of pastoral care (Oates, pp. 194–99). Teachers and counselors also know the value of basic friendships with youth, but these must be within limits. We can be friendly with teens, but not hang out with them at home. Parents ideally raise and release their teens with such sensitivity that parents maintain friendships with their teens. However, to shepherd an adolescent through a crisis, friendship is just the beginning.

Counselors use a different term. "Therapeutic alliance," the traditional medical and psychological label, speaks profoundly, but for a parent or minister, it may imply too much distance. In addition to appearing somewhat detached, it sometimes carries a mechanical connotation. Still, a teenager must at some level invest the trust in us if we are to help in a time of crisis. As long as he or she takes an "I don't need your help" attitude, we are limited in our ability to respond. Formal terms like "teacher-student," "minister-parishioner," and "counselor-client" can be descriptive and technically accurate when understood professionally. They capture the structural nature of the relationship. However, adolescents find little meaning in such terms and at times feel a need to be more than just a part of our job. One nineteen-year-old depressed male confessed during our third month of counseling, "You are like my best friend; I can tell you anything." Then he asked, "I'm not just another case to you, am I?"

Many analogies have been used to describe the relationship, yet all of them carry connotations that might be barriers to forming the relationship. Teens who showboat with their peers refer to a counselor as "my shrink." When possible, let the teenager describe the relationship. The important thing is that we build a caring, professional, and warm relationship that says, "You matter and what you do matters." We join their journeys, but we do not give up our authority. We are still the adults, the responsible ones. The nature of the caring relationship should be respectful, durable, flexible, understanding, confidential, and structured.

Respect is more than praise and deeper than admiration; respect involves holding teens in high esteem. Teens are persons, not just troubled children, victims of abuse, kids with an attitude, or discipline problems. See beyond their behavior and feelings to their value as human beings. Show them positive regard in your daily interactions as well as when they need help. Do not take their hurts, fears, injuries, disappointments, and problems lightly. Do not talk down to them, and do listen to their side of the crisis. A healthy respect for teens must be reflected in the public context of teaching, preaching, lecturing, and socializing with youth, long before it is uttered in a more formal counseling context. Show them respect.

Durability of a relationship forms a bond that not only signals the importance of the adolescent as a person, but also aids the adolescent in managing anxieties that arise from being alone in the world. We signal that we are with them for the long haul. Concrete ways of expressing the durability of the relationship involve such things as being certain that the next visit, appointment, or contact is defined before finishing a given dialogue, and continuing to stay abreast of the major developments in an adolescent's world. Frequently, troubled kids are detached from caring adults in their lives. They feel that nobody cares about them. Parents who ignore significant events and do not show up for activities lack durability in their relationships. The pastor who has attended an eighth-grader's graduation ceremony and asked about adjustments to the first year of high school will find it easier to develop a durable relationship in any subsequent crisis. Likewise, a counselor or teacher who checks with the adolescent periodically concerning important events, such as a job interview, a date, or a college visit, signals the durability and ongoing nature of their relationship. You can tell the teachers who have durable relationships by noting the number of students who return to visit them.

Flexibility, a third characteristic of a caring relationship with an adolescent, calls for meeting each adolescent where he or she is and adjusting to the individual's situation. Hang loose, be cool, and do not insist on calling all of the shots. This does not mean giving in to all of a teen's requests, but do change when you can. For example, many adolescents have difficulty being called into an office and sitting for the formal hour of counseling so characteristic of therapy. A flexible teacher, minister, or counselor can have meaningful conversations seated in a recreation lounge, sharing a soft drink, taking a walk, or simply standing and pacing around the room. Not only is flexibility needed in terms of the framework of the relationship; flexibility is important in terms of the emotional and psychological distance between the caregiver and the young person. Although some teenagers respond positively to an open, warm, enthusiastic, caring professional, others will pull back in suspicion and fear. A caring professional also needs to be flexible over time—to move toward or away from attachments with the adolescent, depending on the adolescent's current needs. For example, after three months of fairly intensive counseling, an eighteen-year-old began to reveal intense anger toward his father and stepmother. As I acknowledged that anger and facilitated its expression, I also communicated warmth and understanding. The young man failed to show up for the next appointment, and only after several weeks was he able to talk in an informal way about resuming the sessions. Three months later, however, he did return, explaining that he had felt anxious and frightened when the counseling got too involved. Time resolved this anxiety.

A fourth characteristic of a caring relationship with adolescents is **understanding**. Teenagers are more concerned that they be understood and heard than they are concerned that they be agreed with. In one therapeutic group setting, a fifteen-year-old girl said, "I wish adults knew what it was like to be a teenager just for one day!" Being a teen in any time is a unique experience. Although there are similarities, the teens' world is different from what ours was at that age. Maybe the situation is worse, but it could be better. Every generation of adolescents faces a new world context with unique pressures, but many adjustments remain the same. Although a caring parent or teacher may not be able to say, "I know exactly what makes you afraid," he or she can say, "I remember being afraid when I first experienced a situation like that" (asking for a job, reporting an accident, finding a date, etc.).

A fifth standard in the relationship of caring with youth in crisis is **confidentiality**. Although confidentiality is important in many family and professional affairs, it is particularly crucial when dealing with adolescents because of the fragile nature of their developing self-concept. For teachers, ministers, and counselors, legal issues involved when the youth are still minors dictate the wisdom of confidentiality. Adolescents need to know that their words are private, will be handled professionally, and will not be repeated lightly in conversations with other teens, parents, and helping persons. Adolescents who fail to receive a pledge of confidentiality do not trust helping persons. Very little progress can be made in the face of distrust. However, adolescents need to understand that if they become a threat to themselves or to other persons, the professional friend will have to intervene and communicate with parents and the proper authorities. Also inform them that you must report any suspected physical or sexual abuse.

Optimism is contagious. As a factor in the caring relationship with teenagers, optimism can be the difference in their trying or giving up. Optimism transforms tragedy and is a stance that can be chosen. We can decide to focus on the mess or the recovery and the future. Long-range hope is not easy for teenagers because they experience time as moving more slowly than adults do. Choosing to focus on the bright side can make a difference. This is not blind wishing for things to be better; it is a confidence that responsible reactions can make a difference. Know when to say, "This is not the end of the world as we know it." However, do not offer this hope in place of listening to their pain. If offered prematurely, optimism can feel like a discount that does not take their crises seriously. Be realistic, but expect to get beyond the crises. Parents can help their teens find other activities when one turns sour. Teachers can offer alternatives for failures or rejections. Ministers can believe with them in the power of transformations and conversions. Counselors can explore options for interpretations, decisions, and responses to a painful situation. Experience the agony, but do not dwell there forever.

A powerful, but difficult to manage, aspect of our relationship with teenagers in crisis is **humor**. Laughter is good medicine for the soul. What seems at first to be an uneasy, awkward, or even embarrassing situation can at times be laughed off. Chuckling or giggling at ourselves can be a good ego defense and models taking a humorous perspective for teenagers. Helping teens see the humor in their situation takes timing and understanding in order for it not to come off as ridicule, mockery, or scorn. Suggest that they look for the humor in a situation. Often I ask, "Is there anything funny in all of this?" For example, when our daughter was thrown into the pool with her clothes on at the end of the lifeguarding season, she was somewhat taken aback; but as we retold the story, it became funny and any initial "sting" in the situation was long forgotten. Teachers who can help students see the funny side of their botched experiments, bungled projects, or substandard tryouts lighten the pain. A forgotten take-out order left in the car can be a family crisis or a really funny tale of the growth of hairy fungus in the trunk. Do not tell funny stories about teens or humiliate them by joking publicly about their crises, but help them to see the funny side of the saga.

The final principle involving the relationship between caring adults and teenagers involves an issue of **sexuality**. Male-female relationships and transference (they transfer their feelings for someone else to us) are certainly difficult issues in counseling people of all ages. However, because of the teenager's fragile sexual identity, sexual issues are an even greater concern. The adolescent needs to be reassured and to be able to feel comfortable, whether the caring professional is of the same sex or of the opposite sex. Ideally, male and female teams of caregivers will work with an adolescent in crisis. However, this is not always possible. Because of sexual transference issues, one must be extremely careful in touching and hugging a hurting adolescent. Although there is a therapeutic place for touching and embracing, certainly this needs to be avoided in private settings and used sensitively even in public. Before one touches or embraces an adolescent, the previously mentioned principle of respect would demand that one asks permission. Because adolescents' emotions are likely to be vulnerable, especially in a time of crisis, one must be careful not to manipulate a teen when seeking such permission. I think it is best that even parents ask before offering a hug. Teachers, ministers, and counselors should take special care to seek clear agreement. Be careful to give no reason for a teenager to be confused by your helping. False reporting of sexual advances can damage the career and family of a teacher, minister, or counselor. Be warm, but be cautious.

Also remember that transference and countertransference (we transfer feelings in their direction) issues can be a difficulty in relation to the parent/child role. Caring professionals may be unconsciously tempted to treat adolescents as their own offspring. Such treatment, when outside the awareness of the caregiver, can be extremely dangerous for the caregiver's stability and for the adolescent's progress. Do not become casual with the relationship. Keep clear roles and safe boundaries.

Having observed characteristics of a caring relationship with a teen in crisis, consider how we figure out what is wrong. Teens seldom open up with a clear statement of their dilemma. We may notice a change in mood, activity level, or friendship. We can ask directly, but that is usually met with a grumbled, defensive "Nothing." Trying to figure out what is bothering a confused teenager is almost as difficult as deciphering what to do for a crying, six-week-old baby. How do you guess? Where do you start? How bad is it? Who else is involved? Parents often contact me with a bunch of questions and much anxiety.

Evaluating the Crises

A number of principles relate to the process of evaluating the teenager, understanding the nature of the crisis, and determining the sources of help. Of course, traditional issues dealing with the type of crisis, the definition of the problem, the history of the individual, the impact on the family, the support system available, and the extent to which the crisis has harmed the teenager should be appraised. As in other types of problem solving, we will each use our training and point of view to evaluate the situation. Parents often rely on their life experiences and whatever job training they have had. Teachers will know educational issues and current teen culture. Ministers primarily assess from a theological perspective. Counselors use their professional training and skills. But we should all be aware of the multifaceted dimensions of any crisis and seek information from the teenager or from other professionals concerning psychosocial, educational, vocational, medical, legal, spiritual, and family dynamics.

The **developmental stage** may outweigh the emergency features of a crisis. The initial principle in assessing the issues facing an adolescent in crisis is to remember that one is dealing with an adolescent first and a crisis second. Where is the teen in his or her psychosocial development? Normally we use our information concerning the nature of a crisis as the major template for assessment. However, with adolescents the developmental stage of the adolescent's struggle becomes the major overlying factor in making the assessment. Ask yourself, "What are the big issues for a teen this age?" Although we might be concerned about long-term issues, the teen might be more concerned with a seemingly minor concern. To the teen the minor concern will not feel minor.

For example, in dealing with an adolescent girl whose mother had recently committed suicide, several professionals attempted to work with her in processing her grief, but she continued to deteriorate; she pulled further away from her family, became more involved in antisocial acting out, and even became suicidal herself. Initially, she did not seem interested in discussing either her family crisis, the issues surrounding her difficulties with the law, or her mother's suicide. She seemed preoccupied by a perceived injustice—having to live with her biological father and stepmother. As these issues were explored further, it became evident that her major sense of grief was the loss of a boyfriend in the high school she was forced to leave in order to move to her father's house. She felt guilty for being preoccupied with her boyfriend. Her family and other therapists had assumed that her "puppy love" was such a small issue in light of the other dynamics and pushed it aside. However, when she was able to address her grief over her boyfriend and to negotiate some opportunities to continue to see him, her depression lifted and she was able to deal rather predictably with her grief and her adjustment to a new school. Of more importance, her acting out ceased, and she was able to return to the tasks of seeking an education and getting on with life. For her at this time, the developmental need (dating and learning to relate to boys) was more significant than the grief process. This is not to say her mother was unimportant but that developmental issues are paramount in dealing with adolescents in crisis.

These psychosocial issues provide a tint to emergency crises. Because most crisis research has been done with adults, particularly grief work, the coloring added to the crisis by the adolescent's developmental issues needs to be taken more seriously and some thought given to adolescent grief or adolescent crisis response, which is often different from the norms reported in research.

A second major assessment principle concerns the **multifaceted dimension** of adolescent crises. Few if any adolescents experience a crisis in one area only. The world of adolescents is an interconnected, interrelated entanglement of forces produced by their mental aptitude, schoolwork, vocational aspirations, body growth, medical circumstances, friendship ties, emotional maturity, legal standing, moral development, spiritual maturity, and family relations. Usually no one thing will solve a complex crisis. Careful assessment of a number of dynamics might give clues to the larger picture of what is going on with a troubled adolescent.

A good example was the case of a very prominent young woman from a leading church in her community who was referred for counseling because she refused to go off to college, choosing instead what her professional parents thought was a menial job waiting on tables in a popular, but not elegant, restaurant. After several frustrating sessions, psychological testing revealed that the young woman's mental ability was below average and she was not suited for college. When informed of these results, she was not surprised and confessed that she had cheated on exams and bought reports and term papers for all four years of high school. Even some of her teachers were surprised. She was so guilt-ridden that she could not continue. But she was unable to confess to her parents that she knew she was not college material. Her parents had always told her she could be anything she wanted to be if she tried hard enough. She knew it was not true, but she did not want to disappoint them for fear they would reject her. She chose to deal with their anger at her rebellion rather than with the shame of feeling she was unacceptable to them. Without the family history and psychological testing, the breakthrough in the assessment of this adolescent would have been nearly impossible.

Likewise, consideration of social involvement in **peer relationships** is a significant part of dealing with teenagers. Because of the influence, particularly on middle and late adolescents, exerted by friends, the nature of the peer group must be clearly understood. The absence of a peer group signals a poor prognosis for quick and easy resolution of many crises. Parents should know the friends of their teenagers. If possible, get to know their parents and families. This becomes difficult in an urban setting but is well worth the effort. Teachers can more easily read the peer groups in their schools, but often there is little discussion with the parents. Ministers often see teens only in a religious setting and have limited knowledge of their peer group at work, school, or in the neighborhood.

Know teens as students. Where are they **educationally**? How bright are they? What are their vocational goals? What plans, if any, do they have for their lives? Are these realistic? The resources of a gifted student may be helpful in recovering from a crisis, but gifted students may also be more devastated by their problems because they see the problem as blocking, altering, or eliminating their life aspirations. Usually they are more worried than necessary. A bright young man was convinced that his goal of getting into a great college was ruined when he got a "D" in tenth-grade English. He had not turned in a project because of depression and parental conflicts. He feared that he was not bright because his emotional upheaval made it difficult for him to concentrate. He got back on track and made stellar marks in his junior year. However, some crises do end dreams. One young man who was arrested for assault during his senior year discovered that his conviction kept him out of several colleges. A seventeen-year-old unmarried mother discovered that she could not continue being in the marching band and care for the baby as she needed to. Numerous athletes have career-ending auto accidents or injuries during competition. For some students the extracurricular activities are the key factors in their education and in their future vocational plans.

Remember the significance of **physical issues** and medical problems. Check out the teen's medical condition by asking the family or by arranging for the teen to get a checkup. Parents should insist on a visit to the doctor when a number of crises surface. Substance abuse, sexual experimentation, disturbances in thinking patterns, and injuries indicate the need to see a doctor. Teachers and ministers should be aware of any ongoing medical problems when talking with a teen in crisis. Counselors should also check to see if the teen is taking any medications and should routinely look at the impact of physical problems on the crisis and vice versa. For example, I counseled with a depressed, heavy-drinking nineteen-year-old for several sessions before learning that his skin problems were not acne but a rare disease. His hopelessness about this condition greatly impacted his depression and substance abuse.

Legal issues and the ability to accept limits need to be examined carefully. A further assessment principle is to assess the nature of controls and limits in the adolescent's environment. Who and what determine the adolescent's behavior? Although teenagers need freedom, they also need limits. Paradoxically, they need a balance between the two that provides a structure where expectations are clarified, schedules are provided, and routines are maintained. They need enough structure to control their anxiety, temptations, and impulses, but enough freedom to permit their self-development. They have rules at many different levels. The family, the school, team activities, the church, the law, and nature itself have rules that a teen must consider. When these subsystems vary in their expectations and levels of enforcement, teens can become confused. When they come into conflict outright, teenagers become frustrated, upset, and angry. "It is not fair that my parents bought me a cell phone and pager to stay in touch, but I can't take them to school," moaned one junior. Look at the teen's awareness and attitude toward the rules in his or her world. How does this fit with the crisis? The use of time, another important ingredient in assessing the structural context of the adolescent's world, can greatly impact her or his response to a crisis. Teens need freedom and stability. One youth psychiatrist argued, "Religious youth cults are an alternative family structure for youth who find themselves lacking a viable family structure" (Pattison, p. 278). If teenagers do not feel enough structure and limits, they will seek out other forms. However, if the limits are arbitrary, unfair, or meaningless, then they are likely to rebel, revolt, or even riot.

This stance is likely to bring legal repercussions. When a teen faces legal problems, get legal counsel. Advise teenagers about the consequences of not taking court proceedings seriously. One honor student from another culture received what he thought was an unfair traffic citation. He refused to pay the fine and had a court date. Of course, he did not tell his parents. On the appointed date and time, he went to court alone and waited. When he was not called within the first two hours, he returned to school because he had a major exam in calculus. Imagine his and his parent's shock when a police officer arrived that evening and arrested him. The predicament was resolved with probation, public service, and fines, but this uninformed teen might have been placed in jail because of his inability to handle the crisis alone. I am still amazed at the casual, cavalier, and indifferent attitude that some rebellious teens take toward legal problems. "The cops will never take me," one boasted; "I can whip two or three at a time." "I am not afraid of youth detention or prison," another crowed. "Those perverts in there will be sorry if they ever touch me." A number of adolescents need assistance with understanding the legal issues involved in their crises and the legal risks they are taking.

Religious ideation of adolescents needs to be assessed in relationship to adolescent **spiritual issues.** Teens vary widely in their depth of religious thinking. How they practice faith and what they believe are important. However, faith is not so much about what they believe as it is about how they process their beliefs. One researcher has categorized faith development across the life cycle. He has suggested that adolescent religion is primarily stage 3, "a synthetic conventional faith" (Fowler, pp. 151–73). This stage is characterized by early formal operations as a form of logic. Teens can think in the abstract, using symbols and propositions to work out alternative solutions to problems. They see the gray issues between the light and dark poles. They have a mutual interpersonal perspective on relationships. They can look at relationships from other people's points of view. An interpersonal expectations form of logic helps them to focus on doing what is right in the eyes of their authority figures and in their own eyes.

Their group (peers' and parents' social class) serves as a bond of social awareness. They see primarily the social issues of only their group. Group consensus is an external locus of authority. If their group says a thing is right, they are relatively powerless to think for themselves and resist that position. "Everybody is doing it" is a basis for authority. Felt meanings become a form of world coherence. Their experience of life is defended uncritically as "the way life is for others." Teens find evocative power in multidimensional symbols. Their symbols are not separated from what the symbols stand for. Symbols, like a cross pendant, are powerful and will be defended against any reinterpretation (Fowler, pp. 244–45).

Another study demonstrates that the modal community of faith is a major factor in the adolescent's development according to the Fowler categories. The "general stage of faith in the community carried over to teens. In churches and faith communities where individual reflective faith (stage 4) was normative, adolescents could also become stage 4 faith persons" (Simmons, p. 201). Because the minister will frequently share in the adolescent's faith system, it might be difficult to see how faith issues can block psychosocial development or how faith issues can serve to nurture and promote growth through resolving the crisis. Parents will need to observe and listen to get at these faith issues. Lecturing and arguing seem not to help. Public school teachers may be at a disadvantage in discussing faith issues. All professionals should work with the faith system of the teenager and avoid pushing their beliefs onto the youth.

Religious issues that frequently arise in crises with youth are the adolescent's

- concepts of authority,
- stage of moral development,
- value system,
- understanding of goodness and evil, of sin and forgiveness, and of his or her own relationship to God.

Look at what is going on in the **family** as you examine the issues with a teenager in crisis. Even the parents need to stop and ask, "What could this have to do with our family situation?" Teachers should keep up with family concerns when helping a student in crisis. One sophomore complained to me, "You say to ask my parents about this problem; in my opinion, my parents are the problem." Ministers have the advantage of seeing all ages in their parishes. A minister is more likely to know and have a previous relationship with the family. We need to remember to assess how the family and the teen's problems interrelate. Counselors have training in family dynamics and should routinely consider the interaction between the crisis and the family. A later chapter will spell out in detail some of these interactions.

Helping teens in crisis must involve a wide array of factors that work with the family background. This means not only the parent(s) and siblings living at home but the extended family of grandparents, aunts and uncles, stepparents, stepbrothers, and stepsisters. Also, in a family history the adolescent's perceptions of a relationship need to be assessed apart from the information given by other family members. A teenager lives by his or her own perceptions, not the conclusions of others. Look at the facets of a crisis through his or her eyes, but also examine what is going on from various angles of vision. Build a three-generation family tree and look at the teen's relationships with each person listed.

Responding to the Crisis

Building a caring relationship and evaluating the crisis are not enough. Help the teens or refer them to someone who can help. Parents, teachers, and ministers often assert, "I did not know what to do, so they are coming to see you." More than a few counselors send teenagers my way with a reluctant statement like, "I do not see how you can work with this age group. They are not my area." Some school counselors avow, "My job is to help them with academic planning and discipline infringements; I don't do personal counseling." This is fine as long as those who need help can find it someplace. The main discussion methods of intervention come in the remaining chapters, but a few initial basics fall into the category of any caring relationship.

Make Referrals

First, know and respect your own limits and refer teenagers to others when wisdom dictates. Parents especially need to be willing to tell a teenager that a problem needs outside help. Make an appointment and stay involved. Whether you are a teacher, a minister, or a counselor, you may find that the crisis may call for expertise beyond your training or may demand more time than you can realistically offer. The adolescent may hook you in a positive or a negative manner. Don't play Lone Ranger and neglect other members of the caring team. When you do make a referral, do so in a clear, direct, and caring fashion that avoids rejection. Explain why and to whom you are making the referral. Then follow up in a short period of time to see how the referral process unfolded. Show that you still care.

A second principle of responding to adolescents in a time of crisis is to **listen, listen, and listen**. Sometimes just listening means a lot. It reduces the stress and may give teens the courage and energy to do something positive. Listen to their hearts. Hear their feeling tone. Patience in listening to adolescents often requires teachers, ministers, and counselors to adjust the regular therapeutic fifty-minute hour to include a number of briefer sessions or a few extended ones. At times there is a need for seemingly marathon sessions, during which the adolescent, especially early in counseling, is permitted to talk through the confusion surrounding the crisis. Sometimes this will not be at convenient times; some adolescents seem to function better in the late evening. As we listen, we need to hear not only the thoughts and the content of the conversation but, of more importance, the affective responses to events. Listen for clues to the decisions and intentions about their behavior in light of both thoughts and feelings. What are they considering? Secret plans are revealed in language designed to reach out for help. Listen in a way that will assist them in understanding how their thoughts and feelings shape their behavior and how they can be responsible for their thoughts, aware of their feelings, and therefore responsible for their own behavior. Don't be afraid to follow clues and hints as you read between the lines. Listen to what the words imply.

Third, **respect their worldview**. Hear what they mean and what the issues mean to them. Be sure that you understand adolescent symbols, terms, and concepts of reality in listening with them. This involves more than understanding their slang and jargon. It means more than knowing their favorite types of clothing, rock groups, or movie idols. One needs to know how a given adolescent comprehends the world of reality. Listen carefully to their terms, values, attitudes, norms, and comprehension of the real world. What are their operating presuppositions? Where is the injustice in their world? What is not fair? How bad is this situation? Stop, focus on them, and show consideration for how they see things. Understand their worldview, but remain squarely in touch with your own. Accept them; you do not have to copy them.

A fourth response involves **collaborating in decision making**. Help them to decide. One cannot tell adolescents what to do and expect instant change. However, one can teach adolescents when they ask. Collaborating with teenagers means that they are ultimately responsible for their growth. They understand that what happens to them is primarily their own responsibility. Helping them accept responsibility for themselves strengthens the helping professional's therapeutic process. At times they need encouragement to move ahead with a chosen course of action. Let them know the peril, but help them remember that risks are the road to seeing their dreams come true. Tell them that life is about choices, and they are responsible for theirs. We are each responsible for ourselves. Help them consider the potential consequences of options. Even offer alternatives for consideration, but tell them that the choice is up to them. Of course, there are limits to this response. One cannot permit self-destructive acts, criminal behavior, or abuse of others. Within reason, collaborate with their decisions.

A fifth response concerns **finding value** in their personhood. Teens do count for something. Help them in making meaning out of life and life's events. As an adolescent tells his or her story, relate it to other stories (or to the songs, poems, books, scripture, or even movies that make up the symbolic belief system). Caring adults can interpret, reflect, and facilitate new ways of thinking about the teen's own crisis story. Because many adolescents in modern society will be ignorant of classical literature—ancient Greek or Roman tales, particular ethnic legends, and even scripture stories—some teaching may be necessary. However, songs, literature, movies, and adolescent folklore can also be used to assist the adolescent to find meaning in his or her current life circumstances.

A final response deals with the **approach to the unpleasant side of crises**. Crises can be messy, filled with hurt, and laced with anger. Provide a safe place for adolescents' nasty feelings, spiteful intentions, foul words, or offensive actions to spew out. They may need to yell or to cry. Let them express the moment. Then ask them to calm down and collect themselves. Still, do not attempt to minimize their hurt or to whitewash the situation. Adolescents carry a lot of anger. Anger is an external expression of inner hurt. It gets expressed in a range of actions. They are volatile or sullen, depending on whether they externalize or internalize their feelings. The ability to receive an adolescent's anger without being hooked into an escalation or mutual put-down session is a very important part of helping. This may be more difficult for parents than for teachers, ministers, and counselors simply because the parents can choose not to be involved. Having a choice makes a difference. The caring professional is able to facilitate a teen's expression of anger and is careful not to attack personally but to set firm, caring limits. One such counselor repeatedly reminds teens, "I know what I am saying must frustrate you. I hope you will learn to deal with it." Because of the fragile nature of the adolescent's identity in the context of the crisis, ugly feelings can be spurred by simple misunderstandings and by jumping to conclusions. Before facilitating the constructive expression of anger with teens, evaluate the data and check the validity of the hurt.

One concluding reflection on the principles of caring for adolescents in crisis sums up the stance that leads to effective intervention. Parents, teachers, ministers, and counselors who venture into caring for a teenager in crisis should be reminded that three elements surpass the others: faith, hope, and love. "The greatest of these is love" (1 Cor. 13:13b). With teenagers this is especially true! They are in life's major transition period. They are no longer caterpillars and not yet butterflies. You who reach out to them must have an extra capacity to love them.

Chapter 4

Guidelines for Intervention

Methods of dealing with adolescents in crisis vary widely among personality theorists and within special approaches to counseling. The following guidelines define a few approaches that I have found work best with teens. Nothing works for every teenager in every crisis. Be flexible and adapt this information to your style, setting, and ethnic context with each specific teenager. Counseling methods developed for adults need to be adjusted when used with teens. The principles in Chapter 3 provide the framework for such adjustments. We now examine interviewing methods, crisis intervention and problem-solving methods, pastoral psychotherapy (including behavioral and cognitive approaches with teens, meditation and relaxation, family counseling, and transactional analysis), and pastoral-care responses.

Interviewing

In interviewing adolescents, traditional interpersonal factors are especially important. Significant consideration must be given to displaying nonpossessive warmth, interpersonal integrity, and an open, aboveboard approach. The ability to empathize is crucial for counseling troubled adolescents because many of these troubled youngsters maintain a generalized suspicion of and rebellion against such adult authority figures as ministers, teachers, and counselors. As one depressed high school senior barked, "I will never spill my guts to any counselor or shrink or whatever. It is like talking to the principal." A fifteen-year-old cracked, "If you think I am going to tell my parents about this problem, you are the crazy one. They would just ship me away. They won't help." After I identified with her fear and we discussed her parents' previous reactions and her other options, she decided to begin to talk with her parents in a joint session. She stated that she would stop if they started to blow up. To her amazement, they listened rather patiently when she did decide to talk with them, and they negotiated a workable solution with her. After a few guidelines for parents, we will consider methods for adults who help teenagers in crisis.

Parents

Initially there will be a problem or crisis that either you or your child talks about. Begin by being as calm as possible and focus on the problem. Avoid overreacting. Stop, think, and gather your thoughts before you address the problem. Stay away from attacking your child as a person. Refrain from the following:

- Name calling
- Bringing up things from the past
- Accusing your child before you have the full story
- Threatening to harm the child
- Knee-jerk reprisals
- Withholding your love and commitment
- Assuming; Ass-u-me (make an "ass of you and me")

Tell your child why you think there is a problem or ask why he or she does. Your initial reaction will set the stage for how your child will open up and share with you. Suggest that both of you talk about the problem and then discuss options for a response. Suggesting a more formal approach helps the adolescent feel hopeful. Also, being taken seriously tells the adolescent that he or she is important and will be included in considering how to move forward. Basic problem-solving intervention with adolescents has a few modifications from adult crisis intervention. However, the overall process is quite similar.

The first phase in problem solving is **defining the problem** from various perspectives and contracting for ongoing discussion. In working with your teenager, be certain to check out the facts as the story of the crisis unfolds—not that adolescents always deliberately misrepresent the facts, although some will. Their perception and understanding of the adult world are noticeably limited. After you hear the teen's definition of the problem, offer your description of the issues. Attempt to focus on the main issue. Keep issues separated and deal with one at a time. If there are legal implications to the difficulty, a maze of misinformation may need to be checked out. One can validate the facts later by contacting other institutions (school, church, work, etc.) and other parties involved. At a later time talk to any other youth involved and their parents. Let your child know you intend to verify your understanding of the crisis. But for now you want to know how your child sees the problem, and you want her or him to understand your point of view. Remember the principles of caring. Listen, listen, and listen.

Also, in defining the problem, seek to clarify the goals and values of the teenager in relation to those of the family. The adolescent may see the problem as not enough freedom and time for fun, whereas you may see the problem as not enough application to schoolwork. The school report may support or refute either or both. Unclear expectations and commitments to common goals could be the common denominator. On the other hand, parents may see a crisis as the shame that the teen's actions have brought on them in the community, whereas the teenager sees the problem as having to go to court. Although both are an issue, the general problem is how to handle the legal and confidentiality issues (perhaps keeping something out of the media). Until the problems are separated and clarified, no problem-solving methods can be successfully employed. Try to state the problem in one brief sentence (or paragraph) that you and the teenager can agree upon.

Building alternatives as a team is the second phase. Ask the adolescent, "What can be done?" Mutually explore the question "What are our options here?" Hope sets the context for the second phase of crisis and problem-solving intervention with adolescents. Hope permits them to think of alternatives. Basically, alternatives fall into three categories: changing (adaptation of self and environment), tolerating (acceptance of self and environment), and avoiding (one of us could leave). Adaptation involves ways of changing thoughts, attitudes, behaviors, feelings, and beliefs. Acceptance involves alternatives that change the guidelines, rules, and expectations for the relationships; one learns to live with life as it is. Avoidance involves alternatives that change the living structures. In changing, for example, new rules might be adopted, a new school selected, or the situation is changed. (The adolescent can get an abortion or seek to put the child up for adoption, etc.) With acceptance, for example, the parents might decide to permit the new behavior and not see it as a problem. (The adolescent can keep the baby, etc.) With avoidance, for example, out-of-home placements with institutions, foster families, or relatives might be a consideration.

A commitment on the part of the adolescent and the family toward a common goal comes before the defining of alternatives. If no mutual understandings can be discussed, there may be a need for professional counseling, legal intercession, or institutional intervention. If you cannot talk about options with your youth, see a teacher, minister, or counselor. Let the teen describe the issues before you define the problems as you see them. Perhaps the third party can help you and the teenager negotiate to build options. If getting outside help fails, consider legal involvement. Out-of-home placement may be necessary. You cannot just throw the child out on the street. You may need to file an out-of-control petition if the teen absolutely refuses to look at responsible alternatives. Of course, these would be actions of last resort. When you do compile a list of possible alternatives and action plans, it is time to look at each one carefully. Be cautious not to argue about these yet. Agree to consider each one.

The third phase of crisis and problem solving with your teenager is **evaluating alternatives**. Do not blurt out your first feelings or impressions about something; think through each alternative carefully. This involves not only each person's spontaneous emotional reaction but also some serious gathering of data and projecting the possible outcomes of each alternative. The impact will differ for each person. The freedom and openness given by God and promised in the Constitution set a model for listening and evaluating alternatives with respect for each individual's position. Frustrated parents may find it difficult to treat their adolescent with dignity and freedom, and at this point a counselor may need to support the adolescent in this process. However, at other times the counselor may need to support the parents in persuading the adolescent to look responsibly at the evaluation of the alternatives.

In evaluating the alternatives, it is important to remember that an adolescent's time perspectives, values, and needs differ greatly from those of his or her parents. A teen more likely values here-and-now issues and views a month as a much longer time than do adults. Creating in advance the expectations for adolescents that their alternatives will be radically different assists in reducing the shock and tension when real alternatives are discussed.

The process of making decisions is not usually well formulated for adolescents. Guiding is a caring perspective for this step. Draw out their resources for making evaluations. They may need assistance in learning to list positive and negative potential outcomes where thoughts, meanings, feelings, and behaviors are taken into consideration. Otherwise, teens are likely to make a decision based on what feels good from a short-term perspective. This is especially true of teenagers who are still bewildered and confused in the early phases of a crisis. Remember, you are the adult.

After ample evaluation of alternatives, the fourth phase of problem solving, **deciding on a mutually acceptable alternative,** brings some resolution and relief of pent-up emotions. Although making the decisions may be difficult and involve open confrontation and differences, after the decisions are made comes a general sense of relief and excitement. During the time of decision making, talk about which options you as a parent can support, permit, and tolerate. Do not give false hope. Be realistic. You will need to remove some of the previous alternatives from the list because you see them as totally unacceptable. Let the teenager do the same. It is hoped that at least a few of the options will be acceptable to both. Either pick one together or consider combining some that might work. Neither you nor your child will like everything about a negotiated decision; however, in the long run this will work best for all persons involved. The older the youth, the more weight you may want to give to her or his decisions. After a certain age, parents can advise, suggest, and limit support of undesirable options, but we cannot force some decisions.

The caring dynamics of reconciling, informing, and guiding are paramount. When a decision is reached, then the issues are not so stressful. When you and your child agree upon a plan of action, things will feel better. As a sense of celebration or joy are shared, one must be careful not to substitute deciding for the actual implementation of the decision.

The fifth phase of problem solving with adolescents focuses on **implementation of the decision.** Specific responsibilities for implementing the plan are allocated by the adolescent and other involved persons. Who does what, now? What will the parents do? What will the youth do? How and when will these be done? Plan your work and work your plan.

Planning the implementation will be somewhat limited by the adolescent's lack of experience in the adult world. You may need to provide information about resources or institutions that can assist the teen. Most teenagers need a clear, probably written, list of responsibilities or actions in the plan. Likewise, you should give a clear statement of your responsibilities and actions. Summarize each list for clarity of understanding.

It is especially important for adolescents to have regular reinforcement during the trial period of their crisis-resolution plans. The teacher, minister, or counselor can support them in this process. The support (phone, letter, e-mail, or visits) will facilitate their continued commitment to living by the process. They need to be sustained.

Whatever the plan, there can be a time of celebration and joy and an asking of God's strength and blessings for the decisions. Isaiah 40:28–31 has been helpful for some adolescents and parents because it reminds them that they are dependent on a power greater than themselves. Their willingness to confess that fact seems to be a critical factor in the success of working through any crisis, but especially addictions.

The final phase is **reevaluating the effectiveness of the plan.** Regular checkup periods encourage everyone to resolve the crisis. This process serves as behavioral reinforcement for both the parents and the adolescent. Also, it symbolizes ongoing care. Periodically ask, "How do you think this plan is working out? Do we need to make any midcourse adjustments?" If new issues surface, suggest some midpoint corrections. A process similar to that used in initially selecting the plan may be necessary to resolve these new issues that emerge. New options are defined in terms of their problem and the alternatives generated, evaluated, selected, planned for, and tried. Furthermore, in the periodic checkup sessions, an important function in offering hope is to summarize progress. Parents can remind the adolescent of what progress has been made. This plays no small part in encouraging movement toward healing and wholeness. In a later chapter we will discuss problem solving as a part of understanding how families function. But parents cannot do it all. Many times teenagers in crisis need outside help. Here are few guidelines for teachers, ministers, and counselors.

Teachers, Ministers, and Counselors

Something has brought the adolescent to the attention of the school or into your professional care. Occasionally an institution will make the referral, such as in court-ordered counseling; more often, the parents will make the contact. A student might directly approach a teacher, school counselor, or minister, but only occasionally will the adolescent in crisis have enough initiative and ego strength to initiate formal counseling plans. An adult who is regularly around the adolescent in an informal setting can often formalize counseling sessions when problems and crises are being discussed.

When initially interviewing adolescents, you will need more time than usual to clearly introduce yourself, your role in this particular context, and your function as seen by the adolescent. Until the adolescent knows, understands, and trusts you and your approach, very little productive counseling can take place. Adolescents appear to be more comfortable when they have something to offer in the relationship and are not seen merely as counselees. I found that adolescent resistance was not nearly so high when I told them I was also conducting research and would be interested in their comments, advice to parents, and tips for other counselors. I assure them that I will help them get help if I cannot help them myself. Offering a role with dignity and power significantly reduced the resistance in several instances. Take time to build a trusting relationship. If parents grow impatient that the process isn't moving faster, provide reassurance.

As soon as the contract for counseling has been clarified and the relationship formulated, the major interviewing time concentrates on facilitating the adolescent's discussion of the problem. It is time to listen and to listen intently. Exploratory questions, like those introduced by Norm Kagan in his *Interpersonal Process Recall,* are essential interviewing tools for adolescents. Gerard Egan in *The Skilled Helper* likewise provides excellent information on getting at the crisis.

Reframing the problem, clarifying significant and less significant issues, and looking at events from various perspectives are important interviewing techniques with adolescents. Reframing the problem helps the adolescent to focus on the central causative issues and move away from preoccupations with relatively insignificant matters. Distinguishing foreground from background helps the adolescent to focus on the issues in a crisis more clearly. To discover patterns and to understand the relationship in a different light strengthens the young person's hope for progress.

The final interviewing issue with adolescents also originates from their concern for trusting relationships. Adolescents appreciate the opportunity to ask questions as you clarify your continued role and your future relationship with them. Adolescents need a concrete commitment as to when and how you will be in contact. Clear up any questions about contacting you as necessary. Are you open to calls, e-mail, or written communication?

Generally speaking, a teacher must be more deliberate, direct, and in control when interviewing an adolescent. This is not to imply that one can get away with speaking down to or overpowering adolescents, but that one must be very conscious of taking responsibility for the flow and direction of the counseling.

For ministers, the spiritual dynamics most at work in initial interviewing and understanding the problem are assessing guilt, sorting out the truth, and giving and receiving forgiveness. Much blaming during the definition of the problem will involve projections from parents and adolescents as well as peers and other adults. Sorting through the story so all concerned can accept responsibility for their own mistakes can lead to authentic forgiveness and reconciliation.

Counselors have a variety of approaches to consider when working with adolescents in crisis. You may have your own style polished and refined. Still, you may want to reflect upon a few popular approaches.

Formal Counseling

In order to deal with self, family system, and worldviews, adolescents and their families may need deeper levels of intervention than interviewing and problem solving can provide. Pastoral psychotherapy, as the approach to counseling that integrates biblical and theological foundations with a particular school of psychotherapy, works best for ministers. This is integrated with the approaches to therapy that research indicates are successful with young people. For the purposes of this study, we will look at behavior modification, cognitive therapy, meditation, family systems, and transactional analysis. Teachers and counselors will know their comfort level in dealing with faith and spiritual issues. In any case, we work with the belief system that the teenager brings to us. We do not impose our beliefs.

Behavior Modification

Behavior modification is perhaps most successful in treating adolescents suffering from character disorders, substance abuse, or eating disorders. In establishing a behavior modification program, all authority persons related to the adolescent must be committed to and involved in supporting the program. If the adolescent might be institutionalized, all staff must work together for the program to be effective. If the adolescent lives with the family, parents, grandparents, teachers, and other authority persons working with him or her, everyone involved must understand and support the system. Adolescents can be particularly skilled at playing "divide and conquer," where they pit one authority person against another in an attempt to shirk responsibility.

The system basically consists of a list of rules and expectations, with some daily mark by each rule as to how carefully it was followed. We used a calendar and put a smile or frown on each day. The tokens or points were given for each smile. A certain number of points were needed for specific rewards. For long-term goals, like improving grades, we rewarded according to monthly or six-week progress reports.

In setting up a behavior modification program, several instructions are essential. First, the reward system must be something that the adolescent values. I often request a list of wishes and then set up rewards. Although some rewards are gifts from parents, most are trips, privileges, and the use of time for enjoyable activities. Second, there needs to be both long-term and short-term reinforcements. Small immediate and daily rewards can be steps toward a major reinforcement. Third, the program succeeds when paying attention to good behavior goes along with the token or reward. An honest compliment goes a long way. Finally, for adolescents the program is better when there is a combination of four types of responses in the behavior modification program. As seen in Table 1, the responses are (1) turning on a positive, (2) turning off a positive, (3) turning on a negative, and (4) turning off a negative.

TABLE I. FOUR TYPES OF RESPONSES IN BEHAVIOR MODIFICATION

	On	Off
	(1)	(2)
Positive	Pleasure	Loss
Response	Joy*	Grief
	(3)	(4)
Negative	Pain	Relief
Response	Fear	Hope*

Hope and joy are the two greatest motivators. However, they work best when they are interspersed with the loss of a positive and the fear of a negative.

- *Turning on a positive* creates pleasure or joy; for example, for good school grades some parents add a bonus to the allowance.
- *Turning off a positive* creates loss and grief; withholding phone privileges for poor grades also gives more time for study.
- *Turning on a negative* creates pain and motivates by fear; a coach makes a player run extra laps around the field.
- *Turning off a negative* creates relief and motivates by hope; a parent might say, "I helped you clean your room this week because you did such good work at school the past six weeks."

Regular reinforcement of consistent, clear expectations assists the adolescent in accepting ultimate responsibility for the outcome. The attitudes of the counselor and other authority persons working with the behavior modification system can be either "We are really pulling for you to do these things for yourself" or "We are sorry you chose not to do them and not to receive the rewards." The adults are careful not to let themselves be set up as doing something *to* the adolescent. The rewards and punishments are the adolescent's own choices by the behavior that he or she elects.

Cognitive Therapy

Cognitive therapy has an excellent record in assisting adolescents with depression and low self-esteem. In combination with behavior modification, cognitive therapy shows promise for several other issues, such as eating disorders and distorted thinking (Schrodt and Fitzgerald, pp. 402–408). Depression seems to grow worse through a vicious cycle that affects the teenager's ability accurately to evaluate input from peers and the environment. The teenager becomes negative about self, about the environment, and about the future. This produces a lack of hope and a negative self-image that leads to negative feelings and further depression. Cognitive therapy rests on the assumption that the process of acquiring knowledge and forming beliefs primarily determines one's mood and therefore one's behavior (Wright and Beck, p. 1119). If one thinks that one is unacceptable, that others do not care, and that there is no hope to change, feelings of depression follow, and behaviors associated with depression—such as lack of motivation, failure to stay with a task, and inability to concentrate—are natural outcomes. The major thrust of cognitive therapy is to identify and correct negative, distorted information processes. Several cognitive errors are traditional with adolescents. (See *Feeling Good* by David Burns for how self-defeating thoughts can lead to self-defeating feelings that bring self-defeating actions.) Because of the pastoral counselor's ability to deal realistically with hope, the hopelessness of this cycle can be broken. Alternatives for overcoming the depression are not limited to rethinking the data. Although distortions play a major role in teenage depression, these young people do experience some real-life loss and grief.

Typical adolescent thought patterns include helplessness—the "nobody can do anything about this anyway" kind of thinking. "All-or-nothing" thinking, also typical of adolescents in crisis, is demonstrated in such statements as "If I can't have everything my way, I just won't take anything." A third typical distortion is the "always-and-never" type of thinking; "it is never going to be any better" and "I am always going to be this way" are obvious expressions of this hopelessness.

The first task is to identify the automatic, negative thinking behind the depressive emotions. Adolescents may not use the word *depression* to describe themselves but may simply say they are bored, tired, feel worthless, and generally don't want to do anything. As the automatic negative thoughts unfold, the counselor and the adolescent examine them in light of the evidence. Adolescents can be assigned a number of homework tasks to assist in confronting the fallacy of the negative thought. For example, they can keep a list of their automatic thoughts and then a list of what actually happens later in the day. They might think, as they get up in the morning, "Nothing good will happen today." But later that day, as they keep their journal, they will notice several positive things. The record of positives confronts the fallacy of the negative thoughts. A mastery-and-pleasure scale also confronts negative thinking. The adolescent keeps a list of activities and rates them from one to ten to show how well he or she did on the activity and how much fun it was. These records are then used to confront the negative thoughts about those activities. Negative cognitions set the adolescent up for feeling depressed. Reality testing assists the adolescent in moving out of the depression and into some sense of pleasure, joy, and hope. From a pastoral point of view, the adolescent can be challenged that ultimately hope comes not from one's own strength but from one's awareness of being created in the image of God and having the redemptive process worked out in one's life.

Cognitive therapy is particularly helpful with adolescents who in their depression refuse to enter the counseling process and resist the formation of a therapeutic alliance. Cognitive therapy helps adolescents to think more accurately about themselves, their environment, and their future; and as thought distortions are corrected, depression and hopelessness are replaced by hope and a corresponding sense of joy. Hope and joy bring a resulting willingness to join in the counseling process. Productive actions and behavior in turn generate new hope and joy. As in behavioral therapy with adolescents, this cognitive approach is dependent on regular brief periods of reinforcement between the counselor and the adolescent.

Adolescents sometimes develop a negative schema—a basic approach for screening, sorting, and evaluating data that is maladaptive. The schema might be something like: "If I don't have a boyfriend or a girlfriend, I am a nerd or dork." As long as they live by that basic schema, they are setting themselves up for depression. Uncovering cognitive distortions is much easier than uncovering negative schemata (Wright and Beck, pp.1119–20). The schema serves as a premise for interpreting the events of life. It becomes the glasses that distort real life.

Meditation

A third basic method with adolescents is the use of meditation. Adolescents can be taught methods of systematic desensitization and meditation. Their experimenting life-styles makes new experiences easy to introduce. If you have not experienced meditation yourself, secure a tape or find a counselor to guide you through the experience before you attempt to use this with teenagers.

Tell the teens what you will be doing, and secure their permission. Tell them to stop and open their eyes at any point that they become uncomfortable. After they relax their bodies, they might focus their thoughts on a word like *hope, love,* or *joy.* Then they can meditate on their major anxieties or imagine facing a feared activity such as returning to school. Adolescents who suffer from anxiety are particularly encouraged by this approach. It gives them a sense of power and self-control because they feel they have contact with the Power beyond themselves. Also, it gives them the ability to bring a sense of peace and quiet to their lives, which displaces the anxiety. Opposites cannot dominate the same space at the same time. It is important in this process, when the negative feelings are overpowered, to then turn the adolescent to a program of meditation and planning that will bring positive feelings. When the evil demons are cast out, the good spirits must take their place. For twenty-five years I have used, with remarkable success, the meditation and relaxation approach with anxious adolescents.

One adolescent was incapable of attending her school classes and performing such routine tasks as going to the grocery store. With the assistance of relaxation and meditation techniques, she not only returned to a basic level of functioning, but was also able to graduate from high school and college. Much later she told me she still uses this approach to dealing with anxiety on business trips or during storms when she has to fly out of town.

Family Systems

Ministers regularly counsel families and are probably most used to family counseling approaches to psychotherapy. However, family counseling theorists present different pictures of family therapy. Some emphasize family history and personal feelings; others stress current structure and boundaries; still others underscore the significance of communication strategies. Yet all share a view of the family as a system. Rather than seeing events through an individual adolescent's set of assumptions, beliefs, feelings, thoughts, and behavioral patterns, the family counselor seeks to understand the crisis from the multiple perspectives of all members of the family system and to conceptualize the relationship between the patterns of interactions in that system and the crisis events. One asks, "How does this family's system affect the crisis?" and "How does this crisis impact the family?"

In counseling with teens and their families for three decades, I have come to rely on several key ingredients of a family's relationships for insights into the interrelatedness between the crisis and the family system:

1. The **structure** of the family unit captures attention first. Who lives with the adolescent, and how are they related? Does this youngster have sufficient family structure to provide the intellectual, physical, and emotional nurture for growing up?

2. The **open or closed** nature of the system is a second key issue. How

does the nuclear family relate to its extended members, the neighbors, and the community (school, church, business, etc.)? How much interchange of ideas, support, and resources can be tolerated? Does the family have sufficient boundaries to define its own identity?

3. **Communication patterns** and depths among family members and with the counselor arise as a third concern. Can members speak for themselves? Do they discuss only the basics of living together (food, shelter, time), or can they discuss ideas, emotions, hopes, and dreams? What topics get ignored?

4. **Conflict resolution methods** deserve detailed attention. Who has the family power, and what is the method of using it? Who and how many participate in discussions about differences of opinions, varied expectations, and family resources? Are the rules clear, consistent, and open for change as the children mature? What rules apply and to whom?

5. Another concern is the **clarity of the roles** played by the parents and the offspring. Can wife and husband keep their relationship clear without entwining the roles of mother and father? Is any child expected to function in a parent role?

6. One last issue, by no means least, is the giving and receiving of appropriate **affirmation** among family members. Can the parents affirm each other's egos and sustain the marriage, or at least refrain from involving the children in their attacks? When parents are divorced, they should still communicate mutual respect in front of the children. Can parents give an honest compliment (a verbal blessing) to their sons and daughters? Does the family share faith experiences? This is more than attending the same church, temple, or synagogue together. Do they talk about their beliefs? Do they spend **quality time** with the teenagers? One nineteen-year-old, crises-laden teen told me that he felt happy again when he visited his grandmother because "she was excited to see me." He was affirmed by her response.

Family intervention methods vary widely. Basically, the counselor becomes an "adopted member" of the family system and by identification with weaker members of the family restores some sense of balance or homeostasis. By modeling effective communication methods, positive conflict-resolution approaches, flexibility, and warm respect for each person, a caring counselor can significantly influence the family. Jay Haley focuses primarily on changing behavior patterns. Nathan Ackerman's major concerns are to expose and resolve the family's conflicts and then to aid in maintaining its balance. Murray Bowen's chief goal is the self-differentiation of each individual within the relationship and avoiding negative triangles.

Family issues receive repeated attention in the Bible. From the creation accounts in Genesis to the household code of Paul in Ephesians, the scriptures affirm the role and power of family life. As will be seen in the next chapter, teachers, ministers, and counselors can make a major contribution to adolescents and their families in crisis.

Transactional Analysis

Transactional analysis (TA) is an especially effective method for pastoral counseling because it uses a system of self-understanding (parent, adult, child) that is easily communicated to adolescents:

- The child ego state acts on the basis of "I feel" and begins at birth.
- A parent ego message is "I should" or "I should not" and is collected by the child from parents and authority figures.
- Adult ego messages begin around puberty and are the "I think" statements. They reflect the ability to decide the pros and cons of an issue and to act on what one thinks, not on the "feel" or "should" impulses.

Adolescents readily understand the communication theories of transactional analysis and respond positively to the concepts of games and scripts. Parallel transactions, crossed transactions, and ulterior transactions help them sort out their own communication problems. Figure 1 illustrates each.

Figure 1. The Three Types of Transactions in Transactional Analysis

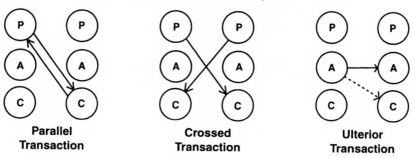

| Parallel Transaction | Crossed Transaction | Ulterior Transaction |

A parallel transaction could be "You should know better" (parent to child) and "Yes, I really am sorry" (child to parent). A crossed transaction could be "You should know better" (parent to child) and "Who are you to tell me what I should know? You shouldn't talk to me that way" (parent to child). An ulterior transaction could be "Would you like to see my room?" (adult to adult), said in a tone that implies "Let's mess around" (child to child). A game is an unconscious interchange between two persons with an emotional payoff for the originator. For example, a teenager who flirts and then gets angry at the response is playing a game. A script is a belief that was learned early and controls one's life. One teen confessed, "I'm never going to amount to much; no one in my family does." Teens need to understand the unconscious nature of games and scripts so as not to feel needless shame and guilt.

Group Counseling

Adolescents live in groups in the classroom, as they hang out, and as they participate in activities. They do very little alone. When was the last time you saw a teenager attend a movie alone? Those who do isolate themselves send a message of "Help me, I am lonely." Teens develop maturity as they learn from each other. They imitate each other's dress, talk, and behaviors. A positive counseling group draws strengths from this process to assist troubled teens grow and become more like adults. Youth learn, accept guidance, and make contracts better with each other than with most adults.

When beginning a group, several decisions hit us straight away. Will the group be homogeneous or heterogeneous? Should we group youth by age, type of crisis, or gender? Sometimes there are no choices. We take whoever shows up. I try to have mixed groups, except for stage of development. I have had success with early, middle, and late adolescent groups with males and females from a variety of families, races, and crisis situations. Not all teens can thrive in a group setting. If they are too shy or too hostile, the group setting might not work. Although many counselors rely on fixed term groups of eight to twelve weeks, I like nondeterminant, continuous groups where new members join as others "graduate." These groups develop an ongoing, healing culture over time. They indoctrinate new members as they introduce themselves, summarize their progress, and recap the group rules. Each new member discusses his or her own crisis and contracts for change and growth. The leadership style in these groups varies with the personality of the coleaders, but generally reflects the caring principles discussed in Chapter 3. It is best to have a male and a female leader for these groups.

Most often we combine group counseling with family counseling. The group leader meets with each member and a parent as needed (weekly or monthly). Confidentiality from the group sessions is observed, but the teen is often urged to share with the group how his or her meeting went with parents.

Parents, teachers, and ministers often have informal groups where healing dynamics can be at work. Use these opportunities to encourage responsible growth. Driving a carpool to swim practice provided my wife and me an opportunity to interact with our daughter and influence her development. As a teacher, formal committee meetings with students, academic team practices, and informal gatherings worked like group counseling if I paid attention to the process. As a pastor and youth minister, I noticed standard group processes and interactions with youth during religious study classes, retreats, and parties. Observing the group dynamics on a hayride, at a prayer retreat, or at drama practice would enlighten most ministers. Group power can be transformational in informal meetings and organized activities as well as in formal counseling groups.

When a new group begins, the youth normally spend time on various formation tasks. They get to know one another, clarify the rules of participation, and jockey for leadership and power. Until these dynamics have been established, most adolescent groups will not function effectively. Take time to tend to these group formation issues before you expect a group of teenagers to do its work.

Other Interventions

Many other methods of intervention are helpful with adolescents. Adolescents respond well to music therapy. The use of music in dealing with adolescents is helpful to assist not only in ventilation but also in establishing a common vocabulary and in understanding the adolescent's values. Drama therapy can do for adolescents what play therapy does for children. **Music and drama** can be listened to, written, discussed, and performed as a part of the therapy with adolescents. Likewise, **art therapy** is effective; adolescents who have difficulty verbalizing and participating in traditional forms of psychotherapy can often be reached through art. In working with adolescents, drama, music, and art all need to be used in conjunction with other approaches to counseling.

An effective method of intervention in any approach with youths is the use of **homework and journaling.** Because adolescents frequently keep a diary and regularly expect to do homework, the caring professional can be creative with a variety of methods of assigning tasks. Asking if it would be possible to see the diaries kept by an adolescent for a number of years might provide an excellent assessment tool (but make special efforts to maintain the confidentiality of these private reflections). Requesting that the adolescent write a personal song, poem, or short story is frequently helpful. Suggesting that the adolescent make a list of the positive and negative possibilities about a given behavior or desired activity can also be helpful. Reading assignments that will assist the adolescent in self-understanding, understanding personality theory, or even understanding the basic principles of an approach to counseling might be productive.

Psychological testing with adolescents needs to be a regular part of the treatment process because teens are changing so rapidly. Psychological testing provides useful cognitive and personality information as it assists in understanding the progress the adolescent has made in the developmental process. Testing instruments will vary from psychologist to psychologist, but pastoral counselors need to have a good working relationship with a psychologist who can test and evaluate adolescents and assist in making therapeutic suggestions. If one is not familiar with a given approach in pastoral psychotherapy, additional supervision and consultation are suggested. Reading a book and trying a new approach can be exciting, but a counselor's effectiveness will be greatly increased by careful, reflective case discussions with other counselors and supervisors.

Faith Responses

For centuries, ministers of the gospel have used certain unique resources and approaches to helping persons. They are still very effective methods of helping adolescents. When used carefully, prayer, Bible study, and religious dialogue all can contribute to the adolescent's response to a crisis.

Prayer

Adolescents in crisis can be asked if they pray and what they pray for. This will give the professional friend not only an insight into their anxiety and concerns but also an awareness of their concept of God and of authority persons. Many modern adolescents seem to have a preoccupation with spiritual matters and even a hunger for such involvement. They are not as interested in organized religion as were their parents. Many religious groups of the 1970s and 1980s composed primarily of young people were a testimony to the attraction of religious issues to adolescents. One psychiatrist thought that the adolescent interest in supernaturalism—belief in demonology, possession, and exorcism—results from dissatisfaction with the Western scientific worldview, a lack of trust in social structures, and a mood of hopelessness (Pattison, p. 227).

The use of prayer in the session can be introduced by asking, "Is it OK if we pray?" Its use can then be developed by asking what the adolescent would like to have included in the prayer. It is helpful to give the adolescent time to pray. The counselor may want to summarize the major themes and to seek God's guidance for the task ahead in his or her own prayer time. Explain that you will be praying for the adolescent at times other than in your sessions.

Bible Study

Although adolescents who have participated regularly in formal Bible study will be familiar with the great heroes, themes, stories, and general theology of scripture, many current adolescents might be uninformed concerning the Bible. Projective questions, which provide the opportunity to name a favorite biblical character, story, or truth, can assist not only in understanding the adolescent's level of religious and spiritual development but also in understanding his or her priorities and self-concept. Although Bible study can be helpful in the formal context of Bible teaching, I have found the most effective use of Bible study for adolescents to be placing the great stories of scripture that teach values and responsibilities in a contemporary setting. Many times a role play or drama of a Bible story can be set up by a counselor in a group context so the adolescents can act out the biblical story and then discuss its meaning. These events are designed to facilitate moral development as well as to assist the adolescent in self-understanding and in empathizing with other persons.

Furthermore, as adolescents tell their own life stories, great stories of scripture can be shared: for example, the accounts of David and Jonathan, of when Jesus chose to stay in the Temple, or of Timothy, the teenage missionary. Teenagers will vary widely in their openness to these stories. If they are hostile, use other stories.

Religious Dialogue

Theological discussion provides an opportunity to talk with adolescents about their own presuppositions as to the role of God, the church, and others in their crises or in their own perceptions of self. Adolescents need opportunities to explore and examine their personal beliefs about God, the universe, creation, personhood, morality, values, and the way persons relate to God. Many times, at the basis of a crisis is an unspoken and unexamined belief. For example, one young woman who had been molested by a teacher was unwilling to go back to school and unable to function, even after being released from a psychiatric setting. She maintained only that she was not blaming the teacher; then, after several sessions, she was able to say that she blamed God, because God had put the sexual appetite in the man who had molested her. In study and understanding, she came to see that God does not control and manipulate persons and that it was not God's intention for men to sexually molest teenage girls. With that insight and understanding she was soon able to return to church, finding social interaction much less threatening. Now she can believe that she lives not in a universe where God wills that teenage girls be sexually molested, but in a world where God's will is much more loving.

In working with adolescents it is particularly helpful to avoid being drawn into theological arguments. Ultimately, information can be shared, dialogue processed, and experiences pointed out, but the adolescent will have to discover his or her own faith system. A caring counselor points the way, listens to the questions, and encourages the faith journey.

These guidelines for intervention will get you started in responding to teenagers in crisis, but you will do well to seek regular feedback and consultation. Ask other parents how they deal with issues. Consult with an adolescent specialist. If you do ongoing counseling with teens, find a professional supervisor to review your cases. Do not be a Lone Ranger.

Chapter 5

Family Problems

Family problems invade most families on a regular basis. Strong families solve or contain them and go on with life as usual. A crisis exists when demands upon a family equal or exceed its resources. There isn't enough time, money, space, or love to go around. Usually, an added load precipitates the crisis; events such as moving, illness, job loss, pregnancy, accident, legal problems, war, fire, storm, or unexpected bills are examples of added stress. However, for a family with adolescents, their rapid changes produce a seemingly unending state of crisis. As adolescents adjust to their new bodies, brains, and feelings, they move to declare independence through a personalized self-identity, and all but the most gifted families will experience upheaval.

Even young Jesus caused his parents stress. Recall that a crisis was precipitated for the parents of Jesus when they learned he had not traveled with them on the return trip from Jerusalem. After three days of searching, they found him in the Temple. His mother's words, as recorded in Luke 2:48, are: "Son, why have you treated us so? Behold, your father and I have been looking for you anxiously." The early adolescent Jesus speaks to them about pursuing his own mission and asks, "Did you not know that I must be in my Father's house?" They do not understand, but he returns with them to Nazareth. They coped with the stress.

Even parents contribute to the stress. Parents often are not prepared to invest the energy necessary in tending to the teens' transitions toward adulthood. Reacting to the stress, teens can make it worse. Teens usually are not aware of their role in the conflict. They blame mom or dad for just about everything—except at school, where they blame the teachers. The reciprocal nature of the parent-child relationship is recorded in Ephesians 5 and 6. Ephesians 5:21: "Be subject to one another out of reverence for Christ" sets the foundation for understanding 6:1–4. The responsibility of offspring is to obey, honor, and respect their parents. There is also a responsibility of parents to nurture and discipline with such caring sensitivity that they do not provoke children to anger. Maintaining the reciprocal nature of adolescent-parent relationships greatly facilitates crisis intervention at all levels. Each step is a two-way affair. The assessment level begins by looking at both parental and adolescent issues. Seeking alternatives becomes a responsibility of both parents and teens. Counseling, education, and care focus on the adolescent, on the parents, and on the family as a unit greater than the sum of the parts. This chapter examines family dynamics in a crisis context, family stressors, and family resources.

Family Dynamics

Any discussion of family dynamics depends on basic assumptions about the nature of personhood and the point of view of the parents, teacher, minister, or counselor. Focus on three components of family dynamics as they impact the teenager's identity struggle. These three—family **promises, role expectations,** and **core values**—affect the teen's self-image, the parents' relationship, and the family identity.

Adolescents and their families who have a sense of mutual promises that bond them together, common expectations, and personal values grounded in a shared faith have resources for facing crises and solving them in ways that produce family growth and strong, confident, competent youth. Adolescents who lack a sense of family promises of support, who sense low or confusing role expectations, or who lack (reject in some cases) family core values not only experience more crises but also have fewer resources for coping with a crisis.

The Identity Triangle

The identity triangle was first introduced in the family systems theory by Nathan Ackerman. It advocates creating reciprocity and homeostasis in the identities by maintaining a healthy balance between the identity of the teen, the identity of the parental pair, and the identity of the family (see Figure 2). Ackerman wrote about the identity of the married pair, but the shift away from traditional family units of husband, wife, and their kids necessitates looking at the relationship of the parents. One cannot assume that they are married to each other. Individual identity or self-concept constitutes the answer to the question "Who am I?" It includes the youth's body image, role definition, personality style, and whatever else makes up one's self-definition. A youth said, "I'm a fifteen-year-old boy who enjoys sports, likes girls, hates school, tolerates my family, and delivers papers." A sixteen-year-old troubled teen described herself as "one tough bitch who hates my family but loves to dance, fight, and try new stuff." Their radically different self-images set the stage for different relationships with parents, teachers, ministers, or counselors.

The identity of the parental pair focuses on the blending of the father's and mother's identities into their style of marriage or relationship. The boy's parents reported, "We are a typical yuppie couple who have all we basically need, but we have lost contact with our son." The girl's mom and dad were divorced. Both wanted her to live with the other; they said, "She is old enough to know right from wrong, and we are tired of her junk. We have enough problems just trying to pick up the pieces of our break-up!"

Family identity passes from generation to generation and carries the family's self-concept and community image. The boy's father complained: "What would people in my hometown think if they knew a Newton had been in trouble with the juvenile authorities? Why, we are the foundation of the church!" The girl's mother reported that she did not want the grandparents to know of her daughter's new attitudes and life-style because "it would be disgraceful." But, she added, "We hardly know our neighbors; I do not care what they think!"

Three significant dynamics help a family in maintaining its identity resources in the face of a crisis and through the transition of children through adolescence:

1. The family *promises,* covenants, commitments, and rules that are implicitly or explicitly evident
2. The family *expectations,* dreams, calling, and goals for the adolescent and the family
3. The family *values,* centeredness, and the degree to which the family is focused on its religious traditions and core values.

As these three overlap the identity triangle, as seen in Figure 3, balance and optimum tension in the various components are paramount. A family cannot give in to living only for the teen's self, or to becoming so focused on the parents' relationship or lack thereof, or to living to keep up the family image regardless of the needs of the youth. Two additional issues, represented by the double lines connecting each of the points, are **communication and conflict management**. Each of these will be examined in detail later in this chapter.

Figure 2. The Identity Triangle

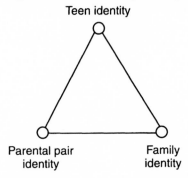

Teen identity

Parental pair
identity

Family
identity

Family Identity

A healthy family that exists intact over a number of years develops a strong identity. If over a number of generations its members maintain a residence in a general locality, that identity will be communicated in society. However, modern-day, "on-the-move" families have little or no identity in their new social communities and receive little reinforcement or resources from the community. For example, the Rowatt family, having lived three generations in a small southern Illinois mining town, has an identity in that community tied to the vocation and family life-style of all three generations. However, when my wife and I and our preschool twins lived in an apartment in Dallas, Texas, for three months while consulting with Park City Baptist Church, we had little or no family identity in the new community. People did not know what we valued or who we were before we left for another community. Now, because we have lived twenty years on the same street in Louisville, we have a new but stable identity. There was very limited interaction with the Texas community and almost no support, except for a few persons also involved in the church. In Louisville, a transplanted family identity has taken root and found support among friends and neighbors.

When one child was hospitalized in Dallas, the crisis rested on our shoulders with little support from the community. However, when a member of the family was hospitalized in our small Illinois mining town, there was a multitude of flowers, cards, phone calls, and personal visits from community members with long-lasting relationships with the family—a much greater support system. Now in Louisville, the support grows. The family identity is a significant factor in counseling with adolescents in crisis. It can be a major support, or it may be a burden for some teens trying to escape its impact. This identity can help teachers nudge students toward their

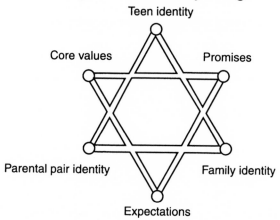

Figure 3. The Identity Triangle

Teen identity

Core values

Promises

Parental pair identity

Family identity

Expectations

potential, but if the family is new, teachers have little to draw on. Likewise, ministers who know the youth's family have a decided edge in caring for the youth in crisis. The stronger the family's identity, the greater the influence. This can backfire, as in the case of a teacher who unfairly compares a teenager to an older sibling who attended the school earlier.

Parental Pair Identity

The identity of the parents, like that of the family, has a community and a cultural dimension. Nevertheless, for the crisis' sake, the most significant component of the parental pair's identity is how the adolescent perceives it. If the parents are perceived as a mutually committed, highly competent functioning team, the adolescent will consider them as a resource in time of crisis. Divorced and single parents still need to work together in the task of parenting. This positive image may be based on the adolescent's lack of awareness of the couple's problems, especially when the couple is not open; however, tension is usually difficult to camouflage. An adolescent can quickly determine that his or her parents are getting along and respond with trust and hope. When the parents talk openly and work collaboratively, the adolescent can face crises more confidently and effectively. When the parents are in a state of continual conflict, the teenager moves toward crisis.

A second perception of the marital pair is as opponents. When adolescents view their parents as opponents, the youth will frequently form temporary coalitions with one parent or the other and try to play the resulting power struggle for private gain. Not only will this add to the crisis dimension of an adolescent's life; it will slow the maturation and self-identity process. It can trigger regression. Furthermore, when external crises arise, the adolescent will be less confident in turning to either parent for support. The parents' inability to collaborate will decrease their power as a resource and their ability to guide their offspring toward maturity. When parents attempt to use teachers, ministers, or counselors to take sides in their family disagreements, the teenager is the loser. The teen will not know whom to trust.

A third identity model is the functional-dysfunctional model. When the adolescent perceives one parent to be functional and the other dysfunctional, the adolescent will usually collaborate with one parent and will correspondingly develop either a functional or dysfunctional self-concept. If an adolescent collaborates with the perceived functional parent, there is the danger of enmeshing identities in that relationship, causing potential difficulties in peer relations and limiting the adolescent's own identity formation. This develops the risk of emotional or physical incest. If on the other hand the identification is with the perceived dysfunctional parent, the adolescent will probably model parallel dysfunctional behavior that will precipitate a number of crises. For example, in an alcoholic family, a teen who identifies with the drinking parent is also likely to turn to substance abuse as a way of acting out and avoiding stress. Not only does this limit the adolescent's individual identity formation, but it also adds to the stressors in a crisis. Several times in group therapy teens have disclosed that they know friends who smoke pot or drink with a parent. In a few cases, teachers have been arrested for substance abuse with their students. If you cannot help these kids, for sure, do not harm them!

When the adolescent sees both parents as dysfunctional, the result is confusion and disarray. With little positive role modeling, the adolescent almost invariably takes on a dysfunctional identity unless, through other relationships (teacher, minister, foster parent, case worker, or counselor), the teen receives unusual nurture and discipline for movement toward adulthood. Dysfunctional-dysfunctional situations merit strong consideration for out-of-home placement in times of crisis. When out-of-home placement facilities are poor or nonexistent, some churches provide alternative living contexts for adolescents with two dysfunctional parents. In some cases, boarding schools serve this function. Long-term hospitalization has become almost impossible because of the health-care insurance situation in the twenty-first century.

When a parent has divorced and remarried or is living with a lover, adolescents are less likely to perceive the parental dyad as functional, especially if the stepparent's age is close to that of the adolescent. When adolescents are brought into blended families, extended family counseling is highly recommended. More than a few blended family parents find that crises erupt when their children reach puberty.

Teen Identity

Although Ackerman primarily addressed the self-identity of any individual, self-identity in our context is from the perspective of the adolescent. The teenager's self-identity is reinforced primarily from family role and functioning; however, secondary reinforcement comes from personal achievements and the youngster's relationship to teachers, counselors, coaches, counselors, other family members, and to the peer group. Youth who have a job begin some identity formation around the kind of work they do. The self-identity of adolescents is also tied to their body images and to their acceptance of their sexuality. If they are uncomfortable with their maleness or femaleness, their identities will be correspondingly confused. Not only does the lack of positive self-identity appear as a developmental crisis; it can add to the likelihood of an adolescent's acting out behaviorally and precipitating an emergency crisis. Young people who are diagnosed as emotionally disturbed, depressed, or having conduct disorders show more self-image disturbances than do other adolescents. Emotionally disturbed adolescents show not only self-image deficiencies but also patterns of deficiencies correlated with the type of disturbance.

From a theological point of view, self-image can be reinforced for adolescents from the doctrines of creation, incarnation, and redemption. Adolescents who believe they are created in the image of God tend to feel better and often take more interest in self-care. Religious teachers and ministers can support the belief that the body is the dwelling place of the Spirit. Likewise, believing that God entered into the form of a person, even an adolescent person, can sustain a teen's self-concept. A belief that God so loved the world (including the adolescent world) that he gave his only-begotten Son that whosoever believeth should not perish but have everlasting life can project a positive sense of self. For Jewish youth, the bar mitzvah and bas mitzvah blessings uphold a positive sense of self.

Adolescents need to be able ultimately to affirm "I am a person of worth created in the image of God (male and female)" to live abundantly and to love and serve others (see *Being Me* by Grady Nutt). Disturbance in the family (divorce, death, prolonged illness, or unemployment) negatively affects personality development. Religious faith supports positive personality development even during family crises.

One study of adolescence prepared at Catholic University showed that the most positive subgroup for self-image was African American adolescents, and an earlier Gallup youth survey revealed that African American teens attend church more often. Ninety-three percent of African American teens and 85 percent of white teens markedly agree or mostly agree on the response "I take a positive attitude toward myself"; 68 percent of African American and 49 percent of white teens had attended worship in the past week. Of course, attending is not the same as being actively involved and engaged in worship.

In discussing this finding with a number of African American men (pastors, athletes, and businessmen), I discovered that they were not surprised. They felt that African American teens receive negative press and are largely misunderstood by most white professionals. They pointed to the strong role of religion in African American history and the high esteem given in the African American church to the pastor. One former NFL player said that African American ministers are role models for African American males just as sports heroes are, but are more available and accessible. In some sections of the country, African American teens have strong support groups for religion, music, sports, and education. More African American professionals are returning to their communities to provide resources for less fortunate youth.

An African American youth in a support group at the hospital refused to talk about his feelings for his mother and offered "I'm tough and mean" language to defend himself against peer pressure to share. After the group met, he handed me a touching note of explanation. This unchurched youth lacked the ego strength to share his love for his mother, but the feelings were present and could be shared with a religious leader. A biracial young lady revealed that she could choose to present herself as Hispanic, African American, or Asian American, depending on the circumstances. She said, "I'm all of these and more. I can be whichever is best. God is not any color. Now I am black."

Promises

"My mom could care less what I do," announced one troubled teen, "so why should I?" Another stated, "My dad loves me no matter what I do, but I won't do anything to disappoint him." As stated earlier, Ephesians 5:21 places a covenant at the center of family relationships. Mutual, voluntary commitment is espoused by the writer of Ephesians. "Be subject to one another" demands that parents and children, like husbands and wives, enter a covenant of 100 percent commitment. This is not based on one another's desirability or worth but on reverence for the relationship to the Christ. A covenant is a promise based on the nature of the covenant maker, not on the conditions of the relationship or the nature of the recipient. The covenant is communicated first to the child through the parents' keeping of covenants in marriage. By the time the child reaches adolescence, she or he is capable of making a mutual covenant with the parents. Such covenants and contracts call for mutual respect and for negotiation of the rules, regulations, and expectations of both the parents and the teenagers (Eph. 6:1–4). Adolescents who live in a covenant relationship with their parents experience fewer crises and are more capable of managing the crises that do arise.

Expectations

Teens need a chance to give back to society. They should be expected to do service hours, to help each other, and to go on mission for a good cause. Matthew 16:25 paradoxically states, "For whoever would save his life will lose it, and whoever loses his life for my sake will find it." A sense of calling may inform the family and the marital pair's identity long before the child is able to conceptualize vocation. But for adolescents, a sense of calling is a way of conceptualizing vocation, an informed perception of their sense of giftedness, their resources, and talents. They find a sense of self by asking how those gifts can be dedicated to service to God and to the betterment of society. A sense of calling asks them to use their resources sacrificially to serve humanity. Adolescents who have a sense of motivation to help society or to serve their country or to seek a profession are more highly motivated and less likely to be in crisis. Those who lose themselves in their sense of calling find themselves from the sense of identity formation. Numerous teen magazines run true stories of teens trying to find some meaning from confessing their mistakes and begging others not to make the same mistakes. Laura, a young repentant inmate, told of how she killed a peer in a drunk-driving accident at age eighteen. What angered her the most was that neither her imprisonment nor the other girl's death changed anything. Her friends continued to party in irresponsible ways (*Teen People,* August 2000, pp. 122–28). Her parents go to schools and churches reading letters from her and trying to stop others from drinking and driving.

Core Values

Centeredness is the degree to which one's identity personally is rooted in one's relationship to the Power beyond one's self. However this relationship is described, be it in "Higher Power" language of the Twelve Steps of Alcoholics Anonymous, in the traditional Christian language of piety centered in Christ, or in terms of transpersonal psychology's understanding of being centered within Self, the dynamic is the same for adolescents. The center of meaning provides values for their experience of change and crisis. From their centeredness they develop a positive sense of self-identity. The content of faith experiences and the stage of religious experience as defined by James Fowler are closely interrelated in their effects on self-identity formation. Stage alone does not determine identity.

Teens' values cannot be judged on externals such as dress, jewelry, or hair. Get to know them as individuals. Ask what seems unfair in the world. What would they like to change? Who angers them most and why? Listen to the themes of injustice and their views of proper relationships. I have yet to meet a teen who did not value fairness and freedom. Often values are more assessable through stories and case studies. Share an incident with them and ask, "What would you do and why?" Listen to their anecdotes for clues to their value base. Are they motivated by fear of getting caught, fear of pain, a desire to be respected, a commitment to follow the rules, a need to be responsible, or a wish to be loving to all persons? They may have little or no desire to do what is right. Training values into a wayward teenager takes time and modeling, not lectures and preaching. Often life situations are their only teachers, as was the case of the girl in prison for killing another girl in a drunk-driving accident.

Family Stressors

A number of dynamics figure prominently in the role of family stressors in adolescent crises. We will discuss internal factors and external factors. Effective communication and successful problem-solving methods facilitate efficient management of crises.

Effective communication and the ability to have a functioning, open, and mutual conflict-resolution process depend on the degree of cohesion between the self-identity, parental identity, and family identity, and the interrelatedness of promises, expectations, and values.

Effective communication between parents and among family members is crucial during the adolescent period. Good communicators speak clearly and openly about a variety of topics, share not only thoughts but also feelings, and are in touch with verbal and nonverbal signals. I tell adults that the three keys to good communication are listen, listen, and listen. Listen to the youths' words; listen to their tone or feelings. Listen to their unmet needs for love, respect, freedom, and self-worth. Listen with your head and your heart.

Capable families employ a problem-solving method that openly invites input from all family members and is egalitarian, not authoritarian, in nature. Strong families set limits and maintain some executive function in the parents. A parent, teacher, or minister who lacks the capacity to set caring, firm limits adds to the anxiety and confusion of adolescents in crisis. As the adolescent matures, participation in conflict management can increase in the decision-making stage of selecting the alternatives to be pursued, as discussed in Chapter 4. Ultimately, as the adolescent assumes a differentiated self-identity, she or he assumes personal responsibility for decision making, and the adults move into a consultative, supportive, collaborative mode of relating.

Internal Factors

The adolescent's family appears as an ever-changing, somewhat confusing, and often fear-filled unit. The family brings some crises upon itself. These crises erupt from internal conditions of the family system.

Major internal stressors on the adolescent's family are these:

- The struggle for dependence vs. independence
- The maintenance of distance vs. closeness
- The planning of family time around a dysfunctional or functional parent

External stressors attack from beyond the family. These have to do with events such as these:

- Illness of a family member
- Death or suicide of a close relative or significant friend
- Divorce of the parents or actions of a stepparent
- Redefining family roles and expectations

In interviewing a number of adolescents, **dependence vs. independence** surfaced in one way or another as a major concern. They said things like, "Our parents need to understand that we have minds of our own. They can't choose our friends. We can think for ourselves." On the other hand, in interviewing parents, the other side of the dependence/independence struggle was a frequent complaint. Parents would lament, "They are associating with a crowd that's not good for them. They talk back! They don't respect us. They're trying to act too old for their own good." In the last decade of the last century, parents complained that teens did not spend time with them. In this century, the tables are turned, and the teens are lamenting that their parents are too busy to find time to support the teenagers. Teens desire quality time, not control from parents and concerned adults. They ask for ministers and teachers who are interested in their future but who respect the right of the youth to define that future for themselves.

In reviewing cases of adolescents admitted to a psychiatric inpatient facility, I discovered that all but a few mentioned family dependence/independence issues as a part of the crisis. Family problems and family stress, although not necessarily the precipitating factor in the hospitalization, surfaced as a dynamic along with other factors. In a multidimensional assessment process, family dynamics almost always need separate, focused attention. Therefore, family-oriented pastoral counseling is a necessary resource that churches need to provide. Because of the demanding nature of a pastor's responsibilities, few pastors can afford the time for in-depth family counseling. Counseling centers or special church staff members are needed to fill the gap and to assist families in appropriately blessing their teenagers' movement toward independence. Educators likewise are wise to include the family dynamics in any attempt to address special needs of a troubled teen. Of course, the problem has been in getting those parents to care enough to work with the schools. More local control of schools and stronger parent-teacher organizations have helped some. Whereas some parents hold on too long, others let go too soon.

The struggle between parents and adolescents for **distance vs. closeness** should not be confused with dependency. Youngsters who spend very little time with their parents can still be dependent on their parents for their identity, whereas those who spend a great deal of time around their parents might be quite independent from their parents in their thinking, feeling, and functioning. Distance and closeness focus not so much on time together as on the ability to share affirmation, develop emotional intimacy, and discuss ideas, dreams, and plans. Intimate families have regular, planned, structured activities and share personal conversation together. When a crisis comes, the communication and decision-making skills developed help in managing the crisis. The closeness provides a caring context for crisis resolution. As a fifteen-year-old victim of sexual molestation put it, "I knew my parents would always be there for me no matter what happened." One thirteen-year-old stated, "I knew my dad would help me out of this trouble because he always listened to me when I was upset." However, a sixteen-year-old pregnant teen worried for seven weeks before telling her parents for fear that they would "get ballistic and kick me out."

Distance is particularly difficult in the modern American Anglo family because of the pursuit of economic advancement. Fathers are frequently uninvolved at home, and, unless special attention is given to the dynamics of managing a two-career marriage, mothers often are less available than were mothers of previous decades who did not go out to work. Children who have limited bonds with parents are prime candidates to become crisis-laden adolescents. Distance can arise from a lack of emotional bonding caused by extended periods of illness, substance abuse, or times of separation (for example, as regards those in prison or the military). Some children miss forming a bond early and suffer tremendously in adolescence. However, as the electronic revolution and the information age spreads, more parents are able to telecommute and do their work at home. Some believe that the home-schooling phenomenon adds to the level of intimacy between parents and teens. More research is needed on the long-term benefits and problems when parents serve as private educators.

Dysfunctional parenting refers to parents who have not sufficiently formed their own self-identity and who themselves participate in deviant, antisocial behavior. For example, alcoholics, drug addicts, and those institutionalized for extended periods of time in a mental hospital or prison may be dysfunctional parents. Family stress caused by the dysfunctional parent distresses not only the relationship but also the structure of the family. An adolescent who grows up with an inadequate family structure lacks the context for developing a positive self-identity. In my estimation, over 50 percent of patients in psychiatric institutions have dysfunctional parents. Patients who lack a family structure have the poorest prognosis for recovery. Of the several internal factors producing stress on the family, having a dysfunctional parent creates more lasting negative effects on adolescents than any other factor. Teenage children of addicted parents are more likely to be in crises with their own addictions. Curiously, some resilient teens become overachievers when their parents are dysfunctional. These teens usually have a neighbor, relative, teacher, minister, or counselor who serves as a parent substitute.

External Factors

External stressors on the family, such as the extended illness of one parent, produce a time of crisis for the adolescent. Although these factors usually cannot be prevented, the negative effects can be alleviated.

In **serious illness,** the structure, style of parent interventions, and general family rules and expectations are frequently thrown into disarray because the family's energy and concern are focused on the hospitalized parent. If the parent is critically ill or injured, the adolescent may for the first time be forced to consider the possibility of the parent's mortality. Adolescents may fill the vacuum created by the attention of the family on the ill member by declaring more independence. The stress from the illness may generate enough anxiety that youngsters begin to act out by taking risks, turning to drugs or alcohol for quick relief, or experimenting sexually. Substance abuse is a common way of "managing" the pressure. If teens can turn to positive resources—other family members, caring teachers, a church leader, or professional friend—they are better able to manage the stress and not create further crises for themselves and their families. They need accurate information about the illness, a plan for intermediate supervision and care, and clear guidelines about expected behavior.

In the case of illness or accident for the teen, the crisis may have immediate disruptive effects and long-term developmental consequences. Teenagers often obsess about the consequences of being hospitalized on their status in the peer group or on their relationships with friends or lovers. Arranging for continued contact helps. In some cases, when those "friends" were part and parcel to the crisis behind the hospitalization, parents are cautioned to limit and closely supervise visitation. Work with a professional counselor to set realistic guidelines. Illness or accidents may interrupt normal development. One nineteen-year-old male confessed that since his long hospital stay, he had fallen behind in his relationships with his friends and felt awkward around other teens. He related better to adults but felt the pain of social isolation from his age group. Often adolescents need activities or jobs that involve regular interaction with same-age peers in order to rebuild confidence.

The **death or suicide** of a family member is a time of grief so overwhelming that unless the adolescent is given regular, almost daily, attention, acting out at an unacceptable level is to be expected. One adolescent whose mother took her own life when he was fourteen wanted to leave home forever. However, after spending a week of almost round-the-clock time with the pastor, he returned to a positive relationship with his remaining parent. Rather than go to an out-of-state boarding school, he attended a private school nearby and lived at home with his father. Another young man was detained for shoplifting a candy bar the day before his mother's funeral. He had plenty of money. Grief often upsets the rational thinking of teens. Expect the unexpected. Provide extra care and supervision. Teens are often most helped by understanding teachers and ministers. Some youth will need peer counseling or professional help.

Divorce, the death of the parents' marriage, is another traumatic experience. With careful crisis management, the adolescent can successfully respond and even grow. However, several dynamics need consideration. Frequently, teenagers will blame themselves and the stress they have placed on the family for causing the divorce. Such borrowed guilt is unrealistic and may help force the adolescent further into crisis. Adolescents need to hear from the parents that they did not cause the divorce. In the confusion of a divorce, adolescents frequently have inadequate information about their parents' plans. Pastoral care and professional counseling need to focus on encouraging teenagers and their parents to speak openly about the future, including the parents' intentions as to marriage, living arrangements, financial arrangements, and so forth. When divorce means moving, there might be major disruption of the peer group. This is a key concern for adolescents. Not infrequently, they will manipulate and play games in an attempt to get their parents back together. These efforts only add to the crisis, in most cases. Joining support groups with other teens and talking with those whose parents have already divorced have helped many. Teachers may want to adjust assignments and work with due dates for teens whose parents are in any kind of crisis.

Remarriage brings unique stress to families with teenagers. For adolescents, **stepparents** and **blended families** mean adjustments. These remarriages can lead to strong families, but it takes work to overcome the issues with teens. Discipline and setting rules can be difficult if the non-biological parent has not developed a deep, mutual friendship with the teen. "You are not my boss; I do not have to do what you say!" barked one fifteen-year-old to her stepfather. Generally, the biological parent should handle discipline and rules. When that parent fails to do so, confusion abounds, and crises gush into everyday living. The new parent should first seek to become an adult friend with his or her spouse's teenager. Let any parental role develop naturally from the growing friendship. I prefer the term *friend-parent* to stepparent. This takes time and patience! However, teenagers often turn to other adults for parental advice (teachers, ministers, neighbors, parents of peers, or counselors). One sixteen-year-old actually told the coleaders of his therapy group that they had "raised him for the last year and that his parents had been too busy with their own crises to give him much attention."

Another sticky area for blended families concerns visitation with a non-custodial parent and relating to stepsiblings. Every family identity operates within its own set of rules. When teens visit the other home, adjusting to the changes can be disturbing. One thirteen-year-old quit doing homework and refused to visit his father on weekends, "because Dad's new wife makes us all clean her house while she is at work. At our new home the cleaning lady vacuums the whole house, even my room," he boasted. After considerable renegotiating, an acceptable list of chores was developed for both homes. The boy settled down and got back to his school assignments. If the rules are not the same for teens living in the same house, they become agitated, irritated, or hostile. "This is not fair!" remains the most common call to battle for teenagers. If a stepbrother or stepsister gets more freedom, spending money, clothes, or attention, problems will surface. Jealousy is normal, but work to reduce these tensions by being as fair as possible. Trade an advantage in one area for a break in another. For instance, one might get to attend a private school, but the other gets extra use of the car.

Clear boundaries, separate belongings, and fair rules will go a long way in stabilizing the relationships of teenagers forced into a house by the marriage of their parents. Regular family conferences can provide a forum for tensions to be resolved before they develop into a crisis. Parents, remember that your marriage will continue after the teens leave the home. Be extrasensitive, flexible, and tolerant until that day. However, blending the families will be a lifelong task of planning weddings, birthday celebrations, and holidays.

Defining roles is a further external stressor for adolescents. Teens resist being pushed into narrow choices. In families where the male or female role is closed to redefinition, adolescents who do not follow their parents' choice of roles have additional conflict. For example, a housewife who finds her role quite fulfilling might experience conflict with a teenage daughter who chooses to pursue a profession and rebels against an assigned role as homemaker. Likewise, a son who disdains athletics may feel parental pressure as he seeks a career in music, drama, or art. A parent's support for the freedom to be oneself aids teens in coping with role pressure. Teachers, counselors, and ministers can help reduce the stress by interpreting the role conflict with the parents. Open communication and discussing alternatives will help, but it is difficult to overcome the noxious effects of inflexibility.

Family Counseling Resources

The first task for teachers, ministers, and counselors with families and adolescents in crisis is to establish rapport while **assessing the dynamics** of the crisis. Other adults can and should be involved in family counseling, because we see the family cycle from birth to death and have ongoing defined relationships with families. It is easier for the minister who already relates well to the family to intervene in an ensuing crisis in a positive way. However, caution should be taken not to presume upon the relationship and to contract openly for any crisis counseling. Because ministers sometimes lack adequate training or sufficient time or may overidentify with the family, long-term crisis counseling may need to be referred to specialized family counselors. Teachers are often reluctant to become involved in family problems, but often a request for a family conference to discuss the student's performance at school can begin a process of healing.

Assuming that a counselor continues in the crisis intervention at some level, the task of assessment can be facilitated by the family dynamic model introduced earlier in this chapter (see Figure 3). The first task in assessment is to look at the identity triad to ascertain the identity formation level and faith development of the adolescent, the family, and the marital pair. Focus not only on the strength of each of these but also on the clarity of boundaries between them. The counselor needs to be particularly alert for confusion of boundaries between the adolescent and the marital pair; partners occasionally emotionally, if not physically, use an adolescent as a mate substitute when the marriage lacks substance. Counselors might notice a negative triangle when conflict arises among the parents and a teen. Members may set up a persecutor, victim, and rescuer triangle that destabilizes the relationships. The teen may employ this in a game of "divide and conquer."

Furthermore, the counselor needs to assess the level of commitment and the clarity and reciprocity of the nature of the promises between the adolescent and the parents. Next, assessment turns to a sense of understanding of expectations or mission for the family as a whole and for the adolescent in particular. Expectations impact the adolescent's involvement in academic pursuits and clarify his or her identity. Finally, the counselor will want to assess the adolescent's values or attitudes toward a personalized faith system. What does the adolescent believe? How does this affect the way the adolescent is relating to the crisis? The counseling mode of sustaining as presented in Chapter 1 is a key perspective during the assessment process. Some persons become impatient when help isn't immediately forthcoming.

A significant part of adolescent counseling involves assisting the family and the adolescent in **developing some simple communication rules,** such as respectfully listening to one another until each person has finished talking, checking out assumptions before acting, and interpreting nonverbal signals without clarification. The counselor will also want to aid the family in expanding its communication to deeper levels so that members can send and receive clear signals about their thoughts, beliefs, and feelings. In working with communication, the counseling mode of informing and guiding is paramount.

The counseling perspective of healing and reconciling blends with that of confrontation as the counselor assists family members in **dealing with their methods of resolving conflicts.** Although all families experience conflict, healthy families can define the conflict, mobilize their resources, and grow through creative responses. Such functioning families define their problems and mobilize resources for coping with the conflict until resolutions can be found from external resources. Families with dysfunctional relationships may or may not be able to define the problem, however, and their relationships begin to deteriorate. Isolation replaces intimacy as the conflict mushrooms. Dysfunctional families begin to disintegrate structurally as the conflict continues unresolved. Matthew 18:15–22 provides one approach to conflict management that openly faces differences, puts reconciliation as a primary goal, and uses a peacemaking process for resolving the conflict. Simple negotiation skills of ventilating feelings, defining problems, and seeking alternatives, incorporated with the attitudes displayed in Matthew, will greatly enhance the family's possibilities for resolving conflicts. Be alert for those negative triangles that lead to side taking and avoid the major issues.

Clarifying values and negotiating rules call upon the counseling mode of guiding and confronting. The counselor needs to assist both the adolescent and the parents in confronting one another's expectations and inconsistent values and then guide them in the process of establishing mutually agreed-upon expectations, rules, and foundational values. The older the teenagers, the more input would be expected from them when negotiating rules and expectations. Although a number of parents remain too rigid in their rules and are unilateral in establishing expectations, too many parents err in the other direction. They do not set firm, caring limits or spend enough time in family activities for the adolescent to model the parents' values. Adolescents become anxious and overly experimental when given more freedom than they can handle.

The behavior in the adolescent unit in a psychiatric hospital improved dramatically when patients were simply placed in a routine with firm limits and clear expectations for appropriate behavior and schoolwork were set. Because each adolescent develops at his or her own pace, there is no way a universal set of rules can be established for all. The rules must be renegotiated periodically around the formula of increased freedom with increased responsible behavior and responsibility for self.

Adolescents and parents struggle to discover a unique balance of law and grace as they model the struggle of human freedom and destiny. Parents must be careful, on the one hand, not to play God with their teenager's future. On the other hand, they need to be careful not to be so distant and withdrawn as to appear unconcerned, apathetic, and uncaring. Some critical decisions need mutual ongoing negotiation, such as when the adolescent will seek employment, how the adolescent chooses friends, what family resources are available to entertain those friends, and what are to be the adolescent's continued dating relationships and vocational decisions.

In a crisis, the family may need assistance in reassessing these issues in light of the crisis issues. "What effect does this crisis have upon the young person's development?" is a key question for the family to resolve.

A sensitive response calls for teachers, ministers, and counselors to be involved and available to the family but for the family members ultimately to make their own decisions as to the structure, relationship patterns, intimacy levels, and identity formation that are uniquely theirs. A caring professional may be helpful in clarifying alternatives for out-of-home placement or boarding schools if the family structure needs to be redefined. Certainly a minister needs to be of assistance in clarifying the nature of faith relationships and parent-child relationships. There will be many disappointments for both adolescents and their parents. As the minister facilitates reconciliation through confession and forgiveness, family units can be maintained. However, in families that insist upon scorekeeping and projecting blame, much confrontation of both sides will be needed. Teachers, ministers, and counselors have an important role in responding to family problems. We help families solve their own problems.

Chapter 6

Sexual Problems

*T*eenage bodies undergo a sexual revolution. They become capable of reproduction. Their glands erupt into explosive stimulators of strange new emotions. One study reported that the average fourteen-year-old boy thinks about sex once every ten seconds. That may be an exaggeration, but not by much. For some teens, life is all about appearing attractive to the opposite sex. Teachers can spot those who are heading for trouble months before a crisis unfolds, yet few can do anything to interrupt the process of trouble waiting to detonate. Ministers offer programs, but those who need them most fail to show up. In fact, it seems that peer attitudes are more significant than religious affiliations for those who do get pregnant (Corcoran, pp. 611–12). Predictably, recent studies indicate that nearly a third of single births are to teenagers. Parental attitudes do make a difference. So do expectations that education is important. Teachers and ministers can support those expectations. Rigid parenting adds to the likelihood of difficulty, but feeling emotionally disconnected from parents may contribute to an adolescent's waiting to engage in sexual activity.

Sexual problems do not begin in adolescence. The issues begin at an early age, when correct sex information, attitudes, and behaviors are not taught in the home. Teenagers who have received accurate information from mom and dad and can talk freely about values and sexual relationships are less likely to be in difficulty. A major factor in a girl's early pregnancy is being physically or sexually abused as a child. One study suggested that as many as 68 percent of teenage mothers had been sexually abused (Kellogg, Hoffman, and Taylor, p. 293). However, concentrating on the past is seldom of much help at the onset of a crisis. Soon those helping the adolescent must turn to questions about the future. As John W. Whitehead, a Virginia attorney, says about talking with boys and girls about teenage pregnancy:

"I think it is more important to decide where to go from there than to dwell on what has already been done. The teen faces several alternatives, and it is important that parents provide guidance to help their child select the best one" (Kessler, 506–07). Teachers, counselors, and ministers support the teen and the family with information and resources, but the ultimate decisions rest with the teen.

Adolescents worry less about sexual problems today than in the past. They consider sexual activity a private issue for their peers. Likewise, some parents appear less focused on restricting sexual activity. Teen-focused talk shows assume that many sexually active teens are open about their activities. One religious program designed to help teens to wait until marriage to have intercourse has had success influencing teens to delay sexual activity, but the teens who make that promise seem to marry at an earlier age than do sexually active teens. They wait, but not for long. Teachers can support youth in setting solid educational and vocational goals. Teens with educational plans get pregnant less often than do teens with no plans. Ministers can assist youth by offering continued support when they face sex crises. Although an inadequate foundation in sex education may have contributed to the adolescent's problem, sex education and discussions of values are only the beginning point for responding to the crisis.

Report Abuse

All adults who know or suspect that a teen or child has been sexually or physically abused *must report* that information to the proper legal authorities. Normally this would be to an agency like Child Protection Services or the Department of Human Resources. However, one can always call the local law enforcement agency and begin a proper investigation. The failure to report is a crime itself. Ministers, teachers, and counselors should be alert to report any incidents promptly. I have informed the family that I intended to make a report and why. One can also choose to make the report anonymously. Some teens request that no report be given, but you must report once you know or have reason to suspect abuse.

Adolescent Pregnancies

Teenage pregnancy is a major crisis from a variety of perspectives. Adolescent girls are considered high-risk obstetrical patients. Pregnant teenagers often do not complete their education. The pregnancy of an adolescent daughter is a major trauma from the family's perspective. The young father's family also feels the pain. Adolescent pregnancies produce problems for the community. These young mothers are ill prepared for the labor force. They have special needs for the health care of their infants, and they are more than likely to be lifelong welfare clients. Low social economic status is a major risk factor for getting pregnant. Likewise, churches and the theological community face a crisis. They often see adolescent pregnancy as a moral issue but inadequately meet the faith needs of young pregnant women. Having expectant mothers in the classroom creates stress for most middle and high school teachers. Regularly, school systems are developing specialized programs for single mothers and fathers.

The sheer magnitude of the problem for Americans can be overwhelming. The United States has an adolescent pregnancy rate that is over 50 percent higher than any other industrial country in the West. The rate of adolescent pregnancy in the United States for fifteen- through nineteen-year-olds is 96 per 1,000, compared with 14 per 1,000 in countries like the Netherlands. The high American pregnancy rate is attributed to a lack of adequate sex education, a lack of adequate access to confidential contraceptive services, and confused messages about sex, including a bombardment from the media. A 1988 review of 2,293 adolescents who participated in a teenage pregnancy program sponsored by the Louisville and Jefferson County Board of Education and the Department of Obstetrics at the University of Louisville School of Medicine showed that medical problems could be overcome but concluded that "the social and psychological consequences are not so readily corrected" (LaVery, et al., 36).

Teenage mothers are at higher risk for premature childbirth, and their infants are at higher risk for disability and morbidity. Parents and other caring adults can help by securing adequate medical care as soon as possible. These young parents need child-rearing education. They are more likely to abuse their babies.

A University of Pennsylvania study in 1987 paints a gloomy picture for the children of unmarried teenagers: "The offspring of teenage parents are doing substantially worse academically, emotionally, and socially than the children of women who had their first child after age 20" (Hoge, 17). Over half the children, most of whom were in their late teens at the time of the follow-up, had repeated a grade in school, and nearly half had been suspended or expelled from school within the last five years. A large proportion admitted they regularly used drugs or alcohol, and 16 percent had attempted to run away from home. Although special attention needs to be given to teenage mothers and fathers, extreme long-term follow-up care must also be given to their offspring if crises are to be reduced for future generations of youth.

Few churches address adolescent pregnancies except to deliver strong moral admonitions against them. The fathers frequently face many frustrations. Even those who want to have contact with their offspring or want to get married find few resources outside their own families to assist them. These young parents need child-care assistance, job training, and social support from other parents.

Several issues are critical for counseling unmarried pregnant adolescents. Ministers tend to focus first on the guilt issue. A counselor should not project guilt from a personal value system onto an adolescent. Some girls view their pregnancies as badges of honor and do not begin counseling by discussing guilt. Others begin with anger as the key issue. Questions about self and identity formation are perhaps the most significant long-range issues. A pregnancy may be an attempt to foreclose on an identity as mother or to forfeit self-differentiation from the family by fulfilling the family's wish to bring a child back into the system. For some, getting pregnant is a way of escaping a bad situation at home. In many cases, the baby becomes a hostage of either the adolescent mother, who needs a plaything to love, or the grandparents, who are attempting to meet unmet marital needs. The demands of raising an infant exceed most teens' maturity level. They need help from family, teachers, and the church. Furthermore, the case worker or counselor dealing with adolescent pregnancies needs to address several pragmatic issues immediately. Does the teenager have a comfortable place to live? Is there a need for reconciliation and healing with her family? Does she have medical, legal, and financial care? What provisions are made for her education?

Although most counselors will choose to address alternatives such as abortion or adoption, these may not be the key long-term issues for the adolescent. Whereas pro-life groups would rejoice with the statement of John Whitehead that the first step is to discuss the Bible teachings about the sanctity of human life and to help the teens consider that abortion is not at all an alternative, others say that addressing such an authoritarian statement to the adolescent has very little impact. Sex education and lecturing them in general has been less effective than sitting down with them and seeking to understand their value system. They should be encouraged to look at their situation in light of their knowledge of the options and their personal values. At that point they can begin to make their own decisions. Sixty percent of pregnant teenage girls go ahead and give birth out of wedlock, and 96 percent of these young mothers keep their babies.

Many teachers and counselors will be in touch with services for adoption and with resources such as school clinic programs or special high schools for pregnant girls. Unless ministers have worked regularly with the community on such issues, they will need first to acquaint themselves with the available resources for abortion information, adoption services, marriage, keeping the child, or the grandparents' raising the child.

When a plan has been established, many significant issues still remain. The adolescent girl may have to deal with changes in the relationship to the father of her child; she may also have to deal with the loss of the child itself and the change of her self-image. One study found that most expecting teenagers had experienced a major grief just prior to getting pregnant. These young women need grief counseling. They also need economic assistance, job recommendations, and opportunities for social activities with other teens.

Counselors and teachers need to focus on developmental issues that are often overlooked: how the pregnancy affects formation of self, the differentiation from parents, the plans for education and vocational development, the relationship to peers, the understanding of God, and the development of one's faith. Furthermore, the issues of future sexual activities and developing a mature attitude about one's body are vital. Because a large number of teenagers deliver by cesarean section, the impact of the scar should not be overlooked. That, like a pregnant body image, can have a more traumatic effect on the psyche of the adolescent girl than discovering she was pregnant in the first place. The fathers need counseling about the legal and financial issues. Frequently the father feels an obligation to the mother, but feels attracted to other girls. Many get confused and depressed.

A seventeen-year follow-up study of pregnant adolescents found that three factors most critical in successfully adjusting to life after having delivered a child as a teenager were continuing with education, being able to limit births of subsequent children, and achieving a stable marriage at a later point in life. Perhaps the crucial initial factors are parental support and being accepted in a community of faith. One set of researchers think that a lack of emotional connectedness with families contributes to an adolescent's engaging in sexual activity to fill the void (Corcoran, p. 611).

Parents of teenagers expecting a baby need to work together to provide adequate medical care, economic assistance, child-care information, emotional support, educational opportunities, legal consultations, forgiveness, and acceptance. It takes the support of a team of adults to nurture the new parents and their baby. This is true if they choose abortion, keep the child, give it up for adoption, and/or get married. In economically disadvantaged families, a parent of the teen may raise the infant. With ample support, teen mothers can grow through the experience.

A single mother who had given birth to her son at age eighteen told me several years later that she had just won the outstanding chemistry student award in her college graduating class. She is preparing to enter graduate school. Her parents provided an apartment attached to their home and offered her spiritual, emotional, and financial assistance. They have maintained a positive relationship with their grandchild. He is "at home" in their local congregation. This successful young woman underscored that forgiveness, not judgmental condemnation and anger, is needed by churches before they can begin to minister to pregnant adolescents. She now is happily married, has another child, and directs a special program for unwed mothers.

Sexual Abuse

Rape and sexual abuse (homosexual and heterosexual) traumatize children and adolescents. Although statistics are difficult to compile, most specialists agree that the number of reported cases of sexual abuse of children and adolescents has increased dramatically in the past decade. Estimates are that 15–40 percent of all females under age eighteen have been sexually abused or assaulted! (Kellogg, Hoffman, and Taylor, p. 293). Special police units focus on catching Internet predators who attempt to lure underaged partners to meet them. The mostly unregulated "net" has opened the teen's bedroom to the world. The number of teenagers involved in porn has increased dramatically in my counseling practice. Stories of date rape and the rape of persons under the influence of drugs appear regularly in news stories. Often broadcast reports carry horrifying accounts of attacks on young gays. It appears that sex and violence have become connected in evil schemes.

The incidence of sexual abuse inside and outside the family is much higher for females. Stepfamilies are probably even more vulnerable to the stresses from abuse, because their boundaries are less clear. Incestuous impulses between adolescents and opposite-sex parents are more likely to increase, particularly in conflicted families. A previously special and loving relationship between a daughter and a father could evolve into a mutually hostile one as a way of protecting the daughter from becoming provocative or the father from becoming possessive.

Like pregnancy, sexual abuse has a major impact on the development of self-identity as well as on a young person's relationship to the parents. Children and adolescents abused by someone other than a parent or stepparent will often distance themselves from their parents and wonder why they weren't better protected. One youngster told of trying to refuse to go to a particular house where she was being abused. Her mother forced her to go and never seemed to suspect that abuse was the issue. Parents who themselves are dealing with unresolved midlife sexual issues will have added conflicts with their adolescents and are especially ill prepared to deal with issues of abuse and teenage sexual identity. Parents should see that abused teens get medical care and begin counseling with a trained professional. Legal consultation may clarify options for prosecution.

In dealing with sexual abuse, teachers, ministers, and counselors need to hear the entire story, deal with accurate information, and support legal as well as social intervention on behalf of the adolescent. Remember it is a violation of the law not to report the physical and sexual abuse of a minor. Report the adolescent's story, and let the professionals decide if an investigation is needed.

Some teens are reluctant to report sexual abuse for fear of losing their families, peers, dates, or teachers if they seek help. Fear of repercussions from the perpetrator can also delay reporting. A sense of shame and doubt stops others. Intense anger, often having no real direction or focus, can lead to violence or be internalized in dark depression. A few teens escape into fantasy and hallucinations to avoid the reality of the abuse. One girl said, "I learned to pretend I was someone else when my stepfather would force himself upon me. Now that it's all stopped, I don't know who I really am."

Date rape accounts for the majority of reported rapes. What would make a friend rape another friend? The issues are complex, but miscommunication, lack of understanding the opposite sex, and different expectations contribute to the problem. It seems that many young men do not believe that their dates mean no when they say it. Teach girls to say "No" forcefully, sternly, and clearly. Despite fact-based sex education classes, most teenage boys and girls do not comprehend the difference in arousal rates, stimulation patterns, and sexual needs. They need to be cautioned not to send the wrong message. Males and females report different expectations for a dating relationship. Females more often want a relationship and friendship. Males express desires for physical intimacy. It seems that many girls give in to sex to get love, and numerous boys give a loving relationship in order to get sex. Remember that drugs and alcohol are frequently a setup for abuse. Also, in the twenty-first century, more girls are the sexual aggressors. One confided, "Since I was raped, I have nailed seven virgin guys and have taken theirs." She wanted to stop the abusive cycle and find a meaningful relationship.

Related complications, such as failure in school, rebellious conduct, depression, social isolation, becoming promiscuous, and experiencing hallucinations, are often the precipitating events that initiated counseling. It seems particularly true that adolescents who have lost the capacity to be critical of their parents are often victims of abuse (emotional, physical, or sexual). Teachers and counselors can work together to assist those traumatized toward maturity.

When counseling abused teenagers, reaffirm their worth as persons through the doctrines of creation, incarnation, and redemption. Deal openly with any fears and transference issues before beginning long-term counseling. Usually it is best for female counselors to see girls and for male counselors to see boys, but this is not always the case. There is some evidence that abuse affects one's concept of God as well as the view of one's own parents. Reconciliation and forgiveness usually come in the latter period of dealing with sexual abuse issues. However, sustaining the victim begins with the first hint of abuse and continues undiminished. Although abuse is usually a family issue, this is not the case for rape. Homosexual and heterosexual rapes of adolescents are on the increase as adolescents move more quickly into society and away from the protection of their parents and as sexual gratification becomes a more highly valued goal of life. The use of sex in advertising contributes to underlying attitudes that cheapen not only our view of sex but also our view of what it means to be a person. Rape victims need special attention (available in many community rape relief centers and ongoing peer support groups). Although the minister will want to continue to support the person, referral and professional help seem wisest unless the minister has specialized counseling certification. Members of the family, parents as well as siblings, also need care and attention. Many times the minister can counsel the family after the victim has been referred.

Teachers need to be flexible in fitting homework and teaching goals to the needs of students when they return to the classroom. Some may want to transfer classes or schools in order to get a new start. Protect them from taunting or teasing. Assist them in focusing on the future and overcoming the past. Be understanding, accepting, and supportive.

Sexual Harassment

During the last decade the issue of sexual harassment charges made the headlines of American news stories from Tail Hook to President Clinton. Although the headlines were about the mistreatment of young women, many teenage females suffer from harassment at work, school, and church. As women have secured new and expanded roles in sports, the military, and places of employment, some males have hassled them more. Adolescent males are also victims. The media have reported numerous harassments and even murders of gay and lesbian teenagers during the past decade. Any unwanted sexual comment, advance, or touch is sexual harassment. Several teens have complained about harassment at work, school, and play. Harassing phone calls, the plague of the twentieth century, have been joined by harassing e-mails. Internet attacks are difficult to trace and escape legal regulations for the most part.

The core of harassment is treating another human being as a thing, not a person. Attacking another is a means of forcing the individual into submission. It is aimed at bringing shame to another as an expression of anger and rage. These are not expressions of love but of resentment. Victims need support in reporting harassment and in seeking to stop the harassment.

Parents can support their teen's right to be treated with respect by valuing the teen as an individual. Keep the lines of communication open by being an interested listener and a nonjudgmental conversationalist. Support the teen's right to stand up to verbal abuse and harassment.

Teachers should educate students about school policies and be firm in not allowing harassing remarks in the classroom. Give and demand respect. Enable students to report offenders. Support those who have been victimized. Be careful, because false reports do exist. Have clear understandings about touch and gestures of affirmation. Do not stay alone with a student. Always have a third person present. Leave the doors open during private conversations unless the door has a window. Protect others and yourself.

Ministers can create an environment of respect and can confront harassment openly. Proclaim the value of the person regardless of gender, ethnicity, or orientation. When talking with victims, sustain their efforts to seek justice, and guide them toward legal counsel. Watch that the victim does not become the object of shame in your community. One fifteen-year-old girl refused to return to church after she reported her coach for harassment. She thought the congregation treated her like a leper. Jesus dealt openly and respectfully with women. Some adolescents blame God for their harassment. They may expect to be protected from such, or they are angry that God allows such evil to continue. As always, be prepared to discuss difficult issues of theology as the events of a youth's life give rise to new doubts and questions.

Counselors need to listen to the story of harassment and support the teenager's right to express anger at the perpetrator. The teen may or may not be ready to confront the perpetrator. Let the teen choose when and how to do that. Be alert for internalized shame and self-blame with those who struggle with low self-image. Help them construct the way they want to share with peers and other adults. They may need special support if their case goes to trial or becomes a media event. Be careful about record keeping, and give added attention to issues of confidentiality.

Sexual Promiscuity

The level of sexual promiscuity among adolescents varies from culture to culture. However, most experts agree that parents are unaware of the extent of adolescent sexual activity. Many ministers also do not realize how widespread it is. One middle-school counselor found that 60 percent of the sixth-, seventh-, and eighth-graders in her school reported having had intercourse at least once, and a large number were involved in oral sex. Other studies say that 70–80 percent of high school seniors report having had sexual intercourse, and a significant number, perhaps 30–50 percent, are sexually active and promiscuous. As one adolescent said in protest to her counselor's suggestion that she date several boys in order to find out what kind of person she liked: "You're in the dark ages. Nobody dates around, because if you are dating somebody, you are having sex, and if you are dating around, you are having sex with a lot of people. I don't want to be seen as that kind of girl."

It seems that few adolescents reduce their level of sexual activity. Once they become sexually active, few ever stop. Therefore, education before they start is essential. The lack of adequate sex education is likely to contribute to promiscuity. Many teens experiment with sex "to see what it's like." Training in the home and the attitudes and values of parents seem to be the most potent factors in postponing sexual activity among adolescents. Families in which females are valued as persons and treated as equals with males are less likely to have daughters who will become promiscuous. Males and females with long-term educational goals and meaningful activities postpone their first sexual encounter, and they are less active before marriage or living with a committed partner. Parents who are open to discussion, provide accurate information, and model a healthy theology of sex encourage their adolescents to postpone sexual activity. Excitement, curiosity, and ignorance are key factors in initiating sexual experimentation. Early forced sex leads to early desired sex. Parents should value connectedness with their children and meet their need for attachments without overcontrolling them.

Counselors who work with promiscuous adolescents will also have to deal with their parents' feelings. These may range from anger, guilt, and grief to indifference, amusement, and pride. However, assisting adolescents to make personal decisions about their sexual activity and adequate birth-control methods comes early on the counseling agenda. Long-term goals might focus on self-image, emotional bonding with parents, anger at authority, and life direction.

Teachers, second only to parents, set values for most students. Understanding the adolescent's own value system and personality struggle paves the way for showing how to use that value system in a rational, integrated way in making decisions about future sexual activity. As one sixteen-year-old said, "When I have to worry about birth control, it makes me think about the kind of girl I have become, and I don't want to be that kind of girl, so I am going to stop having intercourse—until I'm old enough to handle it." When decisions are internalized by adolescents, the decisions are more likely to influence the teens' life-style and behavior. By using role play, peer discussion, and case studies, teachers can assist students in making wise and responsible decisions about their sexual activities.

Alcohol and drugs are closely related to promiscuity. Parties where social pressure and substance abuse break down impulse control and resistances are notorious for their sexual activity. One fifteen-year-old girl's response to the suggestion that she require her lover to use a condom was, "Hell, I'm so drunk most of the time I don't know who he is, let alone whether or not he's wearing a condom. You don't understand the kind of parties I go to." The multidimensional nature of adolescent crises is demonstrated most dramatically in these areas.

Obviously, self-respect and identity formation issues are key in assisting adolescents who are promiscuous. A lack of childhood bonding and teenage blessings from parents sets the stage for sexual problems. Furthermore, a sense of brokenness in their relationship with their parents, perhaps because of their parents' divorce, can cause a general feeling of distance and loneliness that leads to a sexual search for intimacy. Some feel their parents are unconcerned. One eighteen-year-old said, "My parents don't give a damn anyway."

Adolescents need to understand the dangers of their promiscuous behavior in terms of disease, of being raped, or of being forced into prostitution or pornography. Many ministers are so isolated from street life they have little impact on shaping decisions and behavior of promiscuous adolescents. A few clergy who do get involved at the street level tell of many frustrations but have made some dramatic interventions. Unless we are willing to get involved, to sacrifice some of our office comforts, and to let go of our stereotypes, we will continue to have minimal impact. Educational materials such as those available from the National Center for Missing and

Exploited Children located in Washington, D.C., offer effective church and community programs.

Although many teenagers have had some sexual experience, most are not sexually promiscuous. Derek Miller points out that the majority do not constantly move from bed to bed, as commonly fantasized by some adults. Promiscuity is more a symptom of disturbed, immature adolescents. He goes on to hypothesize that middle adolescents who are unsure of their own identities and have poor impulse control are particularly vulnerable to sexual promiscuity at parties. Too much freedom given to adolescents before they are mature enough to make judgments about sexuality creates a context in which promiscuity will grow. Miller concludes that promiscuous adolescent girls are not usually treatable by outpatient counseling. Assisting adolescents in firming up their identities and in clarifying the structures, relationships, and limits in their families will give them the strength to make decisions about more responsible sexual behavior. Knowing and understanding what the scriptures teach about sex sets a foundation for counseling teens and their families. Remember, they live out of *their* values, not ours.

Sexually Transmitted Diseases

Sexually transmitted diseases (STDs), particularly herpes and AIDS (Acquired Immune Deficiency Syndrome), have created a scare among some adolescents. It remains to be seen if patterns of sexual activity will change for long. Early indications are that more mature teenagers do change their behavior. Unfortunately, the new treatments for AIDS seem to have created a relaxed attitude among youth, and they are taking more risks. In the past two decades, over twenty-five million persons have died of this killing disease. The behavior of more immature teenagers will probably remain unchanged by information about AIDS and other sexually transmitted diseases. After viewing a very frank AIDS film, one group of emotionally troubled adolescents concluded that, although AIDS was frightening, they would not behave differently. Only one in the group said that she would change her sexual activity. The others trusted magical thinking, typified by the statement of one boy who said, "Sex is so much fun, it can't be all bad. I'm just sure I won't get AIDS."

Although education alone will not impact some teens, teachers, parents, and ministers need to continue to get the word out about how AIDS is spread. However, the biggest impact comes in the lives of teens who have a friend with AIDS. Keep the issue alive and encourage personal testimonies whenever possible.

The widespread sexual involvement among adolescents has led Judith

Mishne to quote a New York Society for Adolescent Psychiatry newsletter that sex has become "like McDonald's hamburgers"—that is, it is easy to get, cheap, and essentially tasteless. Mishne urges that "infections spread by sexual contact must be understood by adolescents and by all persons engaged in professional work with teenagers because sexually transmitted diseases are running rampant in America" (Mishne, p. 261). However, all sexually transmitted diseases are not transmitted only by sexual intercourse. Other forms of sexual contact can proliferate disease. The common emotional reaction of adolescents who learn that they have herpes or another nonlethal sexual disease is still shock and a frantic search for a cure. They develop a sense of loneliness and isolation. Upon reflection, anger and fear about the future may set in. It is not uncommon for a "leper" effect to appear and precipitate deep depression and perhaps underlying pathology. Some have become suicidal or have started to live life "on the edge" by routinely taking hazardous risks.

AIDS has moved into heterosexual as well as gay communities. No one has yet been known to recover. Because the disease can lie latent for 3–10 years, thousands of people can be infected unknowingly. Therefore, an adequate AIDS education program that informs adolescents how AIDS *is* transmitted—that is, through body fluids, usually by sexual contact or sharing a needle—and how AIDS is *not* transmitted—one does not become infected through casual social contact—can help. Some groups have predicted that the use of prophylactics or condoms is about 90 percent effective in preventing AIDS. But even then there is a realistic chance of spreading the disease. Although depression and disturbance afflict persons with all incurable diseases, the needs of AIDS patients go beyond that level. Because of their profound loneliness and social isolation, AIDS patients need specialized treatment centers and ongoing care.

Ministers and counselors need to be especially sensitive to the family and, whenever possible, to facilitate open communication and a growing relationship with the AIDS patient. Even planning the funeral requires special sensitivity and attention. It is not uncommon for AIDS patients to be suicidal. Unless a minister has specific training, a referral for professional counseling must be a strong consideration. Patients receive better care when a team of professionals work together in this unique time of need.

Counseling and Pastoral-Care Responses

Several guidelines for counseling and pastoral care need to be underscored as we reflect on helping adolescents in sexual crisis. These strategies need to be integrated into your own style, philosophy, and practice of care and counseling.

1. Focus on the facts. Deal with actualities, check out stories, and avoid catastrophizing from rumors. Because of adolescents' general lack of information about sex and ministers' frequent lack of comfort in discussing sexual issues, it is important to make the extra effort to get specific details about a given situation, set of behaviors, and related medical implications. When talking with adolescents, follow up the specifics of their comments. For example, one young man in a church group said, "Sure, I'm sexually active. I have been for several years." Because he was only fourteen, I followed up in an individual session to see what he really meant. Whereas he seemed to be referring to having had sexual intercourse (the group had been discussing pregnancy), his sexual activity had involved only private masturbation. Although one might be disturbed by his concurrent use of pornographic material, that is hardly the way he would get someone pregnant.

Although many adolescents will say they know a lot about sex, they are less sure of themselves when it comes to actual discussions. Many myths and twisted, distorted facts masquerade as accurate information in adolescent circles. While discussing the facts, avoid detectivelike attitudes and questions. Explore sensitively and caringly the adolescents' information, relationships, and behavioral patterns. Whenever possible, check their story with a third source.

2. Understand their philosophy of sex. Whereas some ministers err on the side of an authoritarian legalism that alienates adolescents in crisis, others may err on the side of insecure permissiveness. Adolescents need an opportunity to discuss their views and to understand biblical views of sexuality. As the immediate crisis issues are resolved, reflecting upon and consolidating what was learned provide an excellent opportunity for future growth. Although most adolescents will rebel against lectures and sermons given in an individual context, they are open for dialogue and serious Bible discussions. These ponderings need to be given in the context of assisting the adolescent to contract for limits and to make some covenants with parents, peers, pastor, and professional counselor. A prominent adolescent psychiatrist suggests that middle adolescents, who are unsure of their identities and maintain poor impulse control, might take a lack of adult supervision and guidance as permission to behave impulsively. He says, "Too much freedom given to adolescents before they are mature enough to make appropriate judgments becomes a license; adults are felt not to care." Although late adolescents might have a more developed sense of internal, value-based impulse control, they still need to stop and think through the physical concepts of love, commitment, and long-term caring relationships. More often than not, late-adolescent girls are looking for serious relationships, whereas late-adolescent boys still view sex recreationally. The feminist movement seems to be lessening this difference, particularly for young women interested in careers.

3. Maintain confidentiality. The issue of confidentiality surfaces with the adolescent, with the parents, and with the larger church and professional community. More often than not, adolescents' confidences are violated. Although legally they may not have certain rights for confidentiality, morally they lay claim to such. Explain in advance to the adolescents what you need to share about them, and with whom and why. Seek their permission. Only if legally required or when it is viewed as endangering someone should a confidence be shared without permission. I encourage adolescents to share information with their parents and other counselors themselves, and I offer to sit with them while they do it. Most see the need and share their crises appropriately. I request that they and their parent sign a release-of-information form before sharing with other professionals.

As a professor at the New York University School of Social Work reminds us, "Confidentiality and the right to privacy is the cornerstone of all effective therapeutic work" (Mishne, p. 276). She strongly warns against sharing any information. This is particularly true with questions about pregnancy, birth control, sexual identity, and sexual practice. Counselors who regularly violate confidentiality issues and divulge information even with the person's best interest at heart will soon find they have lost the trust of the adolescent community.

However, the minister is in the paradoxical situation of being equally responsible to the parents, particularly if the adolescent is in his or her congregation. Great care must be taken to walk a tightrope between protecting confidentiality and being responsible to one's relationship with the larger community of faith. The best method may be to support the adolescent in telling the parent. Many times I have gone to parents in advance to say, "I am asking your teenager to talk with you. I want to ask you to agree to certain ground rules: that you will respect your teenager, that you will listen to the whole story, and that you will work with us to find responsible alternatives to the problem." Preparing the ground in advance in this way often makes adolescent/parent conferences quite productive.

Confidentiality must be limited by the legal responsibility to report sexual abuse and child abuse to the necessary authorities and must be shared with fellow professionals. When working as part of a caring team with an adolescent, we ask the adolescent basically to trust the entire team.

4. Assess the developmental maturity level. The maturity level is the primary factor in assessment, particularly in the area of sexuality. Just as young people enter puberty over a wide variety of ages (perhaps from ten to fourteen), they learn and develop sexually throughout adolescence at different rates. Even though an early teen, twelve to thirteen years old, may be pregnant, it doesn't mean she has a developed view of sexuality or is even comfortable talking about sex. In counseling with adolescents, understanding their developmental level is crucial to planning a treatment plan. Take into account the intellectual, emotional, spiritual, and social components of their sexual identities.

5. Consider sexual crises in the larger context of growth. Teens who are having difficulty sexually need to have counselors, teachers, and ministers who will not stereotype them for the rest of their adolescence. The parents of young adolescents need assistance in not overreacting about a sexual problem. Sexual problems for young adolescents are most likely the result of abuse, experimentation, isolation, and ignorance. Attention should be given to forgiveness and reconciliation with their parents and an opportunity to learn from the experience. With middle adolescents, sexual problems are usually more serious in that they reflect an attempt to define themselves, rebel, and change values. These are not just experimentations. Although reconciliation and forgiveness are still key issues, a more radical stance of healing the brokenness needs to inform our counseling. Middle adolescents who are sexually active are less likely than early adolescents to change their lifestyles and patterns. This perversion of self involves an inadequate understanding of love and a refocusing on passion as a life-style.

For late adolescents, who are more refined in their self-identity, sexual problems most often reflect attempts to meet their physical needs and perhaps an unrealistic attitude that they won't get in trouble. Some really think, "It can't happen to me." Others just do not care what happens. They have little respect for themselves, life, or the future. Late adolescents also need to deal with forgiveness and reconciliation issues, but not only with their parents. They need appropriate places to form attachments apart from the family. A counselor can assist them with plans for independent living. When pregnancy is an issue and marriage is considered, the counselor can help adolescents see that marriage is a chosen commitment, not just a quick solution. Sexual problems can thwart the movement toward independence and create a dependence that is intolerable for both the parents and the older adolescent. The older teen may transfer dependence to a mate or live-in partner in a dysfunctional relationship.

Usually, sexual problems result from attempts to resolve either an internal or external developmental difficulty. After the sexual issues have been resolved, the developmental difficulty may still need attention and follow-up. For example, lonely adolescents may have sex to gain acceptance and friendship. Helping them deal with a resulting pregnancy and then terminating the help to the adolescent misses the deeper issue. Some professionals have felt that even sexually abused teens may have personal issues beyond the sexual crisis. Miller states that "young people who are sexually attacked have often unconsciously provoked or consented to the incident" (D. Miller, *Adolescents,* p. 406). Although one might disagree, at first, and point out that they certainly do not want the pain that comes with the attack, one is still wise to assess the need for deeper levels of counseling after addressing the crisis issue; through loneliness, self-rejection, or alienation a youngster may be seeking attachments in dangerous ways. Nevertheless, it must be underscored that loneliness is not seduction. It is the children and adolescents who suffer. They are victims, not accomplices.

6. Confront the society. Although values will vary within social class and racial structure, there is never an excuse for adults to molest and victimize adolescents sexually. Concerned teachers, clergy, and counselors ought to confront the society and communities when such issues go unaddressed. It is not enough to minister to the victims. The caring professional must attack the social structures that allow this victimization to occur.

Remember that adolescence begins with sexual awakenings. Teens need adult guidance, education, and support to navigate the treacherous waters of the rivers of masculinity and femininity. Some will need intervention and special help when they experience a sexual crisis. Concerned, informed, and sensitive parents, teachers, ministers, and counselors can mean the difference between a life of turmoil and a life of faith, hope, love, and joy. Do not give up on your teenager during a sexual crisis.

Chapter 7

Peer and Academic Pressures

*E*ducation—the acquiring of knowledge, understanding, skills, and critical thinking—is a central task of adolescents. Peers set the context for most learning. Education is more than memorizing facts and gaining knowledge. The deeper elements of education involve understanding how facts fit into patterns, functions, and operations. The goal of this understanding is to be able to apply the knowledge and facts in "real life." I have come to believe that the ultimate goal of education is to teach teens to learn from their own lives and from the lives of others, such as peers, parents, and professionals. However, significant numbers of teens fail to get this big picture. They fail at school and with friends. These struggling teens battle in disruptive relationships with peer groups and adults. Those with relationship disorder frequently congregate with other discontent, disturbed, and delinquent teenagers. They fail to love and accept themselves or each other. Often family problems set the pattern for poor peer relationships. Such teens lack a demonstrated love relationship with their parents or feel pushed to succeed at school. They perceive themselves as not acceptable to peers or parents and perhaps not even to God.

School and friends are major factors in the adolescent identity formation process, so we will focus on the critical issues surrounding peer problems and academic pressures. Appropriate peer involvement seems to be a critical factor not only in self-differentiation and social separation from the family but also in successful negotiation of the tasks of education. Social isolation, a matter of concern to adolescents, is highly relevant to subsequent pathology and school problems (Moore, p. 76). Because of the interrelatedness of peer involvement and the school environment, problems in these two areas frequently overlap. Parents need to keep an eye on the numbers and types of acquaintances; they need to know their teen's best friends. Teachers and ministers can often impact the overall ethos of various peer groups and assist teens in finding positive friends. This "ministry" of introduction strengthens the teen culture. The impact of schools on peer associations makes selecting a school all the more important. Bad friends create family stress and lead to a number of larger social problems. Counselors know to evaluate school functioning and peer relationships, but are often handicapped in changing the context. We can support the adolescent in making changes in both areas. We may need to address related issues such as family problems, depression, self-esteem, fear of failure, and lack of motivation. Such underlying concerns disrupt peer relations and impair academic efforts. Let us examine peer relationships before investigating academic problems.

Peer Relationships

Adolescent peer pressure is still complicated by such social factors as the rapid mobility of society, the increased diversification of school systems, and an exaggerated emphasis on academic performance to the exclusion of vocational alternatives. Furthermore, in the past decade the Internet has linked teens across geographical barriers. An estimated 3.4 million are in chat rooms at any given moment. An increasing number of disturbed adolescents appear so socially isolated as to have only one or two "real life" acquaintances and no close friends. Although they develop a type of cyberspace intimacy, they become further isolated from parents and local buddies, pals, and chums. Many access the web from school. Those without Internet access may feel further isolated. Others manage to stay in touch with pagers, cell phones, and the old-fashioned telephone from home. No person is an island, but some young people exist in virtual isolation from the time they leave for school in the morning until they return in the afternoon. As one teen put it, "I kinda stay to myself and never say anything. That way no one messes with you. Even the teachers leave me alone." One boy started wearing "fang" denture inserts in order to draw attention to himself and to stop people from bothering him. Pain from perceived rejection increases to the level that the teenager acts out and explodes or implodes in an attempt to seek help.

Although a lack of friends will seldom bring an adolescent directly into formal counseling, teachers, ministers, and parents frequently discuss isolation and rejection as one dynamic in other crises. The lack of a friendship network may well be a deciding factor in such emergencies as running away, suicide, sexual promiscuity, depression, and substance abuse. Model good friendships as adults, and teach youth to be friends to each other.

Of course, some teens have too busy social lives and err on the other side of peer problems. They plunge into parties, hanging out with friends and escaping for hours on the Internet. This excessive, party-till-you-drop lifestyle frequently leads to academic failure or underachievement. Furthermore, these teenagers often stray from parent values and may make poor decisions about sexual activities, money, alcohol, drugs, and general safety issues. Parents, teachers, and ministers can attempt to limit such activities, but once they begin, it often takes a crisis to alter these patterns. Counselors hear the crisis story and meet these teenagers after they crash. They may have legal, emotional, or health issues in addition to the misguided attitudes about friendships. It is best if we can prevent or delay the process in the first place. At least confront the concept that living on the edge is acceptable or normal adolescent behavior. The casual acceptance of at-risk social patterns adds fuel to the fire. A party mentality is not the same as having productive, mature friendships.

Friendships are grown, not contrived. The characteristics of durable, constructive, meaningful, and enjoyable relationships develop from a variety of factors:

- Friends stay in touch and spend quality time together.
- Friends talk honestly and listen actively with each other.
- Committed pals solve disagreements before they let anger separate them.
- Friends are slow to anger but quick to forgive.
- Friends criticize softly and affirm loudly.
- Bonded youth share inner fears, hurts, doubts, beliefs, and values.
- Tight teenagers laugh, play, and enjoy life with each other.
- Friends know if, when, and how to change for the other.
- Close peers enjoy similarities and learn to accept differences in the other.
- Friends commit themselves to one another.

Parents

Parents directly and indirectly impact adolescents' attachments to peers. Parents can contribute to isolation or friendship problems by ignoring the teenager's feelings in big decisions like moving (even across town), changing schools, and transferring congregational affiliation. Discuss the effect of such adjustments prior to making a final decision. Grief complicates teen relationships and makes trusting new acquaintances more difficult. Give serious attention to the impact on the teen's relationships with friends. Make an effort to arrange for times for the teens to meet new friends, and work to support their time together. Make every effort to help maintain contact with former "buddies."

As might be expected, the adolescent's relationship to his or her family is a key factor in the capacity to make friends. Authoritarian parents who view parental rights and obligations as superior to the needs of their child adversely influence the composition of their adolescent's friendship groups. Likewise, distant, detached parents damage their offspring's friendship attachments. Consistency in moderate levels of family support and control shows up in friendly and spontaneous relationships with peers (Moore, p. 75). Basically, being a friend to our offspring will assist them in being friends with others. Examine your relationship with your teenagers in light of the characteristics listed earlier. Respect, warmth, flexibility, open communication, and effective problem-solving techniques in the family serve as a foundation for adolescents' relationships with their peers. Remember not to hold on too tight or to let go too soon!

Parents should respect their teenager's rights as well as maintain fair rules. This aids the teenagers to develop confidence and positive self-esteem. Teens must learn to like themselves before they can like others. Extremely authoritarian and overly permissive families set up their children for rebellion. These defiant, disloyal, unattached youth become prime targets for slavish conformity to a peer group (Moore, p. 75) or even become target recruits for cults and other countercultural movements that withdraw from society in communal-type living (Pattison, pp. 275–84). Family relationships greatly impact peer problems. The quality of the attachment between parents and teens is directly related to the teenager's self-worth and satisfaction with life. Conversely, youth with strong parent attachments are less likely to be anxious, depressed, alienated, or irritable (Rice, p. 518).

When parents facilitate a teenager's involvement in school, community, and church activities, they give their teen opportunity for natural friendships to grow. Youth hang out with those who do what they do and go where they go. Parents can support activities that offer constructive friendships for their teen. At times we can encourage them to make the effort to be a good friend. On the other hand, in destructive relationships we encourage our teens in setting safe boundaries and in not being used by others. The main idea is to make friendships something we notice, monitor, and support.

Ministers

Ministers with youth can make a difference by taking initiative toward isolated teens. Including new teens in a youth group can transform lives.

Of course, the group must accept and honor differences and not just celebrate sameness. Ministers can also assist by guiding teens to forgive each other and to live above petty ego hurts and rejections. An emphasis on community and the group as the unified Body of God in the world inspires teens to value relationships. Teach them to love God and to love others as they love themselves.

In his delightful and widely read volume *The Five Cries of Youth,* Merton Strommen offers several worthwhile suggestions for creating a network of peer support for adolescents. He reports that successful church youth workers were judged as persons who could help young people get to know one another, encourage group awareness and sensitivity in everyday life, and find Christ in and through relationships with others. Furthermore, they could become involved and make young people aware of loneliness while developing a team attitude through youth activities. Trying to build a staff community in the church could serve as a model of teamwork (Strommen, pp. 118–21). A part of the ministry of reconciliation is helping youth with forgiveness and acceptance of others. Because of hurt feelings and wounded egos, unresolved anger frequently builds walls in the youth community and works against the interlacing of support. Sensitive ministers work for reconciliation, not broken relationships. An attitude of forgiveness and a personal theology of reconciliation will fortify friendships. Teens and their friends will at times disappoint each other, but that need not be the end of their amity.

Within some larger churches, youth form cliques around schools, economic status, and church interests. Help them understand the pain caused to others by these dynamics. Teenagers also separate themselves according to varied preferences, academic ability, level of social development, neighborhoods, and activities. Strommen found on his survey of four hundred young people that young church members were particularly preoccupied with building better relationships. When asked what changes they hoped for, they mentioned "better relationships" more than twice as often as any other single issue. Surprisingly, it surfaced three times as often as having a better self-concept (Strommen, p. 29). Special lessons, retreats, and workshops should focus on how faith relates to friendships. The message of acceptance and inclusion is throughout the scriptures.

Teachers

Teachers hold a central role in adolescent peer development. By attitudes, classroom procedures, and specific comments, teachers can make or break a youth's image with some groups. Teachers who treat all students with acceptance, respect, and fairness encourage students to do the same. Some schools have so little diversity that minor differences separate the popular crowd from the "wanna-bes." Some schools have found that uniforms reduce conflict and promote acceptance of all students. Certainly, uniform treatment of students promotes a healthier peer environment. Other schools promote individuality and value diversity. Different students will thrive in different settings. Help students find the right school for them.

Teachers should be honest with teenagers about their hopes for inclusion in a particular group, but often a youth's lack of self-acceptance leads to a lack of acceptance by others. Peer rejection can be an erroneous perception on the part of some adolescents. Help them see themselves as others do by confronting their distortions. Because of their pain, distortions of relationships are frequent. Helping teens examine the evidence around peer relationships frequently leads them to see that indeed they are as well liked as anyone else. Many times adolescents exaggerate and worsen their peer problems while at the same time generalizing that everyone must feel negatively toward them. They further fantasize that everybody else has plenty of friends.

Help adolescents maintain their current, real friendships. Teaching them to define a problem, list the options, and negotiate a mutually caring, win-win resolution empowers them in peer relationships. Peer rejection can happen over a rather insignificant matter because young people lack the skills to negotiate differences. Their learned patterns of handling anger might be destructive. For example, they may pull away in coldness, resort to sarcasm, deliver threats, or seek to inflict pain because they are upset. In an irrational mode and from a lack of control, they explode at a friend. Assisting them to understand their anger and to solve problems mutually strengthens their peer relationships.

How to make friends is an important issue for shy, lonely, and rejected teenagers. Respect the personality differences of the introverts and extroverts in your classroom, but work for each student's opportunity to speak and to be heard. Elementary and middle school teachers should discourage and separate cliques as much as possible. Early adolescents are particularly troubled by fears of peer rejection and become preoccupied with notes and rumors and "who said what about whom" conversations. Middle school teachers can offer opportunities for group projects that require pupils to work in varied teams. Middle adolescents are more solid in their peer identification, less prone to overreact to rejection, and frequently experiment with a number of peer relationships. The high school atmosphere offers more opportunities for trips, activities, performances, and games where relationships can grow naturally. High school teachers and college professors can be alert for the new student, the shy pupil, or the socially withdrawn loners. They may need to talk with you privately. However, late adolescents are more likely to settle into a harmonious relationship with their peers, particularly if their friends are welcomed guests in the family system.

Peer support or lack of peer support will evidence itself around conflicts with parents or overdependency upon parents. Because one function of the peer group is to help in the transition from dependency on the parents (Mishne, p. 12), an overdependency on a parent could well indicate the lack of age-group friends.

Cliques and prejudice still dominate some schools. Although adolescents in general seem to be less prejudiced than adults (Strommen, p. 78), race and color are likely still issues. In fact, hate crimes have spread to the Internet in the twenty-first century. Those preoccupied with their own perceived lack of acceptance give little thought to the pain of others. Some yield to the temptation to compromise their values for acceptance. As young people define themselves, it is important to assist them to clarify their own values and interests apart from those of a friend. According to a professor at City University of New York, as adolescents reject particular groups, they reject the particular self-definition that would go with those groups (Berger, p. 370). Adolescents need to know why they reject a particular group (as nerds, preps, punks, head-bangers, brains, or jocks) as well as why they choose a specific clique. As teens get older, peer identification will be less significant in defining self, and they can be expected to become more self-directed. Middle adolescents depend on cliques more than early and late adolescents.

Counselors

Counselors consistently deal with peer relationships because teens naturally move away from their parents and into the world. Several counseling responses need to be discussed in detail. Many approaches have proven successful. However, first the adolescent must see the need and be willing to take the risk. One is wise to wait for the adolescent to make a statement about the need for friends or to report some sense of conflict or rejection. Timing is critical when we introduce the peer issue into the therapeutic agenda. Family counseling will perhaps be needed, along with individual counseling of the teen, in order to make new friendships possible. Anxiety, fear, and shame on the part of the parents may be uncovered in family sessions. A number of parents attempt to manipulate their teenager's social relationships in order to heal some pain from their own adolescence. As one mother confessed, "We want Brook to be popular and active in student government because we both missed out by being too shy." Adolescent growth groups and therapy groups addressing issues other than peer involvements do result in excellent peer bonding and assist in building relationships.

In **individual counseling** with adolescents in a peer relationship crisis, first work to become their friend. Treat them according to the list above. Then focus on encouraging them to set goals for making friends. You might want attend to self-appraisal and self-worth issues along the way, but stay focused on the main issue. However, a depressed or shame-filled youth will frequently feel unworthy. As one attractive seventeen-year-old said, "If I met me at my school, I would not want to be my friend; why should anyone else?" The fear of rejection and a tendency to withdraw will work against experiencing community.

Assisting adolescents to "weigh the pros and cons" before making a friendship decision or accepting a particular interpretation to a set of social events is important in helping them to deal with their perceived rejection. Remember that troubled adolescents are likely to be egocentric, not only in thinking that everyone's behavior is centered on them, but in exaggerating the importance of that behavior. They think of themselves as "right" in most situations because they concentrate on only one side. Feelings of suspicion and persecution augment their cognitive distortions. Carefully confront cognitive distortions. Adolescents are apt to focus on one interpretation to an event and feel personally put down. One girl surmised that because a boy walked by without looking up from his book, "he hates me now." Because of their cognitive abilities for formal and abstract thinking, adolescents can consciously reflect on a given event and look at alternative conclusions and interpretations. As they reframe and view the context of a problem differently, their feelings of isolation and rejection are likely to change. Begin to teach them to think carefully about interpretations of social interactions. Ask, "How else could that be perceived?"

Furthermore, an understanding, caring relationship with a counselor can be a beginning point in building a network of friends. I often ask an adolescent to make a list of current and former friends and to look at their friends' characteristics as a way of finding patterns in their own relationships. When teens realize that most friendships develop secondarily to working on a common task, shared activities, common interests, and even the struggle toward recovery, friendships begin to develop naturally. Sometimes role playing and coaching adolescents in handling frustrating encounters with their peers can assist them. Friendly adolescents in a psychiatric unit tend to recover more quickly than those who remain detached. Some adolescents with deeper personal problems may not be ready for friendships with peers until they are further along in their recovery.

Developing a positive identity apart from a family identity is a key issue for adolescents, particularly those who are yielding to negative peer pressure. Focusing on the formation of the self gives adolescents the capacity to say no when peer pressures encourage them toward antisocial behavior that might lead to further complication of a crisis. The relationship between the counselor and the adolescent can be a powerful factor in identity formation. A counselor who understands transference dynamics and can avoid negative countertransferences can be quite effective in imparting ego strength to a disturbed juvenile. Owning and claiming mutuality of the friendship can empower the young person. When an adult listens to the teen's stories, problems, dreams, and convictions, the teen feels validated.

Family counseling may seem strange to the parents. Some protest, "They have the problem, not us." However, as has been mentioned, the teenager's relationship to his or her family plays an integral role in peer issues. Adolescents and young adults who report secure, trusting relationships with parents also report high levels of social competence and general satisfaction with life (Rice, p. 525). Giving attention to unresolved family conflicts, levels of differentiation, trust, flexibility, miscommunications, affirmation styles, and role expectations will free the adolescent for more productive peer involvement. One sometimes uncovers a deeper level of fear as motivation for the parents' role in the dependency. Many times this will mean confronting parents with their role in setting up the adolescent for broken peer relationships. In critical situations, consider inpatient treatment or out-of-home programs. This is particularly important for any adolescent who has been emotionally abused or for late adolescents whose families are burned out by dealing with them.

Clarifying the family rules may mean negotiating new, more age-appropriate guidelines. Assisting some parents and teenagers with the basics of effective communication can become complicated by the generations of tradition behind the current methods. Discovering conflict management styles and techniques often uncovers weak and/or ineffective ego-defense mechanisms. Any dysfunctional patterns may be at the root of the teenager's problems with peers. Discovering conflicting expectations is essential for family therapy with adolescents who are having peer problems. As long as they and their parents maintain differing social goals, their conflicts usually go unresolved. However, the peer issues will frequently involve confused roles and relationships between the teen and one parent. Marriage issues unresolved by the parents may surface. Avoid dealing with marriage issues in the presence of the adolescent. These need to be dealt with separately. However, confront any enmeshment and "triangleing" between the youth and the parents.

Group therapy works well with middle and late adolescents. For younger adolescents, groups need more of an agenda and perhaps an educational component. Their interactive skills make groups an exercise in maintaining focus and orderliness. Small groups of adolescents who are willing to work on peer relationships and social interaction can be helped effectively with brainstorming, problem solving, case incidents, and role-play situations. Adolescents model for one another more effective communication and relationship skills. Counseling groups expand understanding of one another's attitudes, expectations, thoughts, feelings, and values. Adolescents with poor social interaction skills may be willing to take risks in the context of the group setting when they are not willing to do so in an unsupervised social situation. One such group functioned very effectively in assisting shy teens to participate in appropriate peer involvements. Although most of the role plays, cases, and problems are suggested by the adolescents, some might be initiated by the leader and include biblical stories, such as the story of the prodigal son and his conflict with the elder brother. Sometimes I use stories from a movie or the current news. This not only serves a religious education purpose, but also aids the young people in looking at the value issues behind their peer relationships. Although any of these "rehearsal" techniques can be used in individual counseling, I have found them more effective when used with groups of adolescents.

Peer problems consume large amounts of time for today's youth. Teenagers desire and need friends who care for them and value them as persons. Friendship and love sustain teens through many of the turbulent moments (and months) of transition to adulthood. Too much social activity can also be a problem. Negative peer influences can lead a youth to make unwise choices. Finding the proper balance takes support from parents, teachers, ministers, and counselors. Having examined peer issues, we now turn to consider the related issue of academic pressure.

Academic Pressure

Although poor academic performance is a major concern for parents, educators, and potential employers, the teenagers themselves mentioned a number of other concerns more frequently in their interviews: fear for their personal safety, concern for a lack of respect from teachers, being pushed to succeed, and arbitrary, authoritarian rules. Teenagers also complain about facing too many decisions too early in life and that many subjects often seem irrelevant to life now or in the future.

Few adults understand the adolescent's world at school unless they are regularly involved. Distorted images from news stories often create a picture of wild, out-of-control scenes. These are not the norm. However, memories of our own school days may be just as untrustworthy. Today's high-tech schools have superior equipment and vast library resources. Most public schools reflect the cultural and racial blending of society at large, perhaps with a bit more harmony in some settings. Many private schools reflect homogeneous majorities with limited diversity. The quest for academic superiority and social acceptance among all students can be stressful on less-than-gifted students. The pressure to be at the top snags its own victims.

A nineteen-year-old college freshman insightfully reflected on his high school struggles with academic pressures. He confessed: "When guidance counselors spoke to our class of self-conscious fourteen-year-olds, they shared that colleges liked to see Advanced Placement and Honors classes. It was better to make a 'B' in Honors English than to make an 'A' in regular English. So nobody wanted to take 'regular' English. It was a testimony to being 'ordinary'! . . . My parents and I made a conscious effort not to be consumed by the competitive nature that seemed to infect so many of my peers. I did well in school, but I took classes whose subject matter, not the weighted-grade they offered, interested me. . . . I can't say that I was—or deserved to be—the top student in my class. However, I take pride in knowing that I approached academics as an opportunity to learn, not as a device to demonstrate my worth to the admissions officer of a prestigious university" (Karpinos, e-mail 7-21-2000).

In contrast, a seventeen-year-old girl slit her wrist over getting poor marks in two subjects. She lamented, "My future is over. I have messed up for life." She mistakenly thought that her parents would react with horror to the "B" on her report card. Of course, they suffered greatly at the reality of this misunderstanding.

Luke 2:52 records, "And Jesus increased in wisdom and in stature, and in favor with God and man." Such cannot be said for many troubled teenagers. Although they may increase in stature, they struggle and wrestle unsuccessfully with wisdom. Ministers and parents need to visit the school and participate in school functions. Going to open houses and finding other special times to be in school will awaken most adults to a number of new concerns and will acquaint them with the world of adolescents. Talk with a trusted teacher to get his or her view of the ever-changing world of education in your community. Teenagers spend more waking time in school than in any other one place, and yet academic problems receive very limited attention in many counseling approaches.

Concerned parents frequently complain to teachers or drag their offspring into the counselor's office and begin reciting a list of academic failures. Adolescents are likely to reject blame for their poor grades. They speak of injustices, poor instruction, lost assignments, and they offer a list of creative and inventive other excuses. Students need family involvement and support. However, until they have a vision for learning, they are not likely to accept responsibility for their own education.

Poor study habits, the lack of a study place, inability to organize assignments, and failure to maintain a calendar for planning one's workload all contribute to academic problems for otherwise capable pupils. Having determined that the family is involved and that study habits and place are adequate, one needs next to rule out learning disabilities or being misplaced academically. Some adolescents truly cannot do the work. Programs beyond their ability create intolerable frustrations and produce despair and detachment. Training for a vocation after high school is just as important as college preparation. Teens need teacher and family support to find their place in the working world and to receive the fitting training and education.

However, a large number of adolescents have poor academic performance because they devalue academic work. They lack motivation. With no sense of direction (no dreams or promises) and no specific vocational involvement (no expectations or commitments); but in the presence of a "pleasure first" orientation (no deeper values), a youngster is very likely to fail at school. A popular eighteen-year-old told me six months after high school graduation that in retrospect she would gladly have sacrificed being a cheerleader for acquiring better grades and the opportunity to go to a college of her choosing. The pathways to a meaningful adult life are many and varied. What counts most is not so much which one adolescents choose, but that they choose for themselves and that they follow up with all-out effort. A poster in our youth counseling office reads something like this: Years from now it won't matter what you wore to school, who liked you, or how much fun you had; what will matter is what you learned and how you used it.

A few teenagers have academic problems because their workload outside of school is too great. Grades decline when adolescents are employed outside of school more than ten hours a week. Parents should protect their youth from debts and overcommitment to cars, clothes, and electronic entertainment. Of course, a few have to work to assist with basic necessities. They might want to take fewer classes or seek paying internships. Others might want to serve in the military after high school and have money for college or vocational trade school after they are discharged.

Although parents, teachers, and counselors assess, debate, and fret over academic issues facing today's youth, teenagers offer different viewpoints that might add clarity to the picture. Debating particulars in a given situation usually clouds the image. When asked to discuss academic pressures, adolescents acknowledged the issues mentioned above, but they expanded the list of pressures.

A number of adolescents interviewed in the late 1980s reported fears for their safety. This involved personal fears in traveling to and from school. One girl in Miami confessed, "I'm afraid to get off the school bus and walk home without checking to make sure there are no cars or vans. I don't want to be raped." One young man reported that he was afraid to go to the bathroom at his school because gang members who hung out in the bathroom would extort money and sexual favors. The rash of school shootings of the past decade increased safety concerns exponentially. Many students fear for their lives at school and with reason.

Fears for safety obviously affect academic performance, but, of more importance, they affect the adolescent's physical and emotional health. Adults and administrators involved in schools need to address such concerns as a communitywide problem. Many rural and small-town schools have followed the lead of urban systems in installing metal detectors, and many search for weapons at the least hint of trouble. In fact, this issue was just surfacing a decade ago, but it now looms as such a major problem that I have included a separate chapter on the subject.

Some teens complain about teacher-student relations. They feel picked on, neglected, or devalued by one or more teachers. They gripe: "Mr. X 'disses' all blonds." "Ms. Y plays favorites with the popular kids." "The band director selects our music for the horn section to look good." "Coach Z gives higher grades to members of the team." Parents and teachers have a responsibility to check out the validity of such complaints. If a problem seems valid, talk to the teacher or bring it to the administration's attention without compromising the student-teacher relationship. Frequently, adolescents might protest that the teaching in the classroom called into question a particular segment of their religious education and training. However, it is the rare teacher who will not recognize the student's right to disagree. More often, the perceived challenge to faith is a subtle challenge to think openly and critically about values and beliefs. If a teacher does discriminate on the basis of religion, he or she should be confronted by advocates for the student.

When adolescents discuss authority problems at school, they often define the problem in these terms: "Those teachers have stupid rules and treat you like trash when you dare to question them." Parents and teachers often speak of a youth's lack of respect, sarcasm, and rudeness to teachers, counselors, and principals. The authority issue is frequently two-sided. The adolescent's anger is usually fueled by a perceived lack of respect and interest on the part of the teacher. Teachers who fail to negotiate and listen to the pupil's problems set up a juvenile to rebel or lose self-respect. Educators who can learn to negotiate appropriately and to listen respectfully find that discipline is less of a problem in the classroom. Positive discipline models have done much to improve the teacher's side of this authority problem. On the other hand, a number of teenagers have little respect for authority persons. They learn in angry music, rebellious films, and vicious on-line comments that it is cool to disregard adults in authority.

From the student's side, the authority problem often stems from difficulties in relationships at home. A counselor can fully expect that a similar authority problem will develop between adolescent and counselor. Some students complain that school is like being in prison. When a pupil has been branded a troublemaker and festering issues have gone unresolved for a length of time, it is important to consider the option of changing schools. Obviously, that carries with it the problem of shifting peer groups and of losing the adults (if any exist) with whom the adolescent has begun to bond. Miller suggests that in school systems that move between junior high and senior high at grade 9, rather than grade 8, adolescents are less prepared for the social adjustment. It is best if movement from junior high to senior high is between early adolescence and middle adolescence, at age thirteen or fourteen, not age fifteen (D. Miller, *Adolescents,* p. 121).

Many adolescents with other serious crises see dropping out of school as a solution. The pressures of school, the overwhelming inability to catch up, and peer rejection do not lead to dropping out as frequently as do lack of parental support, pregnancy, and involvement in gangs, drugs, or alcohol. The dropout is a loser and creates problems for society. School dropouts have a difficult time ever adjusting economically. Studies suggest that high school dropouts will earn several hundred thousand dollars less in their lifetimes than their peers who finish high school. In states where the General Education Diploma (GED) is possible before age eighteen, that is one alternative. But dropouts have few choices. After teens have gotten more than two years behind, it is very unlikely that they will return to the classroom and complete their education. Juveniles who drop out of high school and can be geared toward vocational and job training fare better than those who do not seek further training.

The electronic communication age demands more, not less, education to enter the job market at above minimum wage. Females are seeking higher education at increasing levels, and males drop out more often. These undereducated men are likely to find slim pickings in the job market of the future. Many delude themselves into thinking they will find high paying manufacturing jobs or become professional athletes or popular rock stars. One twenty-year-old man who barely graduated from high school was depressed because he could not get a tryout with a pro team and lacked the grades for college. He was depressed with the poor jobs that he was offered in food services or general laboring. Those would be respectable jobs but would not support the life-style of his choosing. He joined the military for training and perhaps money for more education. He pleaded with me to warn younger teens to put effort into getting an education. However, he admitted that he did not listen to similar messages when he was in high school. So what can parents, teachers, ministers, and counselors do to help students with academic problems?

Parents

A central issue can be poor communication and a lack of involvement on the parents' part. Simply by **showing an interest,** such as checking regularly about grades and inquiring about school issues, a parent can nurture the adolescent's school functioning. Also, showing an interest in special projects and performances demonstrates parental support and generates energy for better work. Let the teens know that their work isn't being ignored. Lack of family support is a critical issue in underachievement. However, in certain subcultures of American society, too much family involvement can also be a problem. For instance, in some Asian-American families, the pressure to succeed academically is so great that the adolescents suffer low self-esteem and depression out of proportion to their peers.

Teachers

Teachers have recently received focused, public criticism for socially promoting struggling students. A number of states have initiated mandatory achievement testing. Others offer rewards to schools that reach goals for student improvement. Most states require all teachers eventually to achieve a master's degree; states also demand heavy involvement in continuing education. Teachers argue that better salaries and smaller classes would make a major difference. Larger systems have improved student success with advanced tracks, magnet schools, and alternative programs for individualized learning.

For most cases, this war is won one student at a time! **Do not give up** on a slow learner or a nonperformer. If all else has failed, check out test and performance anxiety, panic attacks due to public exposure, lack of motivation, too much pressure to perform, and learning difficulties (Mishne, p. 167). Special education programs are necessary for several challenged students. Be careful to develop individual educational plans with students and their families. It takes a community of caring adults to help special pupils. Know when, where, and how to refer students for testing and counseling.

Work to inspire students, to awaken their imaginations, and to foster excitement in learning. Your teaching style can impact pupils. We cannot all be a Mr. Holland–type music teacher, or "a captain" as played by Robin Williams in *Dead Poets Society,* or the motherly science teacher in *October Sky*; but we can bring energy, commitment, and professional excellence to our schools. The most powerful force for the future is a student on fire to discover new knowledge. One who does not know and does not care to know is asleep; awaken him or her!

Frequently, Beta Club or National Honor Society groups will **sponsor study sessions or tutoring programs**. Of course, the academically struggling youngster must be motivated enough to want to learn and to trust a peer for help. I have been pleased with referrals to local, for-profit learning centers. Several students have brought up their academic scores in a matter of a few months.

Cheating and copying homework seem to be on the increase in some school systems. Not only does this rob students of learning opportunities; it also sets a pattern and agenda that is detrimental to morale and the learning atmosphere of the whole school system. A clear system of reprimands and punishment may stop cheating at the time but cannot be expected to eliminate future cheating. Students will need positive reinforcement to back up and learn what was missed. They also need a positive approach to **values education**. Some schools have found honor codes helpful. However, research indicates that students are more willing to deceive teachers than previously predicted. The biggest lie a student tells, of course, is the lie they tell to themselves.

Finally, remember that students learn better in a calm, safe environment with respectful and caring instruction. Learn to **control your class**; seek administrative support for a zero tolerance program. If a student continues to be disruptive, place him or her in individual learning situations. Get tough, be fair, be a friend, and demand respect. Motivation and interest get them started; a safe place in which to do hard work keeps them growing.

Ministers

Assisting adolescents to **understand their purpose in life** and the calling of God for their lives adds to the motivation of academic involvement. Education prepares young people for life in general, but a particular goal motivates them to try harder at school. Teens need guidance in discovering their gifts, support in developing them, and confrontation to dedicate them in service to others. A major mission of each teenager is to discover a sense of vocational direction. Guide them in this process. Some will need your support in following their chosen direction. Others may need permission to be free to seek and not make a vocational decision too soon. Most college students change majors three times.

It is particularly difficult when churches also refuse to permit adolescents the freedom to debate issues and to think for themselves. Churches that are willing to **discuss relevant topics** like science and faith issues with their young people find that teenagers can remain faithful while pursuing an education. Likewise, open discussion of values and ethical decisions fosters a friendly climate for learning. In general, adolescent development is nurtured when the environment can encourage intellectual exploration. As Abraham sustained by faith moved toward a new land, the faith of adolescents supports them as they move toward the fertile new lands of education and intellectual exploration.

Academic performance can often be improved by **having guided study halls or using tutors.** One church group provided tutors in an after-school program on a volunteer basis. Peer study groups provide perhaps the best program for tutoring and assisting. Ministers can stimulate that motivation and provide space in the church for such programs.

Obviously, understanding vocational and guidance counseling from the educational viewpoint will assist any minister. However, it is best that the minister works as a part of the team and **refers** adolescents and their families to the school counselor. This assumes a working relationship between the church and the schools. Ministers should get to know the school professionals who teach their parishioners. Learn to work as a team.

Assisting the parents and adolescents in **negotiating appropriate study**

places, time, and habits is an important part of the ministry to the entire family. Because most ministers spend a good portion of their own time in study, perhaps they can share their personal styles. It sometimes helps to talk about self-discipline and the capacity to do what one knows is best even when the playful child in all of us is tempted to goof off. Encourage the parents to provide an adequate place; offer space at the church.

General academic problems go hand in hand with low self-esteem. As a minister assists the adolescent in **finding a positive self-image,** academic crises will wane. Young people who feel accepted by God and blessed by the representatives of God have more energy, ambition, and joy to bring into the classroom. Self-formation is a continuous process and involves sustained attention from the minister.

Counselors

When adolescents come with academic problems, first **check out the family system.** Ask yourself, "What role does the family play in this crisis?" If there is tension in the parents' marriage or if there has been a recent divorce, academic problems are understandable. The parents' stress diverts their attention from school matters. Conflict between the parents infects the teenagers. Preoccupation with grief, anxieties, fear, or anger drains young people emotionally and makes concentrating a difficult issue. Furthermore, evaluating the parents' level of involvement in their offspring's everyday study habits and performance is fertile soil for counseling.

A counselor can interpret viewpoints and **facilitate communication with the parents.** Relieving some stress and increasing the family support creates an environment where academic problems can be addressed creatively. Although some parents need to lower their expectations, others need to assert a whole new sense of direction in their offspring's education. Whereas some teens need to increase their expectations and exert more effort, others need to know how to ask their parents for help. A ministry of reconciliation may begin around school issues but will undoubtedly broaden to include many aspects of the parent-youth relationship.

Perhaps the best-researched and most productive counseling approach to academic problems is **using behavior modification.** Set it up as a consistent, clear, personalized system of rewards and punishments. Dialogue with the adolescent, the school, and the parents for a broad base of support. Recall the four areas of response (Chapter 4): responses can (1) reward good behavior while ignoring bad behavior, (2) take away a privilege and motivate by grief, (3) initiate punishment and motivate by pain, or (4) lift a restriction and motivate by relief. Behavior modification systems will frequently need further adjustments after they are implemented. At first, the monitoring may need to be done daily and involve each teacher and the parents. As the system progresses, the adolescent needs to assume more responsibility for reporting on his or her own behavior. The ultimate goal is to internalize the control system so that the adolescent can face new challenges with only limited assistance.

The Team Approach

Although peer and school problems are a normal part of adolescent development, parents should not underreact. Often teachers close their eyes to such issues until the problems become severe. A minister who notices a problem will do well to call it to the attention of the family and seek to deal with it before it becomes unmanageable. Spotting peer and school problems in the "molehill" phase of development frequently means that limited responses can bring lasting results. When academic problems go unattended during early adolescence, they are all but impossible to address effectively during high school. Likewise, unresolved early-adolescent peer maladjustments lay the foundations for crises of major proportion during middle and late adolescence. Even when the church can't directly assist, ministers can call attention to the problems and encourage families to seek counseling. When parents, teachers, ministers, and counselors work as a team, they and the teens become winners.

Chapter 8

Youth Violence

*C*ould your city be the next target for school violence? Paducah, Kentucky; Moses Lake, Washington; Littleton, Colorado; Bethel, Alaska; Jonesboro, Arkansas; Pearl, Mississippi; Edinboro, Pennsylvania; Conyers, Georgia; and Springfield, Oregon, all stand in a growing collection of cities that witnessed shocking, frantic, vicious acts of school violence. These communities were not expecting a school shooting.

Although the total number of felonious acts by teens against one another decreased during the 1990s (White House Conference Paper, p. 7), the number of high-profile, multiple-victim shootings by teenagers increased. No single strand of evidence accounts for the outbreak of violent incidents. Whereas some blame television violence, video-game mayhem, cartoon brutality, and movie murders, others point to the easy availability of guns, Internet instructions on bomb construction, and lack of school safety. Social researchers point to the deterioration of parental supervision, the blight of poverty, the devaluation of human life, gangs, and the decline of two-parent families.

In his gripping description of interviews with 103 convicted adolescent killers, educator James E. Shaw concludes that youth kill for various reasons, but for many there was a lack of meaningful attachment with their parents, a lack of moral intelligence, and the absence of basic social skills. He went on to detail stories of seeking revenge for being discounted, disrespected, or embarrassed (Shaw, *Jack and Jill: Why They Kill*). The steady diet of violence in today's culture adds to the thought of killing someone.

Diverse ministers debate causes ranging from the removal of teaching the Ten Commandments from public schools, the ban on teacher-led prayers, and the lure of satanic cults, to a lack of attention to the needs of the poor and neglected priorities for funding education.

Theologian David Dykstra from Princeton Seminary insightfully points to the lack of religious foundation in the formation of self-identity among today's youth (Dykstra, p. 19). Counselors and psychologists note the lack of peer support, the presence of aggressive disorders, depression, and personal embarrassments. The truth is that all of these factors could be at play in some of the prominent cases of school violence.

Adolescent violence in the drug-laden, poverty-stricken, gang-infested, public housing projects went almost unnoticed for decades. A few civil rights activists, caring law enforcement officers, concerned urban clergy, and empathetic social service workers called for programs to address the high death rate among inner-city youth of color, but the alarms for assistance did not ring in public ways until middle-class schools became the scenes of similar chaos and ferocity.

Understanding School Violence

A trio of cases illustrates the diversity of the current epidemic of adolescent anger and violence. Three unrelated youths were involved in being removed from their schools because of their threatening conversations about violence or explosives. One was the twelve-year-old son of well-to-do, upper-middle-class, divorced parents. The second, a minister's son, made joking comments about blowing up his school. The third, a poverty-shrouded youth of color, became obsessed with the details of the Columbine massacre and told others that he could do a better job than "those two amateurs" if he were to blow up his school. They represented a wide spread on the social spectrum, but shared similar personal profiles. All three isolated themselves from friends, experienced distance or conflict from at least one parent, expressed shyness, and held a seething anger toward "the in crowd." They and their potential victims were the lucky ones. Someone spoke out soon enough to avert a disaster. Probably none of these three youths would have executed a plan of violence. None had easy access to weapons or a history of violent acts. All three had concerned parents and grandparents and were rather closely supervised. Although they felt isolated and picked on, they did have above-average intelligence and were willing to seek help for better self-understanding and coping abilities.

These three adolescents felt pain similar to that reported by actual assailants, but available resources were brought into play soon enough to make a difference. I think that basically troubled, distressed, shame-laden teens turn on their victims in calculated, revenging acts intended to dishonor, humiliate, intimidate, belittle, traumatize, or kill those who seem different, better off, unfair, more accepted, or superior in some way. Their "psych ache" (Schneidman, p. 4) grows to unbearable intensity, and they explode rather than suffer whatever private inner torment fuels the ache. In doing so, such teens seem to be shifting their sense of inadequacy, shame, mistrust, and depression onto the victims by a calculated act of homicidal rage. It is what the Jewish theologian Martin Buber calls an "I-It" relationship rather than an "I-Thou" affinity. They fantasize that they will find an identity by taking away another's. In an interview from jail, one convicted school assassin remarked, "People respect me now!" (Verlinder, Hersen, and Thomas, p. 34). James Shaw relates a story of a boy who had been "jacked up" by a rival gang member. He later not only shot and killed his opponent, but also dragged his opponent's body down the sidewalk to show his friends. He felt real power from dragging his "prey" back to the group.

Profiles of Violence

What about those who have murdered at school? Numerous peculiar factors distinguish each act of violence from the others; however, the motives of proving something, getting even, and seeking notoriety seem to be consciously or unconsciously at work. Several seem to be connected, copycat phenomena. Some executors do not articulate a clear awareness of their motives; others do. A detailed review of nine prominent school shootings from 1996 through 1999 revealed a multiplicity of features. In all or almost all of these school shootings, specific *personal* factors stood out. The attackers had a history of uncontrolled anger, making threatening remarks, blaming others for difficulties, and previous acts of aggression. Most had bouts with depression, and all had a detailed plan. However, only two had a history of treatment for mental health issues (Verlinder et al., p. 43).

Furthermore, the killers exhibited poor social skills and an interest in violence and weapons; for the most part they lacked close family supervision. All had some triggering event that set their homicidal plans in motion (Verlinder et al., p. 43).

One common element among other students is surprise. Middle- and upper-class peers react with disbelief that such vicious bloodshed could befall their circle of friends. Another unifying ingredient is painful grief. Managing the post-traumatic stress of the friends of victims and of survivors calls for compassionate understanding, patient guidance, and bone-jarring honesty on the part of parents, teachers, ministers, and counselors.

Understandably, adult reactions range from professional concern to personal panic and terror. Parents leap for the panic button to protect their own youth and to prevent their offspring from committing acts of violence. Mothers' Day Y2K brought hundreds of thousands of concerned "Moms" and other gun-control advocates to Washington, D.C., to demonstrate for stricter gun laws ("Mothers March Against Guns," p. 1).

Although multitudes of parents stew over school safety, a few parents seem not to care enough to get involved. They probably are not reading this book. A growing number choose private schools or home schooling, but their youth must still live in the communities where violence erupts in fast-food restaurants and churches as well as in schools. Teachers and school administrators learn physical restraining techniques, search for weapons, and work in an uneasy state of anxiety over their own safety and the security of their students. In May 2000, a seventh-grade honor student shot and killed his teacher after being punished for throwing water balloons. Schools are developing programs for tolerance, installing metal detectors, and banning backpacks. Clergy proclaim love, promote forgiveness, and preach acceptance, but also express distress that the violence erupts in their own sanctuaries (Texas youth meeting). Counselors, social workers, psychologists, family therapists, and psychiatrists struggle to respond to the needs of victims and their families, provide therapy for perpetrators and survivors, and express their anxiety that little is being done to address the root cause of the psychosocial angst of dysfunctional teens. We all know there is a dilemma about providing a quality education for each adolescent and protecting youth from themselves and each other.

Keeping Youth Safe in School

Preventing violence is a complicated matter. Parents, teachers, ministers, government officials, and counselors must work together to create safe communities for teens in which to play, work, worship, and discover knowledge. Striving together, concerned adults can operate as a resource network for assessing needs, designing innovative programs, and addressing problems before violence mars their community. Paducah and Columbine have responded with a multitude of interagency programs, but not until *after* tragedy burst their tranquillity. It can happen in your community, too! I suspect that some communities escape tragedy because they have numerous "safety-nets" to catch distressed, potentially violent, anger-afflicted, suffering teenagers. This is not to suggest that communities that collided with disaster were complacent, but being prepared can help. We must prepare teens individually to cope with conflicted relationships, and we must provide social structures that meet the needs of a whole spectrum of diverse teenagers.

Preparing teens for conflict, confrontations, and painful interactions can make a difference. Dealing with angry, furious, hateful emotions reduces the level of volatility at school. Handling disgrace, shame, and humiliation reduces rage. This diminishes the root cause of much brutality. Building positive self-identity can alter the responses of potential attackers. Parents, educators, ministers, law enforcement officers, and counselors form a front line of defense against physical violence and assaults with deadly weapons.

Parents

Teens who learn at home how to manage embittered passions, how to avoid self-destructive conclusions about their images, and how to sustain a degree of self-respect are less likely to assail each other. Dysfunctional, abusive, quarreling families produce out-of-control teens. The best thing parents can do for their offspring is to get along with each other, talk out differences honestly, and prohibit abusive actions in the home. It may be better to separate than to continue in a strife-engrossed relationship. Research suggests that parents who divorce but learn to cooperate around child-rearing issues reduce the negative impact of divorce on their teens (Barber and Eccles, pp. 108–26). Help yourself first! You can model positive conflict resolution for teens.

Dealing with Hateful Emotions

Assisting teens with constructive approaches to their own anger requires focused attention. Many teenagers do not know how to express basic feelings. Before they can control their behavior, they must recognize the feelings that motivate their actions. They need the ability to "cool off" and to help others gain control of themselves. Teaching de-escalating tactics when confronted by peer rage requires modeling, training, and positive reinforcement by parents as well as by schools, churches, and helping agencies. Teens must learn when to walk away. Parents can stress the value of solving problems with words, not threats, abuse, or weapons. Youth reflect our levels of self-control and our methods of problem solving. They are not born with these skills.

I encourage teens to stop their first impulse. Getting their lives off "automatic pilot" and into their own hands is the first step. If they cannot stop themselves, they are helpless victims of their own emotions. The second step for angry youth is to think of alternative actions. If they can ask, "What are my choices?" or "What have I been told to do?" or even "WWJD?" then they are on the path to peaceful interactions. A third step is actually to do something positive. In many cases, just remaining calm and not responding at all would be responsible. Parents should reward teens for progress in anger management. To be competent, reliable, and trustworthy requires willful, deliberate, and contemplative effort. Parents can shield their youth by steering teens to become competent at impulse control. Revenge is not a smart, productive, or caring response to real or perceived slights, scorn, or even insults. Parents ought to discuss the long-term effects of seeking revenge and of escalating a conflict. Sooner or later, those who live by such tactics wind up jailed, wounded, or dead.

Parents who model and teach positive problem-solving strategies enable their offspring to solve conflicts within their peer groups. In Matthew 18:15–22, Jesus instructs the disciples in the art of resolving conflict person-to-person and in the need to seek outside help if that fails. Private conversation is the first step. The next step is involving one or two others to "talk it out." Finally, the larger group mediates. The goal is to resolve the conflict and to live at peace. If this fails, they are to back off and give each other space.

Moms and dads can talk out options and make decisions after teens cool down. Be positive models as you handle your own anger. Parents can assist teenagers by helping them recall the negative consequences of times when anger was out of control. If juveniles can learn to reflect on their previous actions and to consider the consequence of alternative actions, they can continue to learn from the consequences of their mistakes. Ideally, they first learn by reading or being taught. Practically, most teens learn by observing the mistakes of others. Unfortunately, more than a few must "urinate on the electric fence for themselves" in order to learn. Therefore, youth need to experience the natural consequences of their mistakes. If they get angry and destroy something, they must pay to repair or replace it. If they demolish, ruin, or wreck a personal belonging, do not replace it. Let that be their responsibility. A good rule for teens is "we are each responsible for ourselves." Violent teens often have had a pattern of blaming others for their problems.

Parents can support and attend community and school programs about school safety. Talk to elected officials about your desire for funding for safer schools and secure communities. Promote policies that limit the availability of weapons to teenagers. In one Texas study, 18 percent of fifteen- to seventeen-year-old males admitted to carrying a handgun to school (seven times the national average) (Cirillo et al., p. 321). Most of those said the gun was for protection and shooting an aggressor. Teach your teen to walk away from potentially dangerous situations. Encourage them to report threats to suitable authorities. However, also instruct them to be respectful and kind to students who might not fit comfortably in the peer group. Help them build broad inclusive friendships. Connections, friendships, and empathy make a big difference. Encourage youth to avoid haughty, arrogant, scornful, or rude reactions to intimidating, menacing, and sinister loners. Of course, there are no guarantees that any youth will not be the target for a disturbed, demented assailant. However, connecting seems to help.

Do observe your own teenagers, and guard against their becoming attackers. If they exhibit the characteristics of an assailant, get professional counseling. Protect your teen from temptations. Have trigger locks on all guns, and keep them in a locked gun cabinet. Know the sites that your teen visits on the Internet. Question any suspicious activities with explosives or dangerous compounds. Stay alert so that your teen does not become the next headline in the school violence saga. The Cirillo study reported that more than 50 percent of seventh- to twelfth-grade boys had carried a knife to school (Cirillo et al., p. 321). Limit the access to violent expressions of hateful emotions, and limit the access to bombs, guns, and knives.

Dealing with Negative Conclusions About Self-Image

Parents frequently consult me about their youth's poor self-image, lack of confidence, trouble in making and keeping friends, and related mood difficulties. Teens are at risk if they negatively distort how others view them. If an adolescent lets people tease or abuse her or him, one of two extremes might emerge. On the one hand, the teen might become disgusted with himself/herself and suffer from deep depression. This might produce thoughts of self-destruction. One could become a mark for further peer abuse or violence. On the other hand, the juvenile might let this resentment fester until it explodes in violence. Neither alternative produces the fantasized relief from torment. Assist your child to set clear, firm boundaries that discourage taunting. This may mean moving to a new school. The self-image of adolescents often grows in a group-counseling setting. Feedback from peers bolsters their pictures of themselves.

Assist teens to not overact when something goes awry. Some youth distort shortcomings to the point that anything less than perfection is seen as totally rotten. They may make comments such as "I stink," "I can't do anything right," or "I'm such a loser!" Try to understand their frustration, but avoid fatalistic conclusions about their worth. Accepting shortcomings and imperfections as natural serves as a buffer to self-rejection for teenagers.

Tell them a story from your youth about how you handled failure or rejection. Let them hear that perfection isn't achievable.

In fact, admitting failures and confessing transgressions lead to maturity as a person of faith. Teaching teens to give and receive forgiveness begins at home. Parents can admit their own shortcomings and ask for pardon from their offspring. In turn, the youth grasp the power of forgiveness. It may be something as simple as learning to utter, "My fault," after a minor blunder, or it might mean a serious time of religious confession. Either way, the intended outcome is the practice of admitting wrongdoing without self-rejecting thoughts. As the popular teen Christian adage goes, "I may not be perfect, but I am forgiven." As teens grow in the ability to ask for and accept grace, they release the inclination to reach negative conclusions about themselves. This in turn reduces rage and the urge to get even.

Because alcohol and drug use are frequently associated with adolescent violence, parents can ease the pain for their teens by modeling responsible use of alcohol and limiting their youth's access to alcohol. Drug and alcohol treatments are effective in assisting teens to go straight and to learn to solve problems without escaping into substance abuse. Teen drinking is neither normal nor cute. It makes our kids killers on the road and in peer interactions. Alcohol and drugs cause more problems in the peer group. Even smoking causes depression in teens. Substance abuse does not make one a real part of the group. Teenagers who avoid substance abuse and negative conclusions about themselves more readily adapt to their peer group. Misfits are more prone to become attackers.

Nurturing Self-Respect

Nurturing self-respect begins long before puberty, but the onslaught of physical, mental, and social changes compels parents to readdress this issue. As infants are nurtured physically, they develop basic trust, initiative, and autonomy (Erickson, p. 120). Teens struggle to flesh out a constructive, affirmative, and confident identity. Parents hold the keys to this puzzling interchange. Teens need enough rules, attention, and guidance to feel valued; and to feel trusted, they need enough freedom to make their own choices. Teens secretly want more limits, but in a way that lets them take charge of their own lives. As parents bless their children's freedom, the youth must internalize the rules and become self-regulating. This delicate balance assists teens with self-respect and confidence.

Nurturing self-respect may mean taking more interest in the teenagers' interests, friends, hobbies, and activities. Teens need as much parent time as do toddlers, but they need it in different ways. They need parents to be tutors, chauffeurs, audiences, and fans. Cheer them on and recognize their progress. Listen to their pain and console their losses. Parental involvement was found lacking in the lives of those who attacked peers at school (Verlinder et al., p. 43).

Furthermore, cultivate their dreams. Spend time listening to their wild ideas. Be patient as they sort out the possible from the impossible. Do not let your fears block out or stop their dreaming. Have hope with them. If you sustain their aspirations, they will grow in self-esteem. Avoid telling them how important they are without *showing* them your support.

In a study at the University of Nebraska, researchers discovered that shared faith experience was one significant ingredient in building strong families and rearing durable offspring (Stinnett, Chesser, and DeFrain). Going to the same church was not enough; it takes talking about and participating in common faith experiences. Youth feel important when parents can reveal their faith experiences, struggles, and even doubts. Although some of the school assailants participated in religious experiences, they were not significantly spiritual persons. In fact, they attacked peers who were devout followers of their faith. In Paducah, the attacker fired on a student-led prayer circle. In Littleton, one young believer was reportedly shot when she answered, "YES!" to the question "Are you a Christian?"

Parents can safeguard their teens by equipping them with skills for dealing with anger, by nurturing self-esteem, and by fostering strong faith experiences. Parents can monitor their own teenagers more closely, eliminate access to weapons, and seek professional help for their youths who have violent behaviors. However, teachers, ministers, and counselors each hold a place in the community safety network.

Teachers

Teaching is considered to be one of the oldest professions, along with the law, religion, and medicine. Teachers, like other professionals, receive little automatic respect. They even have come under attack by some parents and students. Yet "teacher" is the term that Jesus frequently chose to describe himself (Matt. 23:8). A first step for each school administrator or teacher is to require respect and deliver it to students. When I taught public high school algebra and calculus years ago, this was more or less a given. Only a few students dared to disrespect a teacher, and they were promptly disciplined. Peers shunned them as "culls" or "outcasts" until they either dropped out to get a job or conformed at some acceptable level. Teachers who respect all students receive more admiration, esteem, and honor. Teachers who ridicule pupils invite contempt and disdain. Give the respect you expect to be given.

However, today even elementary school teachers have students and parents who threaten to gun them down. Classroom time in numerous public schools becomes consumed with the task of maintaining order and protecting students from one another. In six of the nine school shootings mentioned earlier, a teacher or principal was killed. Brave teachers died to save the lives of others. What can teachers do to protect themselves and their students?

Personally, teachers can become trained in the management of at-risk students. Although discipline styles differ widely, orderly discipline reduces at-risk incidents. Teachers need administrators who work as a team to handle violent students fairly but firmly. The use of special schools for potentially dangerous students can remove these assailants from the general population. Caution is advised in evaluating who should be referred to such programs. Specially trained counselors and interviewers need to evaluate the student and the family, and they need to talk with peers. False reporting can cause innocent teens to be harmed greatly.

Teachers need to foster a classroom atmosphere where students feel safe in reporting threatening remarks and exposing plans for attacks. It appears that almost all of the school assailants noted earlier told someone of their plan or had communicated violent intentions. Metal detectors might have helped. Teach students to spot a dangerous peer, and protect those who report suspicious activities. Teach youth that referring a peer for counseling help is not "ratting," "betraying," or "finking out." If students might be singled out for reporting a threat, have a system for anonymous reporting of dangerous incidents. Be aware that just because a youth wears particular clothing (e.g., a black trench coat), she or he is not a suspect. One of my group members was smeared with angry comments just because he was dressed in such a coat and had few friends. He was angered by the insults, but had no desire to harm those who were hissing venomous slurs.

Students often give teachers compositions, poems, songs, and projects that discuss violence and express specific dark feelings that include desires to harm others. Although writing out vicious thoughts might make sense as a part of the ventilation of feelings, teachers should talk individually with the author and consider a referral for evaluation. Encourage creativity and freedom of expression, but do not overlook dangerous intentions.

A variety of programs seem to help. The Violence Prevention Project of the Health Program for Urban Youth reported success in reducing violent interactions among adolescents over a decade ago (Cirillo et al., p. 321). However, more recent programs are more cautious in claiming success in reducing violence among teenagers (Ibid., p. 328). The most at-risk students seem to be those who fight at school and use drugs or alcohol regularly. I recommend a number of programs that can impact the problem of school violence:

- Promote school pride.
- Recognize all groups within the student body.
- Foster tolerance and model respect.
- Discuss right and wrong actions (character education).
- Refer aggressive students for anger-management programs.
- Support weapon-screening programs.
- Publicize the dangers of substance abuse.
- Teach positive conflict-management approaches.
- Use peer-counseling training.

Administrators can implement policies of zero tolerance for threats and fights. Also, smaller classes permit students to form closer friendships and find some acceptance. Teach students that they are their "brothers' and sisters'" keepers. When students know each other personally, tolerance grows. One teen commented, "I sat by him in English, and he isn't as weird as people say; he is pretty normal." Most teenagers desire to love, to be loved, and to be recognized as worthwhile. They need to be recognized for positive actions and to not have to resort to killing to seek respect.

Ministers

Clergy, especially youth ministers, make a difference in the teen culture of schools and communities. Ministers can promote peacemaking and value reconciliation over revenge. "Love others as you love yourself" and "Be angry, but sin not" are worthy doctrines for discipleship. Teachers and youth ministers can conduct classes on coping with anger and can offer opportunities for role play and case reflections.

A Web for Peace

Work as a team to support citywide teen programs. Create a church and community climate that retards, impedes, and obstructs violence. Develop a superstructure of faith-filled caring networks. Grow a web of peacemaking initiatives from within your folk. Researchers suggest that young people need five basic resources in every community (White House Conference, p. 17):

- Caring adults
- Safe places
- A healthy start
- Marketable skills
- Opportunities to give back

Churches can and should be contributing to these needs! Churches that offer training for adults as youth workers also impact the entire communities where these caring grown-ups live and work. Enlist and equip mentors and teen guides who volunteer hours in a variety of youth programs. Churches and communities need to allocate more budgets to youth services and programs.

Church after-school recreation, study, and arts programs provide safe places for teens whose parents are not at home. Early and middle adolescents (ages 12–16) especially need structured situations until their parents can be at home. Churches should be safe places to "hang." More than a few churches lock their doors to keep out "risky kids" rather than creatively program for safe-place activities. More volunteers and staff are needed. Welcome skaters to the parking lot, sponsor sports leagues, promote art shows, musical dramas, puppet shows, and so forth.

A few churches have health-screening clinics, crisis hot lines, and parish nursing programs. Any church can sponsor health-awareness education, promote substance-abuse education and rehabilitation, or provide referral resources for medical treatment. Physical well-being bolsters and sustains spirituality and wholeness. Promote health and combat violence.

Although schools and vocational training programs accept primary responsibility for providing marketable skills to youth, churches can assist. One congregation sponsors a "take a teen to work" week. Another offers training on computers after school. By matching retirees and teens, ministers can offer youth the opportunity to learn new vocations, build supportive friendships, and see models of success.

Teens who minister to others are less at risk for violence. Churches can lead in community service hours and meaningful openings for authentic ministry. Teaching the joy of service and the ecstasy of giving without thought of gain (agape living) leads teenagers into deeper levels of personal meaning and self-confidence. Compassion is the direct opposite of violence. Direct adolescents to work with children, volunteer for Habitat-for-

Humanity–type projects, offer assistance to the elderly, or serve in any place of ministry that lets them give back to society. Mega Ministry, an interdenominational youth program, is sponsoring a ministry that will take one thousand teenagers to three continents for a week of mission work. The teens must first do fifty service hours in their home community. Lead youth to serve others, and give them the experience of respect that follows such service.

Inner Peace Work

As ministers, we promote peace on all fronts. We oppose international injustices, denounce urban riots, combat crime locally, abhor domestic violence, and sow messages of inner peace. By being available to troubled persons, ministers form a front line of defense against brutality. We encourage the abused to stand up and the abusers to sit down and talk it out. We promote inner peace in the name of the Prince of Peace. We must take time to discover and rediscover levels of personal harmony, solitude, tranquillity, and serenity.

When we cannot help, we can refer persons for further assistance. Each church should become a referral clearinghouse for potential abusers as well as for victims. Whenever possible, churches have a responsibility to offer pastoral counseling for concerned parents, distraught individuals, and traumatized families. Churches that have affordable, professional counseling centers assist in reducing violence at all levels.

Teach, model, and preach anger control. Develop a theology of anger with your followers. "Be angry, but sin not" and "Do not let the sun go down on your anger" are good starting places. If you cannot offer a word for anger control, at least do not promote violence in the name of your beliefs and social preferences.

Clergy should be models for acceptance and respect for diversity. Christians have a clear statement in Galatians 3:28: "There is neither Jew nor Greek, there is neither slave nor free, there is neither male nor female; for you are all one in Christ Jesus." Unfortunately, some church leaders promote anger and revenge rather than combat violence. For example, those who promote attacks on those who disagree with their positions reduce themselves and their followers to the level of criminals. Ministers should lead the way in peacemaking. Promote nonviolent interventions.

Troubled souls create havoc. Ministers can respond with a word of forgiveness, love, hope, and new peace. There is a spiritual peace that surpasses rational understanding. Boldly offer instruction and guidance for teens lacking this deeper peace. Most religious publishing houses offer materials in church-based programs for finding interior harmony. Make use of them!

Counselors

Counselors in general will probably see an increase in requests for assessing teenagers who get targeted by someone as a potential threat for committing acts of school violence. These youth might have written a note, a dark poem, or a specifically violent essay. It could be a violent work of art or a drawing that marks them. A few are caught when they threaten someone or get detained with a weapon. Some are real bullies, but many are youth trying to avoid being victimized and tormented by other intimidators.

Those who choose to counsel with teens will see more cases that require an approach to anger control and managing violent feelings, thoughts, and impulses. If you do therapy with adolescents, you will want to seek supervision or consultation from peers who also toil with teen cases. The fast-changing pace of adolescent culture demands teamwork to stay abreast of it. Our counseling counterparts can offer other points of view as well as assist in monitoring our countertransference with us. Compare your guidelines for counseling teens with the ones suggested below.

Counselors are increasingly tapped for noncounseling, professional functions such as speaking at schools, conducting community workshops, and providing "expert opinion" in legal matters. Media interviews and appearances can be especially tricky for persons trained more in listening to the inner thoughts of others than in articulating their own for the public. Get involved, but be as "wise as serpents and innocent as doves" when doing so (Matt.10:16).

Assessing a Violent Teen

When beginning an assessment, first get the facts straight from the referral source. Then hear the teen. Let him or her talk personally before showing interest in the "incident" that motivated the referral. Only after understanding his or her situation and building a wholesome connection will you want to begin with confrontational assessments of risk factors. Even then, ask touchy questions with care. Be direct, to the point, but not fierce.

You need a current list of assessment factors. Appraise those introduced in this chapter. Generally, increased signs of danger point to a higher risk. However, not all warning signals carry the same weight. Being without friends is not in the same league as carrying a gun to school. In the end, assessment is an informed judgment. There are no firm and fast rules with clear-cut points on neat measurable scales. Get a comprehensive and distinct picture, and make a tentative interpretation.

Check your initial assessment by interviewing parents, teachers, and friends whenever possible. Consider using empirical tests along with your clinical impressions. When you decide a teen is or is not a major risk for violence, be cautious about how you communicate your conclusions. Communicate clearly, but do no harm by using careless words. If you have recommendations for specific danger management, state them with clarity and give them only to the proper persons. Remember, the youth is innocent until proven otherwise. A major study of risk factors in schools concluded that the ability of counselors to "predict" which youths would become violent is "poop" (Verlinder et al., p. 49).

Not all risk assessments begin with a referral; a teen may hint at being dangerous during your counseling sessions. Treat such comments as seriously as you would suicide statements. Adolescents in crisis seldom present with a single crisis or concern. Be alert for threatening remarks even when given in a seemingly teasing context. Making assessments often leads to doing the counseling.

Counseling with Potential Assailants

Your own style will serve you best; however, a few issues may be different with teens that might harm others. Take a careful history of previous abuse or altercations. What do they consider cruel, and what is just having fun? Take special time to establish harmony and understanding between you and them. Use their own statements and values to confront gently their unrealistic thinking. Later let them know the tragic consequences for them as well as for others, should they ever become violent. Through stories, group role plays, situational case discussions, and calm feedback, teach alternatives to brutality. Challenge any notion that savagery will bring fame or positive gains for them.

On a scale of one to ten, have the youth rate both their inner pain and their rage at specific persons or groups. Assist them to see others as persons of worth. Often a diverse group-therapy program can assist with this slow process of identification and empathy.

Teach positive conflict-negotiation procedures. I teach an easily recalled "A, B, C, D, E," method:

- Accept the problem together. Help the teens to hear the problem from both sides.

- Brainstorm options for resolution. Make a list of widely different responses to the conflict.
- Choose a possible solution together. If the teens cannot talk together about the choices, have them evaluate the options privately and construct a list of possible solutions. See if any solutions are on both lists.
- Do it! The fourth step is to just do it. Try the agreed-upon alternative. Act differently and see what happens. Teens frequently report amazement at how they can grow and perceive startling responses from "those other people."
- Evaluate the new approach. After a few days or a week, ask the teens to evaluate their new behaviors. If the results are disappointing, look for something to modify or start over at "A" and work through the process again.

When change begets personal gains and profits, we celebrate and reinforce the new persons they are becoming. Reward the teens' growth with affirmation and attention. Teens should not feel that they have to seek revenge on someone in order to be respected. Real respect grows out of being responsible.

Counseling the Survivors

The Post Traumatic Stress materials seem to describe most completely the counseling of those who were wounded or witnessed the attacks. Because teens are still forming identities, it is important to help them return to their normal routines after a time of mourning. Avoid labeling them in relation to the trauma. Give support in debriefing groups, and provide individual and group therapy as needed.

Spend ample time hearing the teens's stories. Hear their feelings, but eventually shift to their stance toward the future. Assist them to find ways to be concrete about their mourning. Plant a memorial tree, create a scholarship, erect a plaque, or plan new programs. Then select images for remembering the past and moving into the future. As they build new friendships and expand their own identities, they embrace the future with new hope. The tragedy may accelerate their normal development. They see life differently. However, they still need attention to the routine teen issues of dating, separating from parents, and getting an education for the future.

Listen to the youths' deeper questions. These may surface around dreams. Disturbing, shocking events can trigger philosophical and faith questions. Why did this happen? What makes people mean? Why me? Where was God when the shooting broke out? Teens are naturally restructuring their worldviews. Tragic events hasten the process. Be prepared to listen to their searching. Avoid quick, simple answers. Remain calm in their stormy doubts. We need to journey with them into a search for new faith.

Be alert to traumatized teens who could sink into depression, surge into acts of revenge, or plunge into substance abuse. The pathway to recovery will be arduous, and the temptations for a quick, easy fix will be attractive. Nevertheless, attend to their energy for recovery and stay focused on their progress. All too often, one tragedy becomes the precipitating event for a series of misadventures and a life of disaster. The youth will never forget the trauma, but they can recover from the blow and lead a productive, rewarding life. This will take time. Listen, listen, and listen to their stories. Be prepared to do so for months and years.

Faith Restructuring

In conclusion, we know that teen violence at schools escalated during the past decade. It may be leveling off, but we need to stay on top of this problem. By working together, parents, teachers, ministers, and counselors can impact today's violent youth situations. More focused research is needed to understand why one teenager snaps and becomes a murderer and others turn away from their violent thoughts and plans. The Secret Service released a report in October 2000 that suggested that most attackers gave ample warnings of their intended violence. Adolescents need help in negotiating the treacherous transition from childhood to adulthood without killing or being killed. The three teens that I mentioned at the beginning of this chapter have not harmed anyone. One young man graduated from an alternative school and began college at a nearby state university. Another has successfully transitioned back into public schools and is at grade level. The youngest just began high school and has ceased aggressive behavior toward peers. He made above-average grades in conduct for his last semester. All three have improved relationships with their family members and function normally with friends. Thus far, their growth points toward productive lives as young adults. Others are not so fortunate; they are in jail, crippled for life, or dead. May all of your "wild ones" bloom and bear useful fruit.

Chapter 9

Depression and Suicide

*D*epression becomes such a normal part of the growing-up process that detecting severe depression in adolescents becomes difficult. Adolescents, like children and adults, are likely to become depressed at some point. Daily ups and downs are not depression. Extended periods of gloominess, melancholy, or sadness indicate something is off beam. When you wonder to yourself, "What is wrong with that kid?" think, "Perhaps he or she is depressed." Every time someone feels down isn't a crisis. However, when the depression becomes so heavy as to impair the ability to function, it enters the crisis stage. Someplace along the range between a little sad and depression, a point is crossed and a crisis begins. And although depression is not the only factor in understanding the etiology of suicide in adolescents, it is perhaps the most common.

In the past three decades, the suicide rate for teens has risen sharply. It is the third leading cause of death among teens (Culp, Clyman, and Culp, p. 828). Yet young people often see depression and suicide as not of major concern, perhaps because they are not extensive problems. Although it is estimated that around 400,000 adolescents attempt suicide annually in the United States, most youth ministers and teachers are hard-pressed to name any students who had tried to kill themselves. When it is your child who attempts to kill himself or herself, then the crisis seems enormous. Parents and counselors see the crisis close-up on an individual basis, but may not be aware of the extent of the problem until an attempt is made. Exact figures may be unobtainable because many attempts are not reported, and others are listed as accidents. Parents, teachers, and ministers need to be more alert for potential crises in this area.

Figures do not begin to tell the painful story of depressed and suicidal adolescents. Not all depression leads to suicide; not all suicides are prompted by depression. However, depression heads the list of factors that push an adolescent toward self-destruction. We will discuss aspects of adolescent depression and then explore the dynamics of suicide. Guidelines for assisting depressed and suicidal youth conclude these sections. Parents, teachers, ministers, and counselors should inform one another when suicide is an issue. Knowing how to balance confidentiality issues around depression and reporting data in suicide situations require sensitive assessment. When in doubt, seek consultation, but err on the side of safety for the youth.

Adolescent Depression

Mild depression seems common for most teenagers, but can be associated with a number of maladjustments and traumatic stress reactions. Knowing when depression is a normal part of an adolescent's adjustment to life and when it signals severe problems is a crucial skill. Basically, when the depression has a negative effect on the adolescent's relationships and ability to function at home, school, work, or play, the depression deserves to be treated. Certainly, any time the depression is accompanied by suicidal gestures or ideation, the adolescent needs professional treatment. Depression may mask itself in several ways, and whereas no single behavioral change need be viewed with alarm, a cluster of symptoms usually indicates severe depression.

Depressed adolescents typically become inactive, drop out of peer relationships, spend large amounts of time alone, barricade themselves in their rooms, go out of their way to avoid family contact, and escape for long periods into the world of electronics (television, telephone, music via headphones, surfing the web, and video games). Depressed adolescents show little initiative and project an "I don't care" attitude toward much of life, especially work and school. There is likely to be either a loss of appetite or a preoccupation with eating, especially bingeing on junk food. Likewise, either lack of sleep or too much sleep can denote depression. Generally there is a lack of physical exercise and a decreased energy level, marked by frequent complaints of being tired. Depressed adolescents do not think clearly and are less perceptive of events in the world around them. They draw into themselves socially and cease to function productively at school or at work.

Adolescent depression comes from a wide range of possibilities. Certainly, heredity and personality type seem to play a large role in why some persons become more depressed than others. Internal factors such as physical illness and hormonal imbalances need to be checked out by a physician. Nevertheless, it seems that many causes of depression are external. Consider events such as a sense of rejection, a major disappointment, or a recent loss. Any disappointment for a teenager, such as not getting a job, being cut from a team, not making the play, being bypassed for a choir solo, or not getting first chair in the band tryouts, can precipitate depression or worsen an already existing depressive state. Breaking up with a boyfriend or girlfriend devastates many teenagers. Because early detection is important in treating adolescents with depression, the parents should follow up on all indications of problems. Ministers and teachers may notice a change before the parents catch on to the change. Counselors will conduct an evaluation. Referral to a psychologist for testing may be advisable.

Depression is a normal part of a grief reaction for adolescents, as it is for adults. When assessing a depressed youngster, ask about the death or loss of family members and close friends. Grief often follows a recent move and the resulting uprooting from one's peer group. Another factor is the loss of a relationship as a result of being excluded from a clique or being rejected from a valued peer group.

The **grief from losing a peer in death** deserves special treatment because it affects so many teens. Our family has been rocked to the foundations twice: once when our daughter's best friend from second grade through eleventh grade was killed in a car wreck one cold January Sunday, and again two years later when the captain of her college swim team died in a van accident returning from a meet. One high school in Indiana had four juniors die in different accidents in a nine-month period. The ripples of influence from a teen's death reach the extended family, the community, and the peer group. Few teenagers escape the crisis of having a friend die.

Adolescent grief reactions stretch to many areas beyond depression. Adolescents are bewildered, shocked, and numb at first. In an attempt to get the facts, they often flood the hospital, accident site, or home of the parents. Frequently they feel angry, remorseful, guilty, fearful, and confused. They need structured, open places to talk with each other and to ask any and all questions. Group sessions, team meetings, and organizational gatherings offer a forum for working out initial reactions to their grief. Some need private reflection time to gather their frayed thoughts and deal with unraveled emotions. After they accept the reality of the death and process their feelings, teens face a big decision. They must decide if life can go on in some meaningful, albeit painful, fashion. They remember their departed friend, but look for courage to return to the world of the living. This takes time. For some it lasts months; for others, new issues surface a year or two later. Eventually they form new attachments and life goes on, but never do they forget the deeply loved, deceased friend.

Teens who are grieving want adults who will suffer with them. They need someone to listen for the questions, to watch for the depression, to understand their deeper issues. Often a teen's grief expresses itself in group rituals. They place flowers at an accident site, dedicate a tree, begin a scholarship, or name an event for the friend. They write stories, sing songs, pen poems, and attempt to express the agony of the loss. Some wish they had died in place of their friend. These may struggle with depression or suicide. They may find difficulty returning to school and to studying. They question the value of activities. They need a place to explore their painful thoughts. Caring parents, teachers, and ministers need to talk with these teenagers. Grieving youth may have a host of new philosophical and theological questions. Help them discover new answers rather than give them your advice. Counselors should patiently move through the grief recovery with gentle confrontations and strong support. Remember that depression is a normal part of grief. Other causes of depression may overlap the grief. These can be difficult to separate.

Some forms of depression surface with acts of delinquency and acting out (Mishne, p. 147). When accompanied by isolation, anxiety, powerlessness, and hopelessness, depression often leads to actions that may be self-destructive. Adolescents who are overwhelmed by a sense of failure may have eruptive episodes characterized by extreme impulsiveness. These impulsive acts might get them into legal problems. This type of deep depression is not as often related to a variety of stressors but is more the reflection of an affective disorder. Clinical depression should be referred for professional counseling.

Recent literature urges parents, teachers, and counselors to pay close attention to teenagers' symptoms so that help can be offered early on and can optimistically minimize the chances of more serious problems like suicide attempts (Culp et al., p. 828). Most students seek help from a minister or school counselor. Only four in ten who seek professional help see another professional such as a social worker, psychologist, psychiatrist, or family therapist. Parents, teachers, ministers, and counselors must work as a team so that depression can be addressed before it leads to a suicide attempt.

Parents

The first step for a parent of a depressed youth is to care. Take time to notice and to **listen** to her or his concerns. Teens won't want to talk immediately and may attempt to shove your concern to the side. Give them time to process alone, but be ready to listen. Do not give quick advice. As one person retorted, "If it were that easy, I would have thought of the solution myself!" Significant attachment to parents decreases depression. Acceptance or rejection from grandparents seems to be of considerable importance to a number of depressed teenagers. I have had several youth who made it through dark, down, depressed periods with regular visits to their grandparents. Some stay for weeks or months. Grandparents listen with seasoned ears.

Work out conflicts mutually with your teenagers. Avoid the temptation to use power and authority to win every conflict. Teens who feel overpowered by their parents become down and hopeless. Living in what seems like oppression can be depressing for them. Ask for and value their opinions when conflicts arise. This does not mean that they call the shots, but that they have a voice in conflict resolutions. Talk about options, alternatives, and negotiated contracts for a win-win resolution.

Help the teenagers to **see the issues in a different light.** If they failed at one goal, what about working harder on another? Hope focuses on a new direction. Stories abound about giving up on one activity and excelling at another—like an injured gymnast who becomes a successful diver. When your child suffers a painful loss or disappointment, emotional support is not enough, according to one private high school president. The parent's job is to assist a teenager to find "a new perspective and to discover new possibilities in the rubble of shattered dreams" (Kelly, p. 113).

Seek consultation from a counselor, pediatrician, psychologist, or psychiatrist to see if the depression needs treatment. Counseling may help before the problem becomes major and perhaps leads to thoughts of suicide. Medications along with therapy have usually been most successful. Talk about the problem with a professional.

Teachers

Tell students what services are available. In one study, around half of high school and middle school students were unaware that counseling was available at school (Culp et al., p. 834). Mention services during other times than in announcements when students are possibly not listening or are doing homework. Use illustrations of persons seeing the counselor. Demonstrate an attitude of respect for those who seek help. At least, resist the temptation to poke fun at students who inquire about counseling services. One student reported being teased in class about seeking a "shrink." Be a professional colleague with the counselors.

Get students to do something. Activity is an important step in overcoming depression. Although many persons will want to wait until they feel like participating in something and thus never get around to being involved, adolescents who can force themselves into action find that the depression lessens and new feelings evolve. Basically, they act their way into new feelings rather than feel their way into acting differently. Work to find a way to involve them in projects, research, and activities at school. Help them find a place to become involved.

Identify and externalize anger. Traditionally, this has worked well for depressed persons. Discussing the causes of the anger is also productive. Expressing the anger through actions such as pounding on a chair or stomping or expressive dancing to music has been less productive with adolescents than with adults, but assisting adolescents with dramatic expressions of their anger has been particularly helpful in depressive situations. This includes their writing a small play or drama and then acting it out themselves with peers taking various roles. Although extremely depressed adolescents may be reluctant to participate in these more active forms of expressing their frustrations, even those who watch seem to benefit.

Pay attention to grief situations, especially the death of a peer. Few schools escape the academic year without a death in the student body. Rituals for those close to the deceased youth can provide opportunities for resolving some grief. Schools have dedicated a page in the yearbook, planted trees, held special convocations, and started scholarship funds. Any opportunity to work through the grief can help. Teachers should listen to the pain, postpone assignments, and rework plans to assist grieving students.

Ministers

Don't come on too strong. An aggressive, intense relationship may frighten a depressed adolescent and cause him or her to withdraw even more. Sensitive, supportive caring on a regular but brief basis is better for building the relationship. Ask the youth if he or she can tell you what is troubling. Do not stop at "nothing"!

Sustaining, the process of walking alongside, is vital in responding to depression. The minister needs first of all to "be there" for the depressed young person. However, other elements of the pastoral perspective come into consideration. For instance, there is a time for confronting the distortions that might lead one to be depressed. Likewise, there is a time for reconciling depressed persons with their community (peers and family). Because depression usually makes decision making more difficult, sharing information and guiding can be expected to be a part of the process. This is particularly true toward the end of pastoral counseling. Of course, ultimately healing the depression is the long-range goal. That isn't unrealistic. Depression decreases when teens find meaningful relationships.

Some methods that have been helpful with depressed youngsters may not be in the standard repertoire of most youth ministers' methods of intervention. However, with careful supervision from trained pastoral supervisors and other professionals, one can begin to employ these techniques. Many pastors have had at least an introduction to pastoral care, and more than a few have had clinical training and will be ready to respond at a deeper level of counseling, as discussed below.

Depression can arise from **unresolved grief.** The minister's work at youth funerals and funerals of family members makes a unique contribution. Find creative ways to address youths' need to grieve the death of a friend. One youth minister held a singing and story time for teenagers the night before the funeral of a beloved "sister" who died in an auto accident. Another gave a teen time to address his reflections about his mother at the funeral. Discuss possibilities with youth early in the grief process.

Counselors

Don't assume that the depressed adolescent became depressed *as* an adolescent. Check out childhood symptoms to differentiate between normal adjustment-disorder depression and pathological depression. How long has the youth felt this way? Get data from the parents. Find and use an adolescent depression inventory to get a picture of the seriousness of the depression. I like the one in David Burns's wonderful book *Feeling Good: The New Mood Therapy.*

Build rapport. In working with depressed adolescents, extra attention needs to be given to the rather nonspecific characteristics of the relationship. Go slow with the intake, and wait for them to trust you before exploring the sadness in detail. Depressed adolescents can be even more difficult and resistant than those with behavior disorders. One needs to take time to build a durable counseling relationship. Warmth, empathy, and congruence are hallmarks of an effective counseling relationship with all persons, but are particularly important in dealing with depressed teenagers.

Music helps. Music is the language in which many teens address their mood issues. Just as Saul was soothed by David's playing the lyre, many adolescents identify with and find release through music. Although certain music addresses their depression, other music suggests new feelings. Body movements, exercise, and dancing can also facilitate mood shifts. Consider involving a music therapist or other expressive therapist in the treatment.

Try cognitive therapy, which has been found to be particularly successful with depressed persons and quite applicable to adolescents (Schrodt and Fitzgerald, pp. 402–08; Wright and Beck, p. 1119). Recent findings indicate that cognitive behavioral therapy reduces depression among adolescents and that treatment gains are maintained over time. The basic tenet of cognitive therapy with depressed adolescents is simply to correct the false perceptions that can cause their depression. Adolescents are likely to have distorted interpretations of events in their environment. For example, a youngster might perceive another adolescent's behavior as rejection and then conclude, "If he [or she] doesn't like me, I'm not worth anything." Thinking "I'm not worth anything" leads to depression. The basic approach of cognitive therapy is to evaluate, through mutual logical reflection, both the data and the conclusions drawn from the data. The therapist assists the adolescent in questioning the data and in looking at alternative ways of interpreting the data. The counselor assists the depressed person in identifying errors in thinking. This is often enough to disprove depressive notions. For example, after evaluation, the youngster feeling depressed might conclude, "He [or she] was probably worried about something and didn't even see me. People still like me. I'm OK!"

Adolescent Suicide

As we turn our attention to adolescent suicide, let us address a few common myths. Ministers, youth workers, teachers, and parents have said to me, "I understand that teenagers who talk about suicide won't do it, and those who don't talk about it are the ones who try it." That dangerous falsehood may lead persons to be unresponsive to suicide talk and to overlook strong hints of suicidal ideation. Any time a teenager openly discusses or offers even veiled conversation about self-destruction, he or she needs to be treated with caution. It is better to err and take such a person too seriously (and be told that you have done so) than to pass lightly over a cry for help. If the teen mentions suicide, respond immediately.

Some youth have observed that their families seem to have more incidents of suicide than do others. They ask if suicide can be inherited. That is a common myth. Whereas depression can be, there is no evidence that suicide is hereditary. However, some research does support the idea that family risk factors exist. Although the research does not prove that family factors cause suicide, there are close ties between a history of family physical or sexual abuse and suicide attempts. Also, poor family communication, loss of a parent by separation or death, and psychopathology in first-degree relatives have been linked as factors. Still the research cannot justify a claim that family factors cause suicide (Wagner, p. 246).

A particularly dangerous myth is that once a person decides to attempt suicide, nothing can change the person's mind. Most teenagers who think about suicide are torn between a wish to live and a desire to escape the pain. Parents have asked me if children who have attempted suicide will eventually kill themselves somehow. Although it is true that a previous attempt puts a distressed youth at risk for another attempt, it is not true forever. One episode does not mean that a teen will ever complete a suicide. In fact, most depressed and suicidal teenagers are helped and grow to be happy adults. Teachers and ministers have inquired if bringing up the subject of suicide might plant the idea in the teenager's mind. Talking openly about the subject will not cause an attempt for someone who is considering suicide. In reality, thrashing out the teen's concerns may increase her or his awareness of attractive options and help to prevent an attempt.

A few facts need repeating:

- Suicidal teenagers usually give significant verbal clues; take them seriously every time.
- Suicide tendency is not inherited. However, it might be a learned, copycat experience.
- Interventions can stop a suicide. Teens want release from the pain of their lives, not from life itself.
- One attempt does not mean that teens will eventually kill themselves. Many get help and grow up contented.
- Talking about suicide won't cause it and may help prevent an attempt.

Most adolescents give clues, express their psychological ache, and talk about their social anguish; however, no two adolescent suicide cases are identical. Some factors in addition to depression that need to be considered in the assessment of a young person's potential for suicide include hopelessness, detachment, loneliness, grief, psychological pain, modeling, presuicidal behavior, and substance abuse. Individually, these in and of themselves do not necessarily denote serious self-destructive thoughts; but when three or more are found together, extreme caution needs to be exercised and suicide ideations need to be checked out. If a person does not have professional training in dealing with suicidal teenagers, a referral for professional help should be offered immediately. However, one needs to be careful not to give the impression of abandoning the teen and bailing out. Reassure the teen that your care will continue undiminished but that you are bringing in a professional counselor to assist. Never exceed your limits and capabilities in counseling—especially when dealing with suicidal tendencies in youth.

Hopelessness

Hopelessness prevails in the lives of adolescents who finally despair to the point of contemplating suicide. Because adolescents live in the here and now, hope for a better future depends on how good things are going today. When depressed, feeling positive about the future seems almost absurd to many teenagers. Because of their perception that time is moving so slowly, long-range help seems of little value. In a similar fashion, because the depression tends to isolate them from peers, they feel hopeless about getting help from a friend. Generally, cognitive distortions about their environment feed this hopelessness. Many times they have given up on themselves and others. In the first place, they do not feel adequate to deal with the crisis, and in the second place, they do not feel worthwhile or loved by other persons.

Detachment

Adolescents who have attempted suicide frequently report several weeks or even months of detached and withdrawn behavior. When asked, "Who is your best friend?" they often cannot name anyone, or they occasionally mention someone who lives many miles away and with whom they have not had recent contact. Although they live in the same house with siblings, parents, and other relatives, they describe their relationships with these persons as cold, remote, and distant. Detachment at school can mean moving through an entire school day without speaking a full sentence to any other person, adolescent or adult. When talking with a detached adolescent, if other characteristics are present, suicide needs to be earnestly discussed and ruled out as one of the alternatives. Just ask, "Are you thinking of ending your life?"

Loneliness

Loneliness, although very similar to detachment, is more than a lack of contact with persons. A lonely adolescent may have contact but perceives the contact to be meaningless. Lonely adolescents feel unloved by parents and peers. Loneliness is a perception of the lack of meaningful attachment to any significant other. One youngster may be very lonely in the midst of a crowd; another, who is living in solitude, may not be lonely because she or he carries a sense of attachment to those who are not physically present.

Grief

Perhaps the most frequent precipitating event in adolescent suicide ideation and attempts is grief over a lost boyfriend or girlfriend. This is particularly true for middle adolescents whose identity formation has stagnated and who find their primary identity in belonging with the significant other. Adults frequently underestimate the pain and grief in the broken love relationships of adolescents. To the adolescent, rejection by a boyfriend or girlfriend feels as painful as an adult experiencing a divorce. In despair, anguish, and anger, shunned teenage lovers frequently turn to suicide. There has been some romanticizing of the relationship of lost love and suicide both in classical literature and in popular media portrayals of teenage life. Any time a breakup occurs in an adolescent dating relationship, caring adults need to be on the lookout for other symptoms and assist in processing the grief.

Psychological Pain

Specific unmet psychological needs can lead to suicide, according to a leading professional in the study of the suicidal mind. Thwarted love, fractured control, assaulted self-image, ruptured key relationships, and excessive anger reflect the major kinds of psychological pain (Shneidman, p. 25). The need to belong, universal in most cultures, emerges as a glaring issue for adolescents. They form social subgroups, cliques, and gangs with persons of similar interests, needs, or activities (good and bad). To be left out or excluded brings intense psychological pain. Failing to reach a goal or being removed from a prestigious position can also produce personal hurt that leads to thoughts of suicide. One beauty queen who lost her crown considered harming herself. The humiliation felt overwhelming. She saw no other escape from the disgrace. Lost love produces confusing, hopeless grief for many teenagers. On the other end of the pain continuum, anger and rage at others may lead to thoughts of self-destruction. Teens desire to get even with someone who caused them hurt. They want to create regret in someone who discounted them. "See how they feel when I'm gone!" barked one seventeen-year-old. "They will be sorry for what they did then. Just let them live with that," he roared.

Modeling

There seems to be a follow-the-leader effect when one adolescent in a community attempts suicide. Afterward, the others in the group are at greater risk. Suicide pacts are not uncommon. Evidence suggests that adolescent suicides portrayed in the movies and on television, particularly in urban settings, tend to precipitate attempts or at least push over the edge those adolescents who have already been contemplating suicide. When adolescents view suicide-related films, it is best that they have an opportunity to discuss their thoughts and feelings with their parents, teachers, minister, and counselor. Adolescents, like adults, are also more likely to attempt suicide if the pattern has been established in a previous generation by a relative who chose self-destruction as a way of escaping a problem. Suicide puts the pain on the following generations and implies that killing oneself solves the problem.

Presuicidal Behavior

Adolescents who are seriously contemplating suicide will frequently begin to make ready for their departure. They give away prized possessions and present sentimental objects to friends, lovers, or even their parents. One young man decided to sell his most valued treasure, a reconstructed automobile. Another left several trophies with a friend. Another returned pictures to an old girlfriend. Another expression of presuicidal behavior, saying good-bye, may take the form of talking about going on a trip or discussing being gone. Tidying up can sometimes be a clue. Adolescents will straighten up their rooms, clean their clothes, and put things in place with unusual attention to detail.

Like adults, some presuicidal adolescents appear less depressed. This new cheerfulness may lull others into a false security. A brief interlude of happiness comes from having finally made the decision. Continue suicidal precautions past the time of most concern.

Obviously, suicide statements and suicide notes are serious presuicidal behavior. Not all adolescents leave a note or even take time to say good-bye; however, most do leave a note in which frequently they ask forgiveness and express their love to certain persons. Many notes are similar in nature. A suicide note left by one young man read:

> *Dear Steve,*
> *I'm sorry for what I have done, but Robert and Mom made me think. Will your mom still have wanted us to be friends? I don't know. Tell Missy I love her, and I hope she can still pass Science. Make sure you never be as dumb as I have been. Make friends, and don't let them play that tape before my funeral.*
> *Friends, Jay*
> *(Johnson, pp. 10–11)*

This young man wrote at least five notes to other persons, as well as a recorded tape message. His note to his mother is particularly characteristic.

> *I'm sorry for what I've put you through. I am empty. I just can't face my friends. I want the entire ninth grade invited to my funeral,*

and at the funeral, and not before, play this tape. Please don't play it before if you love me. Also have Tommy fly down if at all possible. Love you. I'm scared. Jay

(Johnson, p. 17)

Suicide notes can express love, anger, grief, or shame. Whatever painful, intolerable feelings that seem to be pent up and inexpressible in life are expressed by the act of death.

Substance Abuse

A dramatic increase in drug and alcohol consumption remains a factor in nonfatal suicidal attempts more than in either suicide completions or natural deaths (Johnson, p. 133). Therefore, new involvement in drugs and alcohol as well as other significant changes in personality may be acting-out behaviors that are signs of suicidal thoughts. They are disguised cries for help. Because many completed suicide attempts begin as cries for help, they must be taken seriously. One can never conclude that someone is only halfheartedly attempting suicide and is therefore at less risk. Alcohol and drugs decrease a youth's ability to control impulses. The capacity to make clear decisions is lost. Therefore, suicidal thoughts may lead to acts of self-destruction when the teen's judgment becomes clouded.

Guidelines for Helping with Teenage Suicide Crises

The interventions and responses that follow focus on the relationship with the teen and are not intended as a comprehensive discussion for a suicide intervention team. Teenagers need family involvement and support. They require open schools that accept and affirm them. Youth desire a minister whom they can trust with their deep fears, hurts, and doubts. Counselors who succeed with suicidal youth exhibit confident warmth, bold openness, and daring honesty.

Parents

Parents can examine the youth's place in the family. Do they feel honored, accepted, and valued in your household? Do not let their hateful, repugnant, and obnoxious acts drive you to wish them dead. If you find yourself depleted and unable to cope, seek help for the family. You may want to consider an out-of-home placement. Any verbal or physical abuse will only add to the problems. In times like these, parenting is a relationship of commitment, not convenience, comfort, and fun.

Predisposing factors. If your teen uses alcohol, drugs, or recreational sex, he or she is at higher risk for suicide. A teen who considers suicide might actually attempt it when his or her impulse control becomes impaired while under the influence of a substance. As mentioned, depression, isolation, and hopelessness add to the likelihood the teen might take his or her own life. Teens think they have no other way out of the inner pain. Problems with the law can also add to their vulnerability. When placed behind bars for the first time, they sometimes try to kill themselves in a moment of panic and despair. A few studies have found that sexual orientation confusion adds to vulnerability, but the reasons are unclear.

Triggering events. If a teenager is predisposed toward suicide, a temporary crisis or any added stress might push the teen over the edge into an attempt. Although any new major negative event could bring the breaking point, several common catastrophes deserve to be noted. As mentioned, breaking up with a lover is the primary triggering event. Failure at school, getting fired from a desirable job, being arrested, accidentally injuring a close friend, or any major, public, shameful event could set off the process. Provide support and care around such raw, distressing times. Watch closely for signs of suicide plans. Be alert to remove any means of self-destruction. Conduct a suicide watch for a few days.

Impulsive moments need to be protected. If a predisposing youth suffers one or more triggering events and begins to plan for a suicide attempt, the teen might go ahead and do it in a moment of low impulse control. Such moments explode into the present with drinking, smoking pot, or using hard drugs, especially ecstasy and the so-called party drugs. When an adolescent is ruminating in his or her room under the heavy clouds of depression and loneliness, something as simple as suicide talk on television or in a movie might initiate this recklessness. Dark, death-wish, hard-rock music could kick off a rash decision to attempt to kill oneself. Even something said in anger by a friend, teacher, minister, or family member might instigate an irresponsible flash. Although these do not cause the suicide, they should be noted as times of vulnerability. Avoid these when possible, and shield the teenager from himself or herself during times of vulnerability.

Get help. What is a parent to do when someone who has his or her whole life to live wants desperately to end it? Find a professional who works well with teenagers. Ask your minister, school counselor, or pediatrician for a referral. Many hospitals have a chaplain who will know a pastoral counselor, social worker, family therapist, psychologist, or psychiatrist who specializes in counseling troubled teenagers. Find help. Call the hot line. Do not ignore the cry for help!

A significant factor in long-range health can be to **bring closure on the**

suicide ideation. There comes a time when the teenager has moved beyond thoughts of suicide, but the family and peers may continue to see a "suicide risk." Give a sense of acceptance, a willingness not only to forgive and forget but also to move on with life in a graceful manner. One teen mused a year later, "I can't believe I did a thing [attempted suicide] like that. I wish people would stop talking about it." Let it drop. After the youth recover and their ways of coping grow, do not continue to treat them as possibly suicidal.

Teachers

A simple, cheerful, focused, warm, and **personal greeting** can make a big difference to a student with suicide on his or her mind. Because suicidal youth are detached, your good spirits and attention can be a significant influence. Your individual greeting may be the teen's only one of the school day. Warmth eludes the experience of many teens. They come to feel and believe that no one cares about them. They interpret care as remembering their name, noticing them in the hallway, wanting to know something about them, or welcoming their presence. A little personal contact can make a huge difference for someone contemplating self-destruction.

Find the positive in the teens' work and find the **hopeful windows** for their future. Noticing their worth offers hope for resolving the dilemma. Giving up on the future sets the mind toward suicide. Discovering clear and optimistic alternatives with the potential to relieve the psychological pain lifts the cloud of hopelessness. A dazzling, new perspective transforms the despair of suicidal thinking. It is like turning on floodlights after a stadium blackout. A whole new world becomes visible.

Caring, getting involved, and forming a primary bond are the most significant ways to help adolescents choose against suicide as an option. However, in befriending suicidal teenagers there are many potential barriers. We must do more than speak of our friendship. Teachers must also **listen to youth** in a way that signals our deep care and respect for them as persons. We need to be cautious not to minimize their concerns. Adolescents may first discuss minor issues to test the level of care before revealing serious problems. Communicate to them the depth of your caring. Become aware of their world. Join them in their race for significance.

Teachers and school administrators can make a big difference by **conducting a therapeutic "postvention"** after the suicide of any youth in the community. Processing the first trauma reduces the likelihood of a copycat, second attempt. Begin immediately after the event and explore students' reactions. Avoid quick, easy answers, and focus on thought distortions and magical thinking. Every school should develop a comprehensive suicide response program. Keep parents informed and involved from the planning stage to the implementation (Stillion and McDowell, p. 232).

Ministers

Suicidal adolescents' resolve to live is strengthened if you **give them an opportunity to tell their life stories.** Getting them in touch with their history and letting them verbalize their own significant events seem to overpower some of the feelings of detachment and loneliness.

Letting the youth discuss conflicts with their parents and their relationship to parents and stepparents is vital. Listen to how they feel about their friends and the youth at church. As they share their history, it is helpful to assist them in interpreting the dynamics of their lives through the gospel story. For example, the loneliness of Jesus in the Garden of Gethsemane might be related to their description of their own sense of isolation and loneliness.

After a suicide attempt, the **ministry of reconciliation** can help reunite a youth with both the peer group and the family. The suicidal adolescent may have multiple broken relationships that need mending. Assist the teen in finding friends at church who will include her or him in activities and perhaps spend time together away from church. A long-range goal of pastoral counseling is to facilitate the building of community and koinonia with the fellowship of the entire church.

Assist depressed and suicidal adolescents to move on with life as an **invitation to a lifelong spiritual journey.** Thoughts of suicide at one point or another in adolescence should not diminish your confidence in their future. They need to be accepted into the community of faith and nurtured along the spiritual journey. They need to live life with the affirmation that they are persons of worth, with the hope that by the help of God they can not only transform their environment but also reshape the future. They are called to live, to love, and to relate to self, life, and God in a manner described in John's Gospel as "abundant living." One suicidal teenager who talked with me for a number of years graduated from seminary and finds satisfaction as a young adult from working with troubled youth. He is happily married and no longer struggles with self-destructive thoughts.

Counselors

Although taking them seriously, caring, and listening to youth are the beginning stages, these responses by no means address the suicidal crisis.

Help adolescents ground themselves in reality. Your attention may give them hope in the short range, but in the long range they need to identify their problems, express the repressed negative emotions around those problems, evaluate the reality of their interpretations and conclusions, and select an appropriate alternative for resolving the problems. Frequently, in their darkest moments adolescents doubt that we care for them; they also distort the intensity of their problems. One very depressed fifteen-year-old girl overheard her parents discussing a financial matter and, without further checking, came to the distorted conclusion that money matters were much more serious than they actually were. Such distortions are not an uncommon basis for actually attempting suicide.

After adolescents have checked out the reality of their interpretations and their understanding of the crisis from those involved, they can **express their feelings** about the real situation. Although they may want to ventilate feelings about their distorted conclusions, only correcting their perceptions, not mere ventilation, will ultimately relieve these feelings.

Because suicide frequently involves the need to "send a message" to significant others, **include all family members** who are living in the household if they will join the counseling. As an expression of anger, the youth may be attempting to get even with or hurt someone. Usually, this person is a family member or close friend. However, this anger is more likely just one symptom and should not to be viewed in isolation. Even when the parents are no longer living together, they both need to be included. If possible, include any stepparents. Engaging the family system helps in discovering the relationships between the adolescent and each family member as well as in assessing the family as a system. Avoid being "triangled" into casting blame or finding fault. Focus on the communication patterns, the methods of resolving conflict, the level of stress in the family, the amount of quality time spent together, the capability for change, faith and values, the capacity of the family to give and receive forgiveness, affirmation, and blessings, and the family's expectations and rules. A family history obviously helps, but wait until the initial trauma gets addressed. The teenager's suicide attempt may be an extreme reaction to dysfunction in the family system, or it may be external to the home situation. In either case, the youth needs family support to get through this crisis.

It is not uncommon to find that the adolescent's actions are actually being subtly encouraged by someone in the family system. Some call this behavior "psychic homicide" (Mirkin and Koman, p. 310). The family not only expects the suicide, but begins to participate in helping make it possible by doing such things as leaving the means of suicide available. The

susceptible adolescent seems to feel that death will serve a sacrificial purpose and actually save the family. Confront such actions and address problems within the family system.

When seeing the parents, **decisions about hospitalizing** the suicidal
adolescent must be made. Most state laws require that someone who
attempts suicide must be hospitalized. Adolescents whose attempts are private and perhaps take place in secluded areas are more serious about dying
than those whose attempts are made around the family or peers, where they
are likely to be found in time. However, neither case should be taken lightly.
Insurance changes in the nineties make hospitalization a last-resort possibility. Many potentially suicidal teenagers are sent home without being
admitted if they have not already injured themselves. The family conducts
its own "suicide watch."

Assist teenagers by **putting the pain in perspective.** Ask them to scale
the pain on a continuum from one to nine. Edwin S. Shneidman, founder
of the American Association of Suicidology, constructed a full psychological pain survey to rate and explore the dimensions of suicidal thinking
(Shneidman, pp. 173–78). He suggests: Ask youth how they related to previous suffering and torment. How did they resolve those crises? What can
they learn for this situation? Ask them to relate an incident of distress and
agony from someone they know. How does that compare to their current
situation? Is theirs not as bad, about the same, or worse? Consider sharing
a distressing situation that has been successfully resolved, but be careful
not to discount the youth's personal pain. Helping teens to gain perspective
can give hope and confidence to face life and to turn from thoughts of
suicide.

For adolescents who see suicide as an escape from an intolerable situation, **seek alternative ways to resolve the pain.** Adolescents have difficulty seeing alternatives for their crises and need the assistance of ministers
and counselors to generate sensible choices. Guiding them during the time
of selecting one or more alternatives means supporting their right to make
decisions. They also need sustaining encouragement in actually attempting
to implement a desirable alternative. An adolescent youth who had
attempted suicide remained distant from the hospital staff and myself for
some time. When he gained enough trust to tell his story, it seemed he had
opted for suicide as a way of relieving his family of the shame of having
him and of his guilt. No one particular event caused the guilt; rather, he felt
a general sense of guilt about himself. The major turning point in his journey was realizing that there were alternatives for dealing with his guilt and
pain. He could feel as good or better than he fantasized he would feel in

suicide. Helping adolescents know that suicide is not a glamorous, painless, easy solution can assist them in deciding for life's alternatives. Dealing directly with shame, guilt, and the disappointment of broken relationships is not hopeless from a theological perspective.

As the adolescent's depression, detachment, loneliness, and guilt improve, she or he is briefly at greatest risk for an actual suicide attempt. Be especially careful to **take precautions to protect adolescents from themselves** at this time. They may need to be hospitalized in a unit where suicide precautions can be ensured. Do not leave them alone and unsupervised for long periods of time. Have the family remove or lock up any weapons. Medications should also be in a secure place. Protective precautions not only prevent an accidental or impulsive suicide; they can also show adolescents the deep sense of esteem and care in which they are held.

Remember that depression and suicide often surface conjointly; however, not always. Think assessment, and take action when the crisis begins to reach a moderate level. Prevention always costs less than trauma. Take action while depression and suicide thoughts remain in the mild stage. Do not ignore danger signals. When parents, teachers, ministers, and counselors work as a team, teenagers usually win the fight against depression and suicide.

Chapter 10

Substance Abuse

"*I*t's not that which goes into the mouth but that which comes out of the mouth that defiles a person," one youth snapped. He went on to proclaim that it was no worse for him to smoke pot than it was for his father to have a martini every evening after work. Regarding the use of alcohol, adolescents regularly point to the biblical teaching of moderation and the practice of Jesus to use wine as they attempt to build a case for their own abuse. Seldom, however, do they quote from Ephesians 5:18: "Do not get drunk with wine," or from Leviticus 1:34 or John 2:10 or Luke 21:34 or Romans 13:13 or any of the passages that speak of avoiding the abuse of substances. However, many current teenagers do not need an excuse; they feel that it is normal to drink, smoke pot, or try a "party drug." They rationalize, "Everybody does it, so why shouldn't I!" This chapter outlines the major factors in adolescent substance abuse, including the misuse of alcohol and drugs and the misuse of food. The deeper approaches to the abuse of alcohol and drugs are similar to methods of dealing with food abusers. Those who overeat and those who refuse to eat, like those who turn to alcohol and drugs, are attempting to cope with a variety of hurtful, shameful, painful emotions in the absence of a support system.

Alcohol and Other Drugs

Although evidence points to a decline in alcohol use among adolescents, one in five youth still reports use of alcohol during the past month. The average age at first use has dropped from eighteen to sixteen years. Around 8 percent of all teenagers admit to binge drinking at least once in the past month. More alarmingly, over half of those also used an illicit drug in the past month. Another study reported that over half of today's youth drink alcohol before age eighteen (Leino et al., p. 208). Moreover, the National Institute on Drug Abuse found that only two in ten high school seniors have not tried alcohol. This should not be surprising in light of the fact that a study in January 2000 reported that one in four children is exposed to family alcoholism or alcohol abuse before age eighteen (National Institutes of Health, p. 1). Although some forms of drug use are down from twenty years ago, new, more dangerous substances have invaded the youth culture. The decline in drug use was lowest in 1992. The slow increase has not reached the peaks of the late seventies. Usage is increasing, but not to the levels of previous generations.

Over half of high school seniors report trying illicit drugs, according to the Partnership for a Drug-Free America. Whatever the numbers say, when your teenager has an alcohol or drug problem, you need to take serious action immediately. Teachers and ministers may be lulled into complacency with news of some decreases in adolescent substance abuse. Adult treatment programs do not work well with teenagers. Counselors have fewer referral options with the closing of many inpatient treatment programs for adolescent substance abuse. Therefore, more teens will need to be treated "in the office."

Nevertheless, startling new research indicates that alcohol and drugs actually hijack the brain of users. The initial rush and good feeling cannot be reobtained without increased amounts—at times, not at all! It will never be that good again—not ever. What is worse, the brain ceases to manufacture its own "feel good" chemicals, and sober life feels worse than before usage began. The youth are trapped unless treatment disrupts this downward spiral into addiction (Bill Moyers, PBS video, *The Hijacked Brain*).

Abuse is widespread, the need for ministry is high, and the responses of most churches are less than adequate. Many ministers lack training in responding to substance abuse crises. Parents have more of the burden for assisting recovery. Schools face defiant, detached students who are strung out, high, and hungover. They are just waiting to drop out. Teachers report alarm that a significant number of bright, affluent, well-groomed teens end up in trouble because of alcohol or drugs. The so-called club drugs are dangerous. Across the country, teenagers flock to all-night dances in warehouses. These raves often offer party drugs that can kill or cause brain damage. The U.S. Department of Justice reports that the number of drug-related deaths have soared to all-time highs in some states like Florida, New Mexico, and California. Understanding the reasons behind alcohol and drug abuse and having a basic knowledge of the effects of alcohol and drugs are the first steps in helping adolescents with a substance-abuse challenge.

Identifying a few common factors may help with prevention as well as with treatment.

Why Do Adolescents Drink and Take Drugs?

Adolescents with various levels of use and abuse describe a whole host of reasons. Many adolescents cannot explain why they first used drugs, including alcohol, because of their lack of self-awareness and their lack of the dynamics affecting their lives. The comment "I just tried some one day, and I guess I liked it and then tried it some more" is typical of many early and middle adolescents who later get hooked on substances. Strong evidence advocates that friends introduce friends to substance abuse. Being with the wrong crowd seduces many unaware teens into their first experience. Even going with a friend to the wrong party can be dangerous. Because some "fun drugs" are colorless, tasteless, and odorless, they are mistakenly viewed as a harmless way to have fun. In reality, they are more dangerous. Alcohol and drugs become an alternative to boredom.

Excitement

Seeking excitement is the first motive that leads to substance abuse. Recreational users will frequently abuse at a party, and soon getting high becomes a regular first step to having fun. Every recipe for a good time begins with a bottle of booze or a joint or some pills. One professor suggests that parent modeling is a major influence on adolescents who drink for entertainment and excitement (Parsons, p. 87). One nineteen-year-old told me that he began drinking in high school because parties became boring otherwise. His drinking worsened in college, when he felt he needed to be drunk to enjoy himself. Failing the first semester did little to sober him up. An overdose did wake up his family to the abuse problem. Another youth told of a bad trip on "mushrooms" that were supposed to make sex more exciting. He suffered memory loss and a new slowness in his thinking processes—hardly his initial vision of excitement! Inhalants are used more by younger teens but have been on the decline. They too lure kids with the promise of excitement.

The search for excitement begins a downhill slide into major addiction. Teens who smoke are more likely to drink and use drugs. Smoking pot is a gateway to the use of harder drugs. Even heroin has marched into the adolescent world. The average age for first trying heroin fell from twenty-six in 1990 to just seventeen by 1997, according to one report. Most teenagers do not know that they can die from an alcohol overdose. They are unaware that

"X" (ecstasy) can cause brain damage and death when overused. Some teens are slipped the date rape drug (Rohypnol) at parties. This odorless, tasteless pill is placed into something as innocent as a pop drink. The teen does not remember anything for up to twelve hours and usually becomes the victim of sexual abuse or rape. Looking for fun in the wrong places is more dangerous than ever. Without doubt, new compounds will filter into the drug picture and offer new problems for those who seek their excitement.

Escape

In addition to those seeking a good time, other adolescents turn to substance abuse as an escape from pain. In essence, they are self-medicating. They want to escape depression or anxiety or guilt or timidity or shame or anger or whatever unpleasant feeling dominates their lives. "I'm not good at talking to girls until I've had a couple of drinks," one young man confessed. "Smoking a few joints doesn't hurt anyone, and it helps me forget the arguing and fighting at home," said a distraught teenage girl. One heroin user blamed school pressure when he alleged, "I felt it was easier to face pressure when I was high." Adolescents escaping from the agonizing realities of their troubled world need crisis intervention and support even more *after* they attempt to escape the ache by turning to drugs and/or alcohol for temporary relief. Those who escape are more likely to become addicts. In a double-barreled way, they are creating new problems through the substance abuse, while at the same time refusing to face their current problems.

Experimentation

A third reason for turning to substance abuse is simply experimentation. A number of first-time users are simply curious about the experience. Frequently, peer pressure will cause those who want to be included in a group or are lonely or are seeking acceptance to respond positively to the taunt, "Oh, come on and try some. It will be fun. Nobody will be hurt." A few early adolescents experiment with older friends. However, middle adolescents, especially in their stage of experimentation, are vulnerable to turning to drugs "just for the experience." Parents need to be careful not to panic and think their child has a major drug or alcohol problem just because he or she has experimented once or twice. Obviously, one would wish that such experimentation were not a part of the adolescent experience, but experimentation is not addiction and is not on a level with regular use. Adolescents who experiment only occasionally can readily be turned from drugs with a positive peer group, family backing, and supportive information about the dangers of drug use. Schools and churches should know that responding early is a key to preventing further use. Counselors can reassure families not to panic on the first experimentation, but to seek help for the underlying problems.

Inherited Disease

Personality difficulties, characterological disorders, and inherited addictive predispositions are a fourth factor in substance abuse. Whereas conclusions are mixed on addiction as an inherited disease, it is known that infants whose mothers are addicts can be born addicted. As Derek Miller defines addiction—chronic intoxication produced by the repeated consumption of a drug—many adolescents become addicted after their parents have already done so (D. Miller, *Adolescents,* p. 442). According to the National Institutes of Health, nineteen million Americans under age nineteen are exposed to familial alcohol dependency.

We have known for decades that "the offspring of alcoholics are significantly more likely than other people to become alcoholics themselves regardless of whether their adoptive parents abuse alcohol" (Kolta, p. 36). However, genetics is not the only question, because over a third of all alcoholics have no family history of the disorder, and only 30–40 percent of the sons of alcoholics have ever become alcoholics themselves. Likewise, family drug usage predicts teenage drug abuse. Whatever the family influence, the need for a comprehensive response remains urgent. Teenagers with anxiety disorders and mood disturbances often turn to alcohol or drugs for self-medication. Most go undiagnosed until addictions have taken control.

Anger

Angry rebellion is a fifth reason adolescents turn to drugs and substance abuse. They will often get drunk or get high as a way of getting even with their parents, a boyfriend, or a girlfriend. It is another way of escaping. When they do not know how to identify and confront their angry, hurt, disappointed feelings and are unable to think through the events in a productive manner, they will often turn to alcohol or escape into the mellow feelings of substance abuse. It is their way of cooling down or chilling when relationships become heated. Rebellious youths' appraisal skills remain low, and their ability to solve relationship problems via negotiation appears nonexistent. Some use alcohol to "have the courage to get mad."

School Problems

Poor social skills are further factors in adolescent substance abuse. Students who think that the pressures of school exceed their ability to cope often turn to drugs or alcohol to escape. They party to forget how bad it seems. Poor social skills begin with youths' inability to maintain a good relationship with their parents. They need something to help them relate to friends. They equate being high with being connected to others. In fact, social problems worsen for most youthful abusers. Over time they lose the friends who do not use alcohol and drugs. At the same time they feel less connected and suspicious of those who do use alcohol and drugs.

Whatever the cause, adolescents can be severely addicted to alcohol and drugs. After becoming addicted, they are in need of serious crisis intervention. Teenagers can suffer major repercussions from a single use of the wrong substance. They especially need swift help. Education, counseling, and support alone are not enough. Medical attention, usually as an inpatient, is most often also needed. Family counseling and a total systems approach based upon behavior modification principles are most effective in assisting the adolescent addict.

Responding to Adolescents Who Use Alcohol and Drugs

Preventive programs based on accurate information about alcohol, marijuana, and other illicit drugs and their effect on the human body and mind appear to be the best approach to adolescents. Parents, ministers, and teachers should keep communication open and maintain a respectful relationship with their youth. Good relationships build positive self-esteem. But although preventive programs serve as the best deterrent to involvement, a sufficient number of adolescents are in need of pastoral care, formal counseling, and crisis intervention.

Parents

A first step for parents is to **set clear rules** that fit your family. Clarify expectations about not drinking or using drugs. Be firm, but do not preach. It seems that adolescent drug users report less parental involvement in their lives. Offer support for them no matter what they do. If your adolescent does drink, assure your teen that he or she can call for you or someone to come and pick him or her up without a hassle. Some parents have found that parents whose adolescents wanted to experiment with alcohol have been successful in educating their children about the use of alcohol and permitting them to experiment by tasting one drink in the presence of the parents. This gives the adolescent an "out" when encouraged to experiment by peers. They can say, "I tried it and I don't like it." Many parents still adhere to teaching total abstinence. Not all teens party and drink. Stop that pattern early.

Get to know their friends. Stay involved with the activities, and insist on meeting friends. Do not hesitate to limit access to suspicious peers. One study reported that teenage drug users stated that their parents do not know their friends. This means more than a one-time meeting. Engage their friends in conversation. Spend time helping them with projects when they are younger. Offer rides, and go the extra mile to take them home after activities. Spend the time before a problem arises.

If problems arise, take abuse seriously and work as a team to **plan an intervention**. Seek guidance from a group like AA to know how to intervene. For example, meet as a group and define the substance problem. Tell the teens what they will lose and how they will be restricted until it stops. Be firm and consistent in limiting their access to alcohol and drugs. "Should I get them out of jail?" I am often asked. Yes, but not out of the consequences. Without consequences they will not learn and change. Do not leave teens behind bars to teach them a lesson, unless they have repeated offenses. Do let them pay fines and lose their transportation. They should cover insurance costs and pay their own court costs.

Limit access to alcohol in the home. Keep your personal supply under lock. In fact, it would be best not to have a private bar if your youth begins to drink. Your modeling will have a major impact on their decisions. You cannot do one thing and expect them to do another. The exception seems to be for light drinkers. If parents stop at one or two occasional drinks, their teenagers seem to learn to wait until they are of age and then to follow this pattern.

Seek a medical evaluation if your teen has a problem with alcohol or drugs. Give teens the facts about the effects of substance abuse. Help them understand their problems and find the resources for other courses of action. Drinking to solve their problems does not work. Assist them to discover what does. Keep an eye on their behavior to see if the abuse returns. Many parents see the signs of substance abuse, but fear asking. Do not be naïve. Consider regular drug screening for your teenager, if he or she has been caught more than once. This might produce distrust and deception, but usually it helps teens to free themselves of casual use. If they are addicted, they will need professional help.

Attend programs for recovery with your youth. Get information about Alanon meetings and become involved. Recovery programs involve the entire family. Do your part, and learn the information for your teenager. Remember that recovery initiates a lifelong, one day at a time process. Understand how your whole family can deal with recovery issues.

Teachers

Alcohol and drug **education** makes a difference for most students, but some are not detoured by information. In addition to planned units on substance abuse, teachers can use illustrations that add to an awareness of the dangers of substance abuse. One student in my therapy group learned in a math class that one joint contained twenty times the lung contaminants as one cigarette. Somehow this information made a greater impact than if it were part of a program on drugs. Likewise, health, chemistry, and biology projects can demonstrate the dangerous outcomes of substance abuse. One school posted pictures of auto crashes on the Internet. Another tested the lung capacity of smokers and nonsmokers in a statistics course.

Teachers should **support organizations** like Students Against Drunk Drivers. Positive peer pressure works. When students educate each other, the impact seems stronger. Statistics influence students when they "overhear" them from a friend. Grassroots projects, like a "do not drink and drive" poster contest, ripple through a peer group like tumbling dominoes. A school in Topeka held a special, student-led, halftime presentation on the dangers of drinking and driving. The Public Broadcasting System produced an excellent series with Bill Moyers that can be shown in schools. *The Hijacked Brain* offered bold new research on how addictions rob users of normal positive feelings and actually reduce pleasure sensations overall.

Take away the glamour. Do not romanticize getting drunk as a way of having fun. Avoid funny stories about abuse. Getting high to have fun reflects a personality problem. If possible, avoid films and novels that portray substance abuse as glamorous or positive. Confront the idea that it is cool to get high. When one teen boasted about smoking pot at 4:20 on April 20, we confronted that as something to be ashamed about, not proud. The peer group was divided in their reaction.

Have tough, zero-tolerance policies for possession at school and at school functions. Refer first offenders for education programs, and stiffen the penalties with any subsequent offense. Expel persistent offenders. Build a reputation for being a clean school. Do not look the other way when students smoke pot in the parking lot after school. Report any persons selling drugs.

Adolescents who are regular abusers will frequently have limited social skills. **Involving them in social skills groups** and teaching them appropriate behavior can be an important part in reintegrating them into the peer group. Remember that experimentation is not the same as abuse. Give sincere students a second or third chance, but stop when the problems continue. Refer problem offenders for ongoing counseling or treatment programs.

Ministers

Because adolescents respond positively to **peer counseling** and group contexts, ministers should support the formation of Ala-teen groups alongside the Alcoholics Anonymous groups in their churches and in the community. Furthermore, ministers should work with communities and schools in developing broad-based chemical-dependency education programs.

Some church groups have assisted parents and children in **forming covenants** and pledges that there will be no drinking and driving. The parents agree to drive to get their teenager and to ask no questions until later. This takes some of the fear from asking for help after realizing a mistake has been made. Stress grace and forgiveness for those who seek help.

Because distance from one's parents is a causative factor, especially in illicit drug involvement, churches can assist in a preventive fashion by **offering education programs that strengthen the overall family life** within their congregations. Family-life education programs that focus the need for quality family time together go a long way in creating an environment where alcohol and drug use is less likely to erupt. Pastoral care issues are important in ministering to adolescent substance abusers, because depression, anxiety, and the inability to express anger frequently contribute to adolescent drug abuse. A minister who deals with those issues from a theological perspective can be of great assistance to the adolescent. Focusing on the adolescent's self-identity from a positive point of view may encourage the adolescent to find the strength to acknowledge the problem of substance abuse and seek further help.

Sustaining and guiding are significant factors in the pastoral care of adolescent drug users. Sustaining the adolescent in the ongoing struggle may even mean being on call in an Alcoholics Anonymous contract fashion if the adolescent is tempted to return to the abuse. Contracts sustain the adolescent who is turning from regular use. Reconciliation is also an important factor of pastoral care with adolescent abusers. Reconciliation in the family system is usually needed. Frequently, the adolescent's relationships with church groups or other friends will be broken, and the minister can serve to facilitate reconciliation in both groups. Reconciliation with peers may mean that the minister serves as a bridge to introduce the former substance abuser into a new peer group and then assists in finding a new role and a new place in the Christian community.

As Alcoholics Anonymous has successfully pointed out, admitting that one is powerless and needs help from a **Higher Power** is an important step in recovery. The pastoral counselor is in a unique place to introduce the adolescent to the Higher Power. Although a manipulative approach would do more damage than good, assisting the adolescent in beginning a sincere faith pilgrimage is a crucial step in long-term recovery from substance abuse. Furthermore, the pastoral counselor can assist the adolescent to deal with the guilt and grief issues that frequently accompany a pattern of abuse. Through honest forgiveness and seeking to clean up relationships and become reconciled with peers and family, the adolescent can find new meaning in life.

A central **theological issue** for counseling with adolescent abusers is that of *personhood*. When personhood can be rooted in a firm understanding of the importance of all humanity, as seen in the creation and incarnation, an adolescent finds a new sense of positive self-worth—a natural high. Assisting adolescents in finding a personhood based in Christian theology helps them to avoid the crises of substance abuse.

A further theological issue—*calling,* or purpose in life—assists adolescents in dealing with abuse issues. As the pastoral counselor seeks to uncover the purpose served by the drinking—for example, control of anxiety, overcoming shyness, experimentation—alternatives are explored. The minister seeks to guide adolescents toward God's deeper purpose in life, to deal with those issues. Wayne Oates provides an excellent discussion of how identity and purpose can be grounded in the Christian faith in his classic volume *Christ and Selfhood.*

When the adolescent has used a substance for relief of intra-psychic pain, an introduction to the *spiritual journey* provides a more productive alternative. Although systematic desensitization and relaxation techniques are not necessarily related to prayer and meditation, they can be. When used in conjunction with Christian prayer and meditation, they have been powerful therapeutic tools in assisting adolescents to feel at peace with themselves and God. Some have reported that their meditative experiences in prayer exceed those previously produced from use of drugs.

Counselors

Contract for recovery. Until teenagers want to recover, focus on the need to decide. Often they will have a time in their mind that they plan to stop using. Push to make that time now. Legal restraints often assist in convincing the teenager to get serious about recovery. I found that testimonies by convicted drug abusers who were serving time was a powerful wake-up call for beginning users, but had little effect on those already in an addiction process. Of course, until they have faced withdrawal, no contract will work. They are powerless over their actions while still under the influence. Contract for recovery after they "dry out." Clean contracts require clear thinking.

Group counseling provides teenage abusers with peer confrontation and support. Long-term recovery is enhanced by age-appropriate peer support. Group therapy can provide ongoing support for handling issues in recovery and can support the decision to stay "clean." Some form of accountability and medical follow-up increases the effectiveness of these treatment programs. Keep the membership constant if possible, and expect regular attendance. Consistency matters. Press for open, honest communication. Testimonies of recovered teens who are further along in the process can be powerful elements of hope for beginners. We have found it helpful to have a male and female coleader in these groups.

Several counseling issues surface with the adolescent who is a frequent user, abuser, or addict. First, **the family must be assessed.** If the parents are also substance abusers, a family systems intervention model is recommended. Treatment for all members of the family in the various programs of Alcoholics Anonymous should be used in conjunction with individual and family counseling. Perhaps one or more members of the system will need long-term institutionalization in a substance-abuse rehabilitation center. However, such resident programs seem to be more effective with adults than adolescents. Some have failed to find statistically significant differences in the outcome of outpatient treatment of delinquent drug abusers as over against inpatient treatment. Nevertheless, work with existing treatment programs whenever possible.

Family structural issues need to be addressed by the counselor when the adolescent abuses drugs but the parents do not. When parents are nonabusers, family dynamics can be more powerful in assisting the adolescent through the process of becoming a nonabuser also. Structural issues that need to be dealt with are the family's ability to set and maintain appropriate limits and the family's commitment to spend regular quality time with the adolescent. Furthermore, the family needs to communicate to the adolescent that they are forming a covenant relationship. This is a particularly difficult issue because the adolescent is in the midst of a struggle for independence. Care and bonding should not be confused with creating dependence. In the context of respect for the adolescent's personhood, such bonding need not denote control.

In addition to family issues, **cognitive issues surface in counseling** with adolescent drug and alcohol abusers. Frequently, adolescents will harbor a multitude of cognitive distortions about adolescence and about alcohol and drugs and their abuse. Such distortions might be in the area of *selective abstraction*, where they would say, "The only way I can have fun at a party is to get high." Another cognitive distortion, *overgeneralization,* might find its way in statements like "I stopped drinking for two days, so

I know I can quit any time I want to" or "Nobody liked me and I never had any fun before I started using, and if I quit my friends will drop me." A third cognitive distortion, *magnification*, can be seen in relationship to substance abuse when the adolescent says something like "I do my most creative work with a little bit of help from the bottle" or "If I quit, it's going to push me over the limit, and I'll never be able to face the problems in my family."

All-or-nothing reasoning, another cognitive distortion, is frequent among adolescent abusers. They will say something like "I can't keep it all together unless I have a few drinks, and if I can't have a few drinks, I won't be able to do anything. I won't even graduate from school." Of course, adolescents personalize the drinking issue when they say, "I'll lose all my friends if I'm not drinking. Everybody's doing it, and they'll reject me if I don't go along." A final cognitive error, *superstitious thinking*, shows the almost magical distortion of some adolescents. "If I take a little bit of this stuff, I have powers beyond anything I can have without it. Just a few drags from the weed and I'm a social butterfly," they might say.

In counseling adolescents, one must be alert for cognitive distortions and confront youngsters with the need to examine the reality involved in their actual substance abuse. When they can see their mistakes in observation and information processing, they can then be led to discover for themselves ways of relating and functioning that do not involve substance abuse.

Behavior modification with adolescents who are substance abusers has been particularly successful when the rewards and tokens are uniquely tied to the adolescent's own values and aspirations. Motivation for treatment, an issue in all emotional problems of adolescents, is a key factor before any behavior modification program can be implemented in substance abuse cases (Derek Miller, *Adolescents,* p. 496). Furthermore, having the complete support of everyone in the adolescent's environment is necessary for a behavior modification program to work. For that reason, inpatient programs may be needed at the start. However, when the schools, parents, church, and friends of an adolescent all support that adolescent in behavior modification, an outpatient program can be especially successful. The actual rewards set up for abstinence and for attaining long-range and short-range behavior goals are not as important as the praise, affirmation, and relationships of peers and significant adults. Many times adolescents have been using the substance itself as a reward. When drugs are replaced by more meaningful, less destructive rewards, adolescent behavior will improve. One set of parents has successfully tied use of a car to continued sobriety.

For occasional abusers, meaningful family experiences and quality time with the same-sex parent frequently serve as the best reinforcement for not using drugs and alcohol. The counselor's role in such behavior modification is to form a contract that includes (1) confrontation of the dysfunctional behavior, (2) clear understanding of the desirable goals, and (3) tokens that support movement toward health. Being available at all times is important when counseling with adolescents under stress; however, it is crucial for abusers (as it is for those at risk for suicide). Finally, remember that substance abuse is much more serious for an older teen than one-time experimentation would be for an early or middle adolescent. Help parents to release their fear that one act of testing the limits means that their child suffers from an addiction.

Food Abuse

As with other forms of substance abuse, the factors involved in abuse of food are complex. Anxiety, experimentation, pressure to be accepted, modeling of peers and parents, power control issues, and lack of self-esteem have all been linked with both anorexia and obesity. The Bible regularly includes gluttony in its list of abuses, although refusing to eat can be taken as religious commitment; fasting is an expression of discipline, and prayer is one of the spiritual gifts. However, gluttony and fasting are both neglected in most literature addressing teenage crises.

Abuses of food and alcohol have long been seen as problems. One of the slanderous statements made about Jesus by those seeking to discredit him was that he came eating and drinking: "Behold, a glutton and a drunkard" (Matt. 11:19). Not all preoccupation with dieting and not all cases of obesity are signs of emotional disorders; obviously, a variety of genetic and biological factors must be taken into consideration. Nevertheless, among adolescents, particularly adolescent girls, a number of eating disorders deserve attention.

The past twenty years produced an explosion of research into eating disorders. Anorexia nervosa, refusal to maintain a minimally normal body weight for age and height, might also include an intense fear of becoming fat, undue influence of body on self-image, and denial of the seriousness of current low body weight. Bulimia, binge eating and then self-induced vomiting that jeopardizes health, also reflects a self-evaluation unduly influenced by body shape and weight. Of course, at times the two come together (Zerbe, pp.10–11). Although there are still many questions to be researched, it seems that persons with eating disorders frequently experience a serious deficit in their ability to recognize and express a variety of feelings. This is especially true in bulimic patients (Garfinkel and Garner, p. 276). Zerbe, director of the eating disorders clinic at Menninger, argued that the life-sustaining unity between the body and spirit becomes disrupted and they begin to wage war on each other. As the battle rages in anorexic and bulimic persons, the body is hated (Zerbe, p. 21). As the unity of the mind, body, and spirit breaks down, the person ceases to thrive and grow. Only 10 percent of eating disorders are in males.

Society pushes females to maintain the ideal body and extols the value of thinness. Models, actresses, singers, certain athletes, and "beautiful people" chase the illusive perfect body image. Gymnasts, divers, distance runners, and other athletes who work to maintain a lean body seem predisposed to an increased risk of developing an eating disorder (Zerbe, p. 137). Also, in many instances food abuse exists alongside major personality disorders. Other psychological disturbances (deep depression, obsessive patterns, high anxiety, and disturbances in primary relationships) are clear signals that a food-abusing youth needs a professional evaluation.

Responding to Adolescents Who Abuse Food

Early recognition of symptoms and acceptance that a problem exists can help prevent food-abuse troubles from escalating. The inner conflicts and self-esteem struggles need to be addressed as soon as possible. Once health is an issue, seek professional assistance.

Parents

Adolescence is the time to become your own person. Parents can **watch the process of letting go** and not hold on too tightly, but they should not become detached. The struggle to remain attached to the family while becoming a separate individual can lead to confusion for both the teenagers and their parents. For some teens, not eating or eating too little becomes a form of control. It is a harsh statement of independence that declares, "You can't make me . . . !" However, for bulimia, the opposite may be the case. These young women desire more parental involvement. They long for emotional nurturing (Zerbe, p. 64). As teens get older, give more freedom but maintain your involvement in their lives.

Accept and nurture yourself and the teen as having both good points and limitations. Get comfortable with the concept of "excellence without perfection." Assist your youth to strive for quality, but do not push for flawlessness. Accepting their strengths and flaws removes the pressure and reduces the heaviness of "measuring up." Dad and mom need to nurture the teen as a person of worth to them and support his or her directions in life. However, avoid the temptation to push teens to grow up too fast or to become "superchildren" who do not make mistakes. Find a balance between encouraging their best and accepting their best effort as "OK." Parental nurture fills the void that might otherwise be filled with food.

Get help from a professional who specializes in adolescent eating disorders. The sooner you seek help, the better. Take seriously the teens' cries for help. One mother was shocked to find that her daughter had eaten a box of cereal in one sitting and then induced vomiting. Only after the sixth occurrence did the mother go for help. Do not wait. Whenever you notice abnormal weight gain or loss, face the issue and address alternatives. Have healthy foods in the home.

Assist your teen in knowing what to eat and when. **Nutritional information** can make a difference. Do not nag or push, but firmly help your teen to make wise decisions. Do not give in to buying junk food, but do purchase healthy food. Those on a limited budget can ill afford to spend money for nonnutritional foodstuffs like chips, sweets, and soft drinks. Fresh fruits and vegetables make a better choice. School food can be helpful if the student will make wise choices. Do not support the teen's choice of unhealthy eating.

Teachers

Teachers serve as **role models** for their students. In spite of discipline problems, a large number of students listen to their teachers talk about life and life-style. This is especially true for younger teens. By talking about her own eating choices, one middle school English teacher had hundreds of students deciding to try to become vegetarians. Teach healthy choices about eating. Raise the youths' consciousness about eating problems, and make suggestions for wholesome choices about food. Confront abuse in a caring, warm, and empathetic approach. Because certain athletes are inclined toward food abuse, coaches should provide nutritional information for their teams. Of course, the coach has more impact if she or he follows the same advice.

Referring teens for medical evaluation is an important step. Sometimes the family fails to see the seriousness of the issue. Know when, where, and how to get help for your students with food-abuse problems. Not everyone who is thin or everyone who is outside some "ideal" weight is in need of counseling. One rule of thumb for identifying anorexic girls is to figure twenty pounds for each foot of height and five pounds for each inch above five feet. For example, a five-foot five-inch female of average build could weigh 125—100 pounds for the five feet and another 25 pounds for the five inches. Anorexia would be considered an issue if her body weight were to drop in a short period of time below 90 percent of that weight—to 112 pounds or less. For example, one youngster lost 13 percent of her body weight in three weeks after breaking up with her boyfriend; her weight loss exemplifies a typical attachment anxiety issue. For someone hospitalized for anorexia, the 90 percent point is a likely goal for discharge. If an anorexic girl drops to 80 percent of her body weight (to 100 pounds for our 125-pound example), severe physical complications can set in; there can be a stopping of the growth hormones, and the menstrual cycle may stop. More than 15 percent *above* normal body weight can also create health problems by putting additional strain on the heart and circulatory system.

Ministers

Ministers who are not aware of the dynamics in food abuse can be a caring friend and refer the adolescent to a professional counselor. Refer when weight falls below 15 percent of normal weight for age and height. Refer if the teen binges or purges more than three times in a month. Be aware that the teen might not reveal the full nature of the problem. When in doubt, be safe and refer.

The concept of self seems to be a central issue for those who abuse food. The self is viewed as an object of disdain, and self-esteem suffers significantly. Ministers working with food abusers, as with other substance abusers, can **focus on self-esteem** issues and one's relationship with God and the people of God. Focus on the body as the dwelling place of the spirit and on the unity of the body, mind, and soul. Because self-esteem issues are so important, some researchers indicate that females should counsel female substance abusers for the benefit of the modeling on the part of the counselor. From a pastoral counseling point of view, encouraging food abusers to have a positive respect for their bodies as a creation and gift from God goes hand in hand with a positive formation of the sense of self. From a Christian perspective, one is acceptable in any body, regardless of color or size. This assertion can be used to confront adolescent preoccupations with an idealized image and a fear of not having an acceptable body.

Remember that anxiety about being good enough haunts these teenagers. **Addressing the anxiety through theological and pastoral**

approaches seems to work quite well. The presence of God can be of great comfort. Teenagers can find guidance in the scriptures. In short, the church as a community of faith can serve as a safe place for teens to face their fears and anxieties. They may need support in seeking independence or nurturing from their parents. In a context of trust and faith in the sustaining power of God, relationships with families and peers can be less fearful and even a source of joy.

Counselors

As counselors attempt to aid patients with eating disorders in **sharing a variety of feelings,** they offer a place where it is OK to say whatever is on their minds. Those who purge may be attempting to empty themselves of bad feelings. We assist not only in identifying feelings but also in directing teens toward appropriate targets. Support them in finding a name for their inner turmoil. Is it anger, grief, guilt, fear, shame, or some other emotion? Next, help them to focus the feeling. Who or what caused this? Whom should they tell? How will they communicate these feelings? Teens need help in engaging the range of intensity of these feelings. On a scale of one to ten, just how strong is the feeling? For example, teens might feel miffed, upset, irritated, angry, mad, furious, or enraged. Let them find their own words when possible. Assisting adolescents in accepting their feelings will increase their self-esteem as well as facilitate their integration into peer group and family structures. Furthermore, the counselor can model effective communication by the way he or she shares and identifies feelings in the counseling session.

Address cognitive distortions. Cognitive distortions and misinterpretations of body image seem to be a consistent factor for food abusers. A dangerously thin teenage girl might insist that she is indeed fat. (She does not mean "PHAT," which for some teenagers still stands for "Pretty, Hot, And Tempting"!) A range of cognitive distortions is particularly strong for anorexic patients. Thomas C. Todd, director of the Marriage and Family Therapy and Training Program in Bristol, Connecticut, has pointed to research indicating that combining cognitive therapy and family therapy has been particularly helpful with anorexic patients. Characteristic distortions are seen in statements like "The only way I can be in control is through eating" (selective abstraction) or "I used to be of normal weight, and I wasn't happy, so I know gaining weight isn't going to make me feel better" (overgeneralization) or "Gaining five pounds would push me over the limit" (magnification) (Todd, p. 235). As the counselor attempts to combine family and cognitive therapy, he or she needs to be particularly mindful of distortions that are reinforced by the family, by family myths, or by family rules. Direct confrontation is frequently resisted by further "not eating" behavior. Therefore, assisting the adolescent to uncover cognitive distortions through examining the evidence seems to work more productively.

Separation and autonomy issues surface in adolescents with eating disorders. Some obese persons seem to fear attachments with members of the opposite sex and use obesity as a symbolic layer of insulation to create distance between themselves and others. Anorexics who are preoccupied with their thinness seem to be attempting to thwart the developmental maturity process in order to remain a child and not have to leave their parents. This desire to retreat from maturity may also be a desire to avoid emergent sexuality that might be seen as a threat to relationships with parents (Garfinkel and Garner, p. 263). When separation and autonomy are central issues, the development of a greater degree of self-identity and differentiation from the family through family therapy methods is important.

Some counselors rely on behavioral modification exclusively when treating teenagers with food-abuse issues. Because of the control and power issues in eating disorders, behavioral methods seem to have inconsistent results. This is especially true when the behavioral treatment has been mechanistically misapplied. There may be short-term results, but long-term change does not happen because of the presence of underlying issues (Garfinkel and Garner, pp. 285–88). In the long term, more holistic approaches appear wise.

Finally, parents, teachers, ministers, and counselors should see food abuse and substance abuse as a part of the bigger picture. In general, healthy relationships with family and peers and significant others make maintaining a healthy body less stressful. Food abuse, like alcohol and drug abuse, can best be understood as an indication that the teen's fundamental sense of self is not intact, and any effort to address the abuse issues needs to speak to those larger concerns.

Concluding Reflections

*P*arents face increasing demands on their time and must make tough choices about their teenagers. Teachers, ministers, and counselors stand in a unique position to respond to the needs of adolescents in crisis. Teen questions about the meaning of life, confusing moral issues, the search for identity, and personal values offer helping adults an unparalleled opportunity. Although limitations exist, the schools, churches, and counseling agencies cannot neglect their responsibility to teens.

One veteran youth minister now in training as a professional pastoral counselor shared an insightful thought. The contemporary needs of youth are not met through quick-fix solutions and campfire-brand spirituality. Youth need adults who genuinely care but also have skills in listening, communicating, and *modeling* the age-old story of God's love in Jesus Christ. Youth need strong bridges of relationship built to weather the storms of time in order to help them live securely and to believe authentically in the concepts of faith, hope, love, and grace. We cannot out-entertain the world of Bruce Springsteen, Michael Jackson, and Madonna, but with skill born of training and grace conceived in Christ, we can care for youth in crisis.

The May 2, 2000, White House conference on adolescents in crisis called for community leaders and helping agencies to focus attention on programs that work. A call has gone out to the entertainment business to stop marketing sex and violence to children and teenagers. Parents, teachers, ministers, and counselors must unite their voices and resources to nurture and protect future generations of teenagers.

Barriers to Overcome

There are numerous reasons given by professionals for not getting involved in the care of adolescents in crisis. Beyond the typical brush-off are some substantial limitations of teachers, ministers, and counselors. Some teachers report being hurt by attempts to reach out. Some ministers will say, "I just don't relate well to teenagers" or "The adults are the backbone of this church" or "I haven't time to concentrate on adolescents" or, simply, "Not many young people come to our church." Counselors often talk of feeling unprepared for the antics, rebellion, and tricks of teenagers. More serious questions are raised around other issues.

The **training** required for responding to the needs of adolescents in crisis may exceed the training provided the average teacher, minister, or counselor. Unless a person has had an opportunity for specialized supervision in counseling and crisis ministry, he or she may soon find that the crisis is overwhelming. Although no one can be informed in all of the areas that confront adolescents in crisis, we can become knowledgeable about basic issues such as adolescent identity formation, sexual crisis, violence, depression, grief, alcohol, and adolescent faith questions. We cannot do it all, but we can become equipped in one or two areas. Furthermore, even if we lack specific training in depth counseling, we can learn how to make a referral for professional help.

The **time** demands on teachers, ministers, and counselors are already heavy, and responding to teenagers in crisis can consume large additional blocks of time and energy. "Crisis ministry will take away from the other needs of my congregation," complained one minister. "I cannot be fair to the regular students and give the attention needed to help those in trouble," complained a veteran teacher. This is true. Busy professionals must make choices, but so does everyone. Usually, time considerations are a matter of priorities. If teachers and ministers cannot themselves deal with young people in crisis, we need to seek additional staff or train lay volunteers who have the time and desire to work with adolescents in crisis. Can we afford to not get involved?

"Ministers are not always **trusted** by teenagers, for a variety of reasons," proclaimed a high school counselor. Typically, some teens are in a process of revolting against external authority. This includes parents, teachers, "the cops," and institutions like the church and school. More than a few are rebelling against God. As one respondent from Hawaii confessed, "It's a real problem in getting youth to see my church as a viable resource." Admittedly, the polarization of American culture into the secular and the sacred does create a barrier for reaching out to distrustful adolescents. Some teachers are afraid to discuss personal issues with teens. They do not want to invite legal problems. Nevertheless, during a time of crisis, adolescents are more willing to accept a caring response from any source. We need to overcome stereotypic projections on the teens' part. We must work to earn their trust.

Ministers, teachers, and counselors do not always trust each other. Sometimes they don't trust and are not trusted by mental health and legal professionals. Because a few individuals have abused privileges and spoken unkindly about others, some professionals are reluctant to welcome teachers, ministers, and counselors onto the helping team. However, if one takes the time to get to know resistant professionals and relate to them from a clearly helping position, respect and rapport among professionals can be earned. Achieved relationships are more durable in a time of crisis than expecting power to be ascribed simply because of one's role. Teens need us all to work as a team.

Schools, churches, and counseling agencies often **lack the financial resources** for the programs needed for adolescents in crisis. "Small churches have limited means and cannot afford the resources to specialize in ministry to youth in crisis," complained an exacerbated pastor. Some school districts barely have the funds to hire teachers. Even though the number of troubled adolescents may be small, their needs are just as important. The resources of the wider community are available if someone will take the time to get involved and build an adequate referral system. By working together we can avoid overlap and can pool resources.

Reasons for Getting Involved

For a variety of reasons, teachers, ministers, and counselors should respond to the needs of adolescents in crisis. Although we are certainly one part of a caring team and must be careful to develop professional interdependence with other professionals in the community, we are greatly remiss if we neglect our responsibility to today's troubled teenagers.

Teachers spend more time with youth than any other professionals do. We know youths' concerns. We have **access** to their lives on a daily basis. Clergy are in an unparalleled professional position by having a relationship with all members of the family. Because of the minister's **access** across generation lines, she or he is more likely to know and understand what the family system was before the crisis. Counselors have been trained to access the inner world of our clients. We can help teens know their own thoughts, feelings, and intentions. We all have special access to today's youth.

The biblical imperative to minister to the "least of these" must include adolescents. By the nature of their **call,** ministers accept responsibility to minister to all persons regardless of social position, race, or age. Only by excluding teenagers from the status of persons can a minister dare neglect them. Teachers and counselors also have a special calling by training and gifts. Our special training and varied perspectives on the adolescent situation demand that we get involved.

Being nonjudgmental and accepting adolescents as persons in process, not finished products, are traits frequently mentioned by teenagers as important in someone they trust. This nonjudgmental attitude does not mean being without values or having an "anything goes" mentality. Perhaps this was best captured in the words of the fifteen-year-old who said of her minister, "She's easy for me to talk with. It's not that she accepts the stuff I do; it's that she makes me feel like I can do better. She's not always just getting on my case, but still points me in the right direction." What a challenge for each of us! How can we guide youth through a crisis to feel they can do better? How do we coach them out of their cocoons at just the right moment?

By way of summary, it appears that a wide variety of individuals and groups will respond to the needs of adolescents. Teens vary significantly. Whereas some appear arrogant, proud, and defiant, others are confident, caring, and involved. Still others are hurt, scared, detached, and suffering. However, enough similarities exist for us to reach out to individuals and to plan programs to meet their needs. Ongoing activities reach most young people, but special, focused crisis-intervention and counseling approaches are needed for those for whom a major change brings danger, not opportunity. Teens who have supportive families and who find caring professionals to shepherd them through a time of crisis can return to their everyday tasks and to normal development. Those whose initial emergencies go untended follow a path of continued troubles and increased dysfunction. Ignored crises escalate and expand.

Being a shepherd with adolescents in crisis is an awesome responsibility. Get all of the help you can. Do not overestimate your abilities, and don't try to do too much alone. Get involved in a consultation group, find supervision with professionals, and join interdisciplinary case conferences whenever possible. As you guide one youngster into adulthood, rejoice briefly and then turn to the next child struggling with the crises of adolescence.

Bibliography

BOOKS

Ackerman, Norman J. *A Theory of Family Systems*. New York: Gardner Press, 1984.

Ackerman, W. Nathan. *The Psychodynamics of Family Life*. New York: Basic Books, 1958.

Aleshire, Daniel O. *Faithcare: Ministering to All God's People Through the Ages of Life*. Philadelphia: Westminster Press, 1988.

Apthorp, Stephen P. *Alcohol and Substance Abuse*. Wilton, Conn.: Morehouse-Barfow Co., 1985.

Arnold, William V. *Introduction to Pastoral Care*. Philadelphia: Westminster Press, 1982.

Augsburger, David W. *Pastoral Counseling Across Cultures*. Philadelphia: Westminster Press, 1986.

Barnes, Jr., Robert G. *Confident Kids*. Wheaton, Ill.: Tyndale House Publishers, 1987.

———. *Single Parenting*. Wheaton, Ill.: Tyndale House Publishers, 1987.

Berger, Kathleen Stassen. *The Developing Person Through the Life Span*, 2nd. ed. New York: Worth Publishers, 1988.

Blackburn, Bill. *Caring in Times of Family Crisis*. Nashville: Convention Press, 1987.

Bolton, Iris. *My Son, My Son*. Atlanta: Bolton Press, 1983.

Borchert, Gerald L., and Andrew D. Lester, eds. *Spiritual Dimensions of Pastoral Care: Witness to the Ministry of Wayne E. Oates*. Philadelphia: Westminster Press, 1985.

Bowen, M. *Family Therapy in Clinical Practice*. New York: Jason Aronson, 1978.

Bugental, James F. T. *The Art of the Psychotherapist*. New York: W. W. Norton & Co., 1987.

Burns, David D. *Feeling Good: The New Mood Therapy*. New York: Signet Books, 1999.

Capps, Donald. *Deadly Sin and Saving Virtues*. Philadelphia: Fortress Press, 1987.

Cavanaugh, Michael. *Biotheology: A New Synthesis of Science and Religion*. New York: University Press of America, 1995.

Clinebell, Howard J. *Basic Types of Pastoral Care and Counseling: Resources for the Ministry of Healing and Growth*. Rev. & enl. ed. Nashville: Abingdon Press, 1984.

———. *Contemporary Growth Therapies*. Nashville: Abingdon Press, 1981.

———. *Understanding and Counseling the Alcoholic*. Nashville: Abingdon Press, 1985.

Cole, Robert. *The Spiritual Life of Children*. Boston: Houghton Mifflin Company, 1990.

Conley, Dalton. *Being Black, Living in the Red*. Los Angeles: University of California Press, 1999.

Corey, Marianne Schneider, and Gerald F. Corey. *Groups: Process and Practice*. Monterey, Calif.: Brooks/Cole Publishing Co., 1996.

Deutsch, Helene. *Selected Problems of Adolescence*. New York: International Universities Press, 1967.

Dunlap, Susan J. *Counseling Depressed Women*. Louisville: Westminster John Knox Press, 1997.

Duvall, Evelyn. *Handbook for Parents*. Nashville: Broadman Press, 1974.

Dykstra, Robert C. *Counseling Troubled Youth*. Louisville: Westminster John Knox Press, 1997.

Egan, Gerard. *The Skilled Helper: A Problem Management Approach to Helping*. Monterey, Calif.: Brooks/Cole Publishing Co., 1994.

Elkind, David. *All Grown Up and No Place to Go: Teenagers in Crisis*. Reading, Mass.: Addison-Wesley Publishing Co., 1984.

Emmett, Steven Willey, ed. *Theory and Treatment of Anorexia Nervosa and Bulimia*. New York: Brunner/Mazel, 1985.

Erikson, Erik. *Identity, Youth, and Crisis*. New York: Norton, 1968.

Feindler, Eva L., and Randolph B. Ecton. *Adolescent Anger Control*. Elmsford, N.Y.: Pergamon Press, 1986.

Fowler, James W. *The Stages of Faith: The Psychology of Human Development and the Quest for Meaning*. New York: Harper & Row, 1981.

Friedman, Edwin H. *Generation to Generation*. New York: Guilford Press, 1985.

Gallatin, Judith E. *Adolescence and Individuality*. New York: Harper & Row, 1975.

Gerkin, Charles V. *The Living Human Document*. Nashville: Abingdon Press, 1984.

Gilligan, Carol. *In a Different Voice: Psychological Theory and Women's Development*. Cambridge, Mass.: Harvard University Press, 1982.

Gilligan, James, M.D. *Violence*. New York: First Vintage Press, 1996.

Glasser, William. *Stations of the Mind: New Directions for Reality Therapy*. New York: Harper & Row, 1981.

Haley, J. *Leaving Home*. New York: McGraw-Hill, 1980.

Hiltner, Seward. *Preface to Pastoral Theology*. Nashville: Abingdon Press, 1958.

————. *Theological Dynamics*. Nashville: Abingdon Press, 1972.

Husain, Syed Arshad. *Suicide in Children and Adolescents*. Jamaica, N.Y.: Spectrum Publications, 1984.

Johnson, Jerry. *Why Suicide?* Nashville: Thomas Nelson Publishers, 1987.

Kagan, Norman I. *Interpersonal Process Recall*. Copyright by Norman I. Kagan, 1976.

Kelly, Brother James M., C.F.X. *Respecting the Man the Boy Will Become*. Louisville: Butler Books, 1998.

Kemp, Charles F. *The Caring Pastor*. Nashville: Abingdon Press, 1985.

————. *Physicians of the Soul*. New York: Macmillan Co., 1947.

Kesler, Jay, ed., with Ronald A. Beers. *Parents and Teenagers*. Wheaton, Ill.: Victor Books, 1984.

Kurtz, Ernest, and Katherine Ketcham. *The Spirituality of Imperfection*. New York: Bantam Books, 1994.

Lerner, Harriet. *The Dance of Anger*. New York: HarperCollins, 1985.

Lester, Andrew D. *Pastoral Care with Children in Crisis*. Philadelphia: Westminster Press, 1985.

Levy-Warren, Marsha. *The Adolescent Journey*. Northvale, N. J.: Jason Aronson, Inc., 1996.

Lovinger, Robert J. *Working with Religious Issues in Therapy*. New York: Jason Aronson, 1984.

May, Rollo. *The Meaning of Anxiety*. New York: W. W. Norton & Co., 1977.

Mayeroff, Milton. *On Caring*. New York: Harper & Row, 1971.

Mickey, Paul, and Gary Gamble. *Pastoral Assertiveness*. Nashville: Abingdon Press, 1978.

Miller, Alice. *For Your Own Good: Hidden Cruelty in Child-Rearing and the Roots of Violence*. New York: Farrar, Straus & Giroux, 1983.

Miller, Derek. *Adolescence: Psychology, Psychopathology, and Psychotherapy*. New York: Jason Aronson, 1974.

———. *Attack on the Self: Adolescent Behavioral Disturbances and Their Treatment*. New York: Jason Aronson, 1986.

Mirkin, Marsha P., and Stuart L. Koman, eds. *Handbook of Adolescents and Family Therapy*. New York: Gardner Press, 1985.

Mishne, Judith Marks. *Clinical Work with Adolescents*. New York: Free Press, 1986.

Moore, Charlotte Dickson, ed. *Science Reports: Adolescence and Stress*. Washington, D.C.: U.S. Department of Health and Human Services, 1981.

Moyers, William. *Moyers on Addiction: The Hijacked Brain*. Public Affairs Television, Inc. 1998 (800-257-5236 for information on ordering).

Nelson, C. Ellis. *Helping Teenagers Grow Morally*. Louisville: Westminster John Knox Press, 1992.

Nutt, Grady. *Being Me*. Nashville: Broadman Press, 1971.

Oates, Wayne E. *Behind the Masks: Personality Disorders in Religious Behavior*. Philadelphia: Westminster Press, 1987.

———. *The Bible in Pastoral Care*. Grand Rapids: Baker Book House, 1973.

———. *Christ and Selfhood*. New York: Association Press, 1961.

———. *The Christian Pastor*. Philadelphia: Westminster Press, 1982.

———. *On Becoming Children of God*. Philadelphia: Westminster Press, 1969.

———. *Pastoral Counseling*. Philadelphia: Westminster Press, 1974.

Oettinger, Katherine B. *Normal Adolescence: Its Dynamics and Impact*. New York: Charles Scribner's Sons, 1968.

Parke, Ross D. *The Family*. Chicago: University of Chicago Press, 1984.

Parsons, Richard D. *Adolescents in Turmoil, Parents Under Stress: A Pastoral Ministry Primer*. New York: Paulist Press, 1987.

Patton, John. *Pastoral Counseling: A Ministry of the Church*. Nashville: Abingdon Press, 1983.

Peck, Scott. *Further Along the Road Less Traveled*. New York: Simon and Schuster, 1993.

Pruyser, Paul W. *The Minister as Diagnostician: Personal Problems in Pastoral Perspective*. Philadelphia: Westminster Press, 1976.

Ross, Richard, and G. Wade Rowatt Jr. *Ministry with Youth and Their Parents*. Nashville: Convention Press, 1986.

Rowatt, G. Wade, Jr., and Mary Jo Brock Rowatt. *The Two-Career Marriage*. Christian Care Books. Philadelphia: Westminster Press, 1980.

———. *Pastoral Care with Adolescents in Crises*. Louisville: Westminster John Knox Press, 1989.

Shaw, James E. *Jack and Jill: Why They Kill*. Seattle: Onjinjinkta Publishing, 2000.

Shelp, Earl E., and Ronald H. Sunderland. *AIDS and the Church*. Philadelphia: Westminster Press, 1987.

Sherrill, Lewis Joseph. *The Struggle of the Soul*. New York: Macmillan Co., 1951.

Shneidman, Edwin S. *The Suicidal Mind*. New York: Oxford University Press, 1996.

Simmons, Randy James. *Content and Structure in Faith Development*. Louisville: Unpublished Ph. D. dissertation, Southern Baptist Theological Seminary, 1986.

Smolin, Ann, and John Guinan. *Healing After the Suicide of a Loved One.* New York: Simon and Schuster, 1993.

Stillion, Judith M., and Eugene E. McDowell. *Suicide Across the Life Span.* Washington, D.C.: Taylor and Francis, 1996.

Stinnett, Nick, and John DeFrain. *Secrets of Strong Families.* Boston: Little, Brown, 1985.

Stone, Howard W. *Crisis Counseling.* Philadelphia: Fortress Press, 1978.

———. *Using Behavioral Methods in Pastoral Counseling.* Philadelphia: Fortress Press, 1980.

Strommen, Merton P. *The Five Cries of Youth.* New York: Harper & Row, 1974.

Switzer, David K. *The Minister as a Crisis Counselor.* Nashville: Abingdon Press, 1974.

Thornton, Edward E. *Being Transformed: An Inner Way of Spiritual Growth.* Philadelphia: Westminster Press, 1984.

Van Ornum, William, and John B. Mordock. *Crisis Counseling with Children and Adolescents.* New York: Continuum Publishing Co., 1983.

Waterman. Alan S., ed. *Identity in Adolescence: Processes and Content.* San Francisco: Jossey-Bass, 1985.

Weeks, Louis. *Making Ethical Decisions: A Casebook.* Philadelphia: Westminster Press, 1987.

White, Ernest. *The Art of Human Relations.* Nashville: Broadman Press, 1985.

Wicks, Robert, Richard Parsons, and Donald Capps, eds. *Clinical Handbook of Pastoral Counseling.* New York: Paulist Press, 1984.

Wimberly, Edward P. *Counseling African American Marriages and Families.* Louisville: Westminster John Knox Press, 1997.

Wynn, J. C. *Family Therapy in Pastoral Ministry.* San Francisco: Harper & Row, 1982.

Zerbe, Kathryn. *The Body Betrayed: A Deeper Understanding of Women, Eating Disorders, and Treatment.* Washington, D.C.: American Psychiatric Press, 1993.

PERIODICALS

Anthony, E. James. Normal Adolescent Development from a Cognitive Viewpoint. *Journal of the American Academy of Child Psychiatry.* 1982, Vol. 21, 317–21.

Barber, Bonnie L., and J. S. Eccles. Long-Term Influence of Divorce and Single Parenting on Adolescent Family- and Work-Related Values, Behaviors, and Aspirations. *Psychological Bulletin.* 1992, Vol. 111, No. 1, 108–26.

Begley, Sharon. Getting Inside a Teen Brain. *Newsweek.* Feb. 28, 2000, 58–59.

Bennett, David S. Depression Among Children with Chronic Medical Problems: A Meta-Analysis. *Journal of Pediatric Psychology.* 1994, Vol. 19, No. 2, 149–69.

Boehm, Kathryn E., et al. Teens' Concerns: A National Evaluation. *Adolescence.* Fall 1999, Vol. 324, No. 135, 523–28.

Cherlin, Andrew J. Longitudinal Studies of Effects of Divorce on Children in Great Britain and the United States. *Science.* June 7, 1991, Vol. 252, 1386–89.

Cirillo, Kathleen J., et al. School Violence: Prevalence and Intervention Strategies for At-Risk Adolescents. *Adolescence.* Summer, 1998, Vol. 33, No. 130, 319–30.

Cohn, Lawrence D. Sex Differences in the Course of Personality Development: A Meta-Analysis. *Psychological Bulletin.* 1991, Vol. 109, No. 2, 252–66.

Corcoran, Jacqueline. Ecological Factors Associated with Adolescent Pregnancy: A Review of the Literature. *Adolescence.* Fall 1999, Vol. 34, No. 135, 603–19.

Culp, Anne McDonald, Mary M. Clyman, and Rex E. Culp. Adolescent Depressed Mood, Reports of Suicide Attempts, and Asking for Help. *Adolescence.* Winter 1995, Vol. 30, No. 120, 827–37.

Dawkins, Marvin P. Drug Use and Violent Crime Among Adolescents. *Adolescence.* Summer 1997, Vol. 32, No. 126, 395–405.

Denton, Rhonda E., and Charlene M. Kampfe. The Relationship Between Family Variables and Adolescent Substance Abuse: A Literature Review. *Adolescence.* Summer 1994, Vol. 29, No. 114, 475–95.

Diamond, Guy S., et al. Current Status of Family-Based Outcome and Process Research. *Journal of the American Academy of Child and Adolescent Psychiatry.* January 1996, Vol. 35.

Erikson, Erik H. Identity and the Life Cycle. *Psychological Issues.* 1959, Vol. 1, No. 1, 120.

Fillmore, Kaye Middleton, et al. Alcohol Consumption and Mortality. *Addiction.* 1998, Vol. 93, No. 2, 183–203.

Gerlsma, Coby, Paul M. G. Emmelkanp, and Willem A. Arrindell. Anxiety, Depression, and Perception of Early Perenting: A Meta-Analysis. *Clinical Psychology Review.* 1990, Vol. 10, 251–77.

Gfroerer, J. C., Janet C. Greenblatt, and Douglas A Wright. Substance Use in the US College-Age Population. *American Journal of Public Health.* June 1997, Vol. 87, No. 1, 62–65.

Graves, Roger, et al. Demographic and Parental Characteristics of Youthful Sexual Offenders. *International Journal of Offender Therapy and Comparative Criminology.* 1996, Vol. 40, No. 4, 300–317.

Heldt, Laura, and David Oliver Relin. I Drove Drunk and Killed Someone. *Teen People.* August 2000, 123–128.

Hoag, Matthew J., and Gary M. Burlingame. Evaluating the Effectiveness of Child and Adolescent Group Treatment: A Meta-Analytic Review. *Journal of Clinical Child Psychology.* 1997, Vol. 26, No. 3, 234–46.

Hoge, Dean. Study of High School Seniors from Monitoring the Future Data. Unpublished essay at Catholic University, 1987, 17.

Jehlen, Alain. The Wealth Factor. *NEA Today.* September 2000, 33.

Kellogg, Nancy D., Thomas J. Hoffman, and Eizabeth R. Taylor. Early Sexual Experiences Among Pregnant and Parenting Adolescents. *Adolescence.* Summer 1999, Vol. 34, No. 134, 293–303.

Kling, Kristen C., et al. Gender Differences in Self-Esteem: A Meta-Analysis. *Psychological Bulletin.* 1999, Vol. 125, No. 4, 470–500.

Klingman, Avigdor. Psychological Education: Studying Adolescents' Interests from Their Own Perspective. *Adolescence.* Summer 1998, Vol. 33, No. 130, 435–46.

Laursen, Brett, Katherine C. Coy, and W. Andrew Collins. Reconsidering Changes in Parent-Child Conflict Across Adolescence: A Meta-Analysis. *Child Development.* June 1998, Vol. 69, No. 3, 817–32.

LaVery, Patrick J., et al. Pregnancy Outcome in a Comprehensive Teenage Parent Program. *Adolescent Pediatric Gynecology.* 1988, Vol. 1, 34–37.

Leino, E. Victor, et al. Alocohol Consumption and Mortality. *Addiction.* February 1998, Vol. 93, No. 2, 205–18.

Matula, Kathleen E., et al. Identity and Dating Commitment Among Women and Men in College. *Journal of Youth and Adolescence.* 1992, Vol. 21, No. 3, 339–56.

Pattison, E. Mansell. Religious Youth Cults: Alternative Healing Social Networks. *Journal of Religion and Health*. Fall/Winter, 1980, 275–86.

Rehearsal Follows Moms 17 Years Later. *Newsletter of the Colorado Organization of Adolescent Pregnancy and Parenting*. 1987, 1.

Reinecke, Mark A., Nancy E. Ryan, and David L. Dubois. Cognitive-Behavioral Therapy of Depression and Depressive Symptoms During Adolescence: A Review and Meta-Analysis. *Journal of the American Academy of Child and Adolescent Psychiatry*. January 1998, Vol. 37.

Rice, Kenneth G. Attachment in Adolescence: A Narrative and Meta-Analytic Review. *Journal of Youth and Adolescence*. 1990, Vol. 19, No. 5, 511–38.

Rudd, David M., and Thomas E. Joiner, Jr. An Integrative Conceptual Framework for Assessing and Treating Suicidal Behavior in Adolescents. *Journal of Adolescence*. August 1998, Vol. 21, No. 4, 489–98.

Schrodt, G. Randolph, and Barbara A. Firzgerald. Cognitive Therapy with Adolescents. *American Journal of Psychotherapy*. 1987, Vol. 41, No. 3, 402–08.

Toner, Robin. Mothers March Against Guns. *The Courier-Journal*. May 15, 2000.

Verlinder, Stephanie, Michel Hersen, and Jay Thomas. Risk Factors in School Shootings. *Clinical Psychology Review*. 2000, Vol. 20, No. 1, 3–56.

Wagner, Barry M. Family Risk Factors for Child and Adolescent Suicidal Behavior. *Psychological Bulletin*. 1997, Vol. 121, No. 2, 246–98.

Werner-Wilson, Ronald Jay. Gender Differences in Adolescents' Sexual Attitudes: The Influence of Individual and Family Factors. *Adolescence*. Fall 1998, Vol. 33, No. 131, 519–31.

Whited, Charles. *Miami Herald*. Dec. 5, 1987, B, 1.

The White House Conference on Teenagers: Raising Responsible and Resourceful Youth. *http://www.pub.whitehouse.gov/uri-res/I2R?urn:pdi://oma.eop.gov.us/2000/5/4/11.text.1*. May 2, 2000, 1–44.

Wright, Jesse H., and Aaron T. Beck. Cognitive Therapy of Depression: Theory and Practice. *Hospital and Community Psychiatry*. Dec. 1983, Vol. 34, No. 12, 1119–26.

YMCA Parent and Tean Study, April 2000.

Index

Printed in the United States
74097LV00004B/289-321

9 780664 223342